*f*P

# Prisoner of Tehran

A MEMOIR

## Marina Nemat

*Free Press*

NEW YORK   LONDON   TORONTO   SYDNEY

FREE PRESS
A Division of Simon & Schuster, Inc.
1230 Avenue of the Americas
New York, NY 10020

FREE PRESS and colophon are registered trademarks
of Simon & Schuster, Inc.

For information about special discounts for bulk purchases,
please contact Simon & Schuster Special Sales at
1-800-456-6798 or business@simonandschuster.com

Manufactured in the United States of America

1   3   5   7   9   10   8   6   4   2

Library of Congress Cataloging-in-Publication Data
Nemat, Marina.
Prisoner of Tehran : Marina Nemat.
p. cm.
1. Nemat, Marina. 2. Women political prisoners—Iran—Biography. 3. Political prisoners—
Iran—Biography. 4. Iran—Politics and government—1979–1997.  I. Title.

DS318.84.N46 A3 2006
365'.45092 B 22        2006050191

ISBN-13: 978-1-4165-3742-7
ISBN-10:      1-4165-3742-2

To Andre, Michael, and Thomas;
to all political prisoners of Iran,
especially Sh.F.M., M.D., A.Sh., and K.M.;
and to Zahra Kazemi

And if I pray, the only prayer
That moves my lips for me
Is, "Leave the heart that now I bear,
And give me liberty!"
Yes, as my swift days near their goal,
'Tis all that I implore
In life and death, a chainless soul,
With courage to endure.
—Emily Brontë

Although this is a work of nonfiction, I have changed names to protect the identities of my cell mates, and I have added the details of other prisoners' stories to theirs, merging lives and reshaping them. This has enabled me to safely tell of life and death behind the walls of Evin and to remain true to what we went through, without putting anyone in danger or invading anyone's privacy—but I'm sure my cell mates will easily find themselves here.

While working on this book, I had to rely on my memory, which, like any other, has a habit of fading and playing tricks. Some things I remember clearly, as if they happened a week ago, but others are fragmented and foggy; after all, more than twenty years have gone by.

In everyday life, dialogue is our main means of communication, and I believe that memories cannot be effectively brought back to life without it. I have reconstructed the dialogue in this book to the best of my abilities and as close to the truth as is humanly possible.

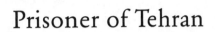
Prisoner of Tehran

# One

THERE IS AN ANCIENT PERSIAN PROVERB that says: "The sky is the same color wherever you go." But the Canadian sky was different from the one I remembered from Iran; it was a deeper shade of blue and seemed endless, as if challenging the horizon.

We arrived at Pearson International Airport in Toronto on August 28, 1991, a beautiful, sunny day. My brother was waiting for us. My husband, our two-and-a-half-year-old son, and I were to stay at his house until we could find an apartment. Although I had not seen my brother in twelve years—I was fourteen when he left for Canada—I immediately spotted him. His hair had grayed and thinned a little, but he was six feet seven and his head bobbed over the enthusiastic chaos of the waiting crowd.

As we drove away from Pearson, I looked out the window, and the vastness of the landscape astonished me. The past was gone, and it was in everyone's best interest that I put it behind me. We had to build a new life in this strange country that had offered us refuge when we had nowhere to go. I had to concentrate all my energy on survival. I had to do this for my husband and my son.

And we did build a new life. My husband found a good job, we had another son, and I learned how to drive. In July 2000, nine years after our arrival in Canada, we finally bought a four-bedroom house in the suburbs of Toronto and became proud middle-class Canadians, tending our backyard, driving the boys to swimming, soccer, and piano lessons, and having friends over for barbecues.

This was when I lost the ability to sleep.

It began with snapshots of memories that flashed in my mind as soon as I went to bed. I tried to push them away, but they rushed at me, invading my daytime hours as well as the night. The past was gaining on me, and I couldn't keep it at bay; I had to face it or it would completely destroy my sanity. If I couldn't forget, perhaps the solution was to remember. I began writing about my days in Evin—Tehran's notorious political prison—about the torture, pain, death, and all the suffering I had never been able to talk about. My memories became words and broke free from their induced hibernation. I believed that once I put them on paper, I would feel better—but I didn't. I needed more. I couldn't keep my manuscript buried in a bedroom drawer. I was a witness and had to tell my story.

My first reader was my husband. He, too, didn't know the details of my time in prison. Once I gave him my manuscript, he put it under his side of our bed, where it remained untouched for three days. I was anguished. When would he read it? Would he understand? Would he forgive me for keeping such secrets?

"Why didn't you tell me earlier?" he asked when he finally read it.

We had been married for seventeen years.

"I tried, but I couldn't . . . will you forgive me?" I said.

"There's nothing to forgive. Will *you* forgive *me*?"

"For what?"

"For not asking."

If I had doubts about speaking out, they vanished in the summer of 2005 when I met an Iranian couple at a dinner party. We enjoyed each others' company and talked about everyday things: our jobs, the real estate market, and our children's education. When the evening air became too cool to sit outdoors, we moved inside for dessert. As the hostess served coffee, she asked me how my book was coming along, and the Iranian woman, Parisa, wanted to know what it was about.

"When I was sixteen, I was arrested and spent two years as a political prisoner in Evin. I'm writing about that," I said.

All color left her face.

"Are you all right?" I asked.

She paused a little and said she herself had spent a few months in Evin.

Everyone in the room fell silent, staring at us.

Parisa and I discovered we had been prisoners at the same time in different areas of the same building. I mentioned the names of a few of my cell mates, but they weren't familiar to her, and she told me about her prison friends, but I didn't know them. However, we shared memories of certain events which were well known to most Evin inmates. She said this was the first time she had talked to anyone about her prison experiences.

"People just don't talk about it," she said.

This was the very silence that had held me captive for more than twenty years.

When I was released from Evin, my family pretended that everything was all right. No one mentioned the prison. No one asked, "What happened to you?" I ached to tell them about my life in Evin, but I didn't know where to start. I waited for them to ask me something, anything that would give me a place to begin, but life went on as if nothing out of the ordinary had happened. I guessed that my family wanted me to be the innocent girl I had been before prison. They were terrified of the pain and horror of my past, so they ignored it.

I encouraged Parisa to phone me, and we spoke a few times. Her voice always trembled as we shared our memories of our cell mates, recalling friendships that had helped us survive.

A few weeks later, she told me she didn't want to talk to me anymore; she didn't want to remember.

"I can't do it. It's too hard. It's too painful," she said, her voice choked by tears.

I understood and didn't argue. She had made her choice—and I had made mine.

# Two

I WAS ARRESTED ON JANUARY 15, 1982, at about nine
o'clock at night. I was sixteen.

Earlier that day, I woke before dawn and couldn't go back to
sleep. My bedroom felt darker and colder than usual, so I stayed
under my camel-wool duvet and waited for the sun, but it seemed
like darkness was there to stay. On cold days like this, I wished our
apartment had better heating; two kerosene heaters weren't enough,
but my parents always told me I was the only one who found the
house too chilly in winter.

My parents' bedroom was next to mine, and the kitchen was

5

across the narrow hallway that connected the two ends of our three-bedroom apartment. I listened as my father got ready for work. Although he moved lightly and quietly, the faint sounds he made helped me trace his movements to the bathroom and then to the kitchen. The kettle whistled. The fridge opened and closed. He was probably having bread with butter and jam.

Finally, a dim light crawled in through my window. My father had already left for work, and my mother was still sleeping. She didn't usually get out of bed until nine o'clock. I tossed, turned, and waited. Where was the sun? I tried to make plans for the day, but it was useless. I felt like I had tripped out of the normal flow of time. I stepped out of bed. The linoleum floor was even colder than the air and the kitchen was darker than my bedroom. It was as if I would never feel warm again. Maybe the sun was never going to rise. After having a cup of tea, all I could think of doing was to go to church. I put on the long brown wool coat my mother had made for me, covered my hair with a large beige shawl, and climbed down the twenty-four gray stone steps leading to the front door, which connected our apartment to the busy downtown street. The stores were still closed, and traffic was light. I walked to the church without looking up. There was nothing to see. Pictures of Ayatollah Khomeini and hateful slogans like "Death to America," "Death to Israel," "Death to Communists and All the Enemies of Islam," and "Death to Anti-Revolutionaries" covered most walls.

It took me five minutes to get to the church. When I put my hand on the heavy wooden main door, a snowflake landed on my nose. Tehran always looked innocently beautiful under the deceiving curves of snow, and although the Islamic regime had banned most beautiful things, it couldn't stop the snow from falling. The government had ordered women to cover their hair and had issued edicts against music, makeup, paintings of unveiled women, and Western books, which had all been declared satanic and therefore illegal. I stepped inside the church, closed the door behind me, and sat in a corner, staring at the image of Jesus on the cross. The church was empty. I tried to pray, but words floated meaninglessly in my head. After about half an hour, I went to the church office to say hello to the priests and found myself standing face to face with Andre, the handsome organist. We had met a few months back, and I frequently saw him at the church. Everyone knew we liked each other, but we were both too shy to admit it, maybe because Andre was seven years older than I. Blushing, I asked him why he was there so early in the morning, and he explained that he had come to fix a broken vacuum cleaner.

"I haven't seen you in days," he said. "Where have you been? I called your house a few times, and your mother said you weren't feeling well. I was thinking about coming to your house today."

"I wasn't well. Just a cold or something."

He decided I looked too pale and should have stayed in bed for another couple of days, and I agreed. He offered to drive me, but I needed fresh air and walked home. If I wasn't so worried and depressed, I would have loved to spend time with him, but ever since my school friends, Sarah and Gita and Sarah's brother, Sirus, had been arrested and taken to Evin Prison, I had not been able to function. Sarah and I had been best friends since the first grade, and Gita had been a good friend of mine for more than three years. Gita had been arrested in mid-November and Sarah and Sirus on January 2. I could see Gita with her silky long brown hair and Mona Lisa smile, sitting on a bench by the basketball court. I wondered what had happened to Ramin, the boy she liked. She never heard from him after the summer of 1978, the last summer before the revolution, before the new order of the world. Now, she had been in Evin for more than two months, and her parents had not been allowed to see her. I called them once a week, and her mother always cried on the phone. Gita's mother stood at the door of their house for hours every day and stared at passersby, expecting Gita to come home. Sarah's parents had gone to the prison many times and had asked to see their children but had been denied.

Evin had been a political prison since the time of the shah. The name brought fear to every heart: it equaled torture and death. Its many buildings were scattered across a large area north of Tehran at the foot of the Alborz Mountains. People never talked about Evin; it was shrouded with fearful silence.

The night Sarah and Sirus were arrested, I had been lying on my bed, reading a collection of poems by Forough Farrokhzad when my bedroom door burst open and my mother appeared in the doorway.

"Sarah's mother just called . . ." she said.

I felt as if I were breathing shards of ice.

"Revolutionary guards arrested both Sarah and Sirus about an hour ago and took them to Evin."

I couldn't feel my body.

"What have they done?" my mother asked.

Poor Sarah and Sirus. They must have been terrified. But they were going to be fine. They had to be fine.

"Marina, answer me. What have they done?"

My mother closed my bedroom door behind her and leaned against it.

"Nothing. Well, Sarah has done nothing, but Sirus is a member of the Mojahedin." My voice sounded weak and distant to me. The Mojahedin-e Khalgh Organization was a leftist Muslim group that had fought against the shah since the 1960s. After the success of the Islamic revolution, its members opposed Ayatollah Khomeini's unlimited power as the supreme leader of Iran and called him a dictator. As a result, the Islamic government declared their party illegal.

"I see. Then maybe they took Sarah because of Sirus."

"Maybe."

"Their poor mother. She was beside herself."

"Did the guards say anything?"

"They told their parents not to worry, that they just wanted to ask them a few questions."

"So, they might let them go soon."

"Well, from what you're telling me I'm sure they'll let Sarah go soon. But Sirus . . . well, he should have known better. There's no need to worry."

My mother left my room, and I tried to think but couldn't. Feeling exhausted, I closed my eyes and fell into a dreamless sleep.

For twelve days after this, I slept most of the time. Even the thought of doing the simplest tasks felt tiring and impossible. I wasn't hungry or thirsty. I didn't want to read, go anywhere, or talk to anyone. Every night, my mother told me there was no news of Sarah and Sirus. Since they had been arrested, I knew I would be next. My name was on a list of names and addresses my chemistry teacher, Khanoom Bahman, had spotted in the principal's office—and our principal, Khanoom Mahmoodi, was a revolutionary guard. Khanoom Bahman was a good woman, and she had warned me that this list was addressed to the Courts of Islamic Revolution. However, there was nothing I could do but wait. I couldn't hide. Where would I go? The revolutionary guards were merciless. If they went to a house to arrest someone and that person was not home, they would take whoever was there. I couldn't risk my parents' lives to save myself. During the past few months hundreds of people had been arrested, accused of opposing the government in one way or another.

At nine o'clock at night, I went to take a bath. As soon as I turned the tap on and the water began to steam, the sound of the doorbell echoed in the house. My heart sank. No one rang our doorbell at this hour.

Turning the tap off, I sat on the edge of the tub. I heard my parents answer the door, and a few seconds later, my mother called my name. I unlocked the bathroom door and opened it. Two armed, bearded revolutionary guards wearing dark green military-style uniforms were standing in the hallway. One of them pointed his gun at me. I felt as though I had stepped out of my body and was watching a movie. This wasn't happening to me but to someone else, someone I didn't know.

"You stay here with them while I search the apartment," the second guard said to his friend and then turned to me and asked, "Where's your room?" His breath smelled of onions and made my stomach turn.

"Down the hallway, first door on your right."

My mother's body was shaking and her face had turned white. She had covered her mouth with her hand, as if to muffle a never-ending cry. My father was staring at me; he looked as if I were dying from a sudden, incurable disease and there was nothing he could do to save me. Tears fell down his face. I had not seen him cry since my grandmother's death.

The other guard soon came back with a handful of my books, all Western novels.

"Are these yours?"

"Yes."

"We'll take a few of them as evidence."

"Evidence of what?"

"Of your activities against the Islamic government."

"I don't agree with the government, but I haven't done anything against it."

"I'm not here to decide whether you're guilty or not; I'm here to arrest you. Put a chador on."

"I'm a Christian. I don't have a chador."

They were surprised. "That's fine," said one of them. "Put on a scarf and let's go."

"Where are you taking her?" my mother asked.

"To Evin," they answered.

With one of the guards following me, I went to my room, grabbed my beige cashmere shawl, and covered my hair with it. It was a very cold night, and the shawl was going to keep me warm, I decided. As we were about to step out of the room, my eyes fixed on my rosary, which sat on my desk. I took it.

"Hey, wait! What's that?" said the guard.

"My prayer beads. Can I bring them with me?"

"Let me see."

I handed him the rosary. He studied it, looking closely at each one of its pale blue stones and its silver cross.

"You can bring them. Praying is exactly what you need to do in Evin."

I dropped the rosary in my pocket.

The guards guided me to a black Mercedes parked at our door. They opened the back door, and I stepped in. The car started to move. I looked back and caught a glimpse of the bright windows of our apartment staring into darkness and the shadows of my parents standing in the doorway. I knew I was supposed to be terrified, but I wasn't. A cold void had surrounded me.

"I have a piece of advice for you," said one of the guards. "It's in your best interest to answer every question you're asked truthfully or you'll pay for it. You've probably heard that at Evin, they have their ways of making people talk. You can avoid the pain if you tell the truth."

The car speeded north toward the Alborz Mountains. At that hour, the streets were almost empty; there were no pedestrians and only a few cars. Traffic lights were visible from a distance, changing from red to green and back again. After about half an hour, in the pale moonlight, I saw the snakelike walls of Evin zigzagging across the hills. One of the guards was telling the other about his sister's upcoming marriage. He was very glad that the groom was a high-ranked revolutionary guard and from a well-to-do traditional family. I thought of Andre. A dull pain filled my stomach and spread into my bones, but it was as if something terrible had happened to him and not to me.

We entered a narrow, winding street, and the tall red brick walls of the prison appeared on our right. Every few yards, from lookout towers, floodlights poured their intense brightness into the night. We neared a large metal gate and came to a stop in front of it.

There were bearded, armed guards everywhere. The barbed wire covering the top of the wall cast a tangled shadow on the pavement. The driver stepped out, and the guard sitting in the front passenger seat gave me a thick strip of cloth and told me to blindfold myself. "Make sure it's on properly, or you'll get in trouble!" he barked. With my blindfold in place, the car passed through the gates and continued for two or three minutes before again coming to a stop. The doors were opened and I was instructed to step out. Someone tied my wrists with rope and dragged me along. I stumbled over an obstacle and fell.

"Are you blind?" a voice asked, and laughter followed.

Soon, it felt warmer, and I knew we had entered a building. A narrow strip of light appeared below my blindfold, and I saw that we were walking along a corridor. The air smelled of sweat and vomit. I was instructed to sit on the floor and wait. I could feel other people sitting close to me, but I couldn't see them. Everyone was silent, but vague, angry voices came from behind closed doors. Every once in a while, I filtered out a word or two: Liar! Tell me! Names! Write it! And, sometimes, I heard people scream in pain. My heart began to beat so fast, it pushed against my chest and made it ache, so I put my hands on it and pressed down. After awhile, a harsh voice told someone to sit next to me. It was a girl, and she was crying.

"Why are you crying?" I whispered.

"I'm scared!" she said. "I want to go home."

"I know, me too, but don't cry. It's not going to help. I'm sure they'll let us go home soon," I lied.

"No, they won't," she cried. "I'm going to die here! We're all going to die here!"

"You have to be brave," I said and regretted saying it right away. Maybe she had been tortured. How dare I tell her to be brave?

"This is very interesting," said a man's voice. "Marina, you're coming with me. Get up and walk ten steps ahead. Then turn right."

12

The girl was crying loudly now. I did as I was told. The voice instructed me to take four steps ahead. A door closed behind me, and I was told to sit on a chair.

"You were very brave out there. Bravery is a rare quality in Evin. I've seen many strong men fall apart here. So, you're Armenian?"

"No."

"But you told the guards you were Christian."

"I am a Christian."

"So, you're Assyrian?"

"No."

"You're not making any sense. Christians are either Armenian or Assyrian."

"Most Iranian Christians are, but not all. Both my grandmothers migrated to Iran from Russia after the Russian revolution."

My grandmothers had married Iranian men who worked in Russia before the 1917 Communist revolution, but after the revolution, their husbands were forced to leave the Soviet Union because they weren't Russian citizens, and my grandmothers chose to come to Iran with them.

"So they're communists."

"If they were communists, why would they leave their country? They left because they hated communism. They were both devout Christians."

The man told me that a part of the Holy Koran spoke about Mary, Jesus' mother. He said that Muslims believed that Jesus was a great prophet and that they had great respect for Mary. He offered to read that part of the Koran for me. I listened as he read the Arabic text. He had a deep and gentle voice.

"So, what do you think?" he asked when he finished reading. I wanted him to continue, knowing that I was safe as long as he kept on reading, but I also knew I couldn't trust him. He was probably a revolutionary guard and a violent man who tortured and killed innocents without remorse.

"It was very nice. I've studied the Koran, and I've read that passage before," I said. My words came out of my mouth slightly jagged.

"You've studied the Holy Koran? Now, this is even more interesting! A brave Christian girl who's studied our book! And you're still a Christian, even though you know about our prophet and his teachings?"

"Yes, I am."

My mother had always told me that I spoke without thinking. She mentioned this when I answered questions truthfully, when I did my best not to be misunderstood.

"Interesting!" the Koran reader said with a laugh. "I'd like to continue this conversation at a more appropriate time, but right now, Brother Hamehd is waiting to ask you a few questions."

It seemed like I had truly amused him. Maybe I was the only Christian he had ever seen in Evin. He probably had expected me to be like most Muslim girls from traditional families: quiet, shy, and submissive, and I didn't have any of these qualities.

I heard him rise from his chair and leave the room. I felt numb. Maybe this was a place beyond fear where all normal human emotions suffocated without the luxury of even a struggle.

I waited, thinking they had no reason to torture me. Torture was usually used to extract information. I didn't know anything that could be of any use to them; I didn't belong to any political groups.

The door opened and closed, and I jumped. The Koran reader had returned. He introduced himself as Ali and told me that Hamehd was busy interrogating someone else. Ali explained that he worked for the sixth division of the Courts of Islamic Revolution, which was investigating my case. He sounded calm and patient but warned me that I had to tell the truth. It was very strange to have a conversation with someone without being able to see him. I had no idea what he looked like, how old he was, or what kind of a room we were in.

He told me that he knew I had expressed antirevolutionary ideas in school and that I had written articles against the government in my school newspaper. I didn't deny it. This was not a secret or a crime. He asked me if I worked with any communist groups, and I said I didn't. He knew about the strike I had started at school and believed that it was impossible for an individual without any connections with illegal political parties to organize a strike. I explained that I had not organized anything, which was the truth. I had only asked the calculus teacher to teach calculus instead of politics. She had told me to get out of the classroom, I had, and my classmates had followed me, and before I knew it, most of the students had heard about what had happened and had refused to go back to class. He couldn't believe that it had been this simple, saying that the information he had received suggested I had strong connections to communist groups.

"I don't know where you get your information," I said, "but it's completely wrong. I've studied communism the same way I've studied Islam, and it hasn't made me a communist any more than it has made me a Muslim."

"I'm actually enjoying this!" he said, laughing. "Give me the names of all the communists or any other antirevolutionaries from your school, and I'll believe you aren't lying."

Why was he asking me for the names of my schoolmates? He knew about the strike and the school newspaper, so Khanoom Mahmoodi must have talked to him and given him her list. But I couldn't risk telling him anything, because I didn't know whose name, besides mine, was on the list.

"I won't give you any names," I said.

"I knew you were on their side."

"I'm not on anybody's side. If I give you names, you'll arrest them. I don't want that to happen."

"Yes, we'll arrest them to make sure they aren't doing anything against the government, and if they aren't, we'll let them go. But if they are, we'll have to stop them. They'll have nobody to blame except themselves."

"I won't give you any names."

"How about Shahrzad? Are you denying that you know her?"

For a moment, I didn't know who he was talking about. Who was Shahrzad? But I soon remembered. She was a friend of Gita's and was a member of a communist group named Fadayian-e Khalgh. About two weeks before the summer holidays, Gita had asked me to meet with her, hoping that Shahrzad would be able to talk me into joining their group. I met with her only once and explained to her that I was a practicing Christian and was not interested in joining any communist groups.

Ali told me that they had been watching Shahrzad, but she had realized she was being watched and had gone into hiding. They had been searching for her for some time and believed she might have met with me again. Ali said that Shahrzad must have had a better reason for meeting with me than talking me into joining the Fadayian; she was too important to waste her time like that. No matter how much I tried to explain to him that I had nothing to do with her, he wouldn't believe me.

"We have to know her whereabouts," he said.

"I can't help you, because I don't know where she is."

He had remained calm during the interrogation and had never raised his voice. "Marina, listen carefully. I can see that you're a brave girl, and I respect this, but I have to know what you know. If you aren't willing to tell me, Brother Hamehd will be very upset. He isn't a very patient man. I don't want to see you suffer."

"I'm sorry, but I don't have anything to tell you."

"I'm sorry, too," he said and led me out of the room and through three or four hallways. A man was screaming. I was told to sit on the floor. Ali said that, like me, the man who was screaming didn't want to share any information but that he would soon change his mind.

Pain-saturated cries filled the air around me. Heavy, deep, and desperate, they penetrated my skin, spreading into every cell of my body. The poor man was being torn apart. The world became a slab of lead sitting on my chest.

The loud, severe impact of the lash. The man's scream. A split second of silence. And the cycle repeated itself.

After a few minutes, someone asked the man if he was ready to talk. His answer was no. The lashing started again. Although my wrists were tied, I tried to cover my ears with my arms to push the screams away, but it was useless. It went on and on, strike after strike, scream after scream.

"Stop . . . please . . . I'll talk . . ." the suffering man finally cried.

It stopped.

Nothing mattered except the fact that I had decided not to give them any names. I was not helpless. I was going to put up a fight.

"Marina, how are you?" asked the voice that had questioned the suffering man. "Ali has told me all about you. You have impressed him. He doesn't want you to get hurt, but business is business. Did you hear that man? He didn't want to tell me anything at the beginning, but he did at the end. It would've been a lot smarter if he'd told me what I wanted to know at the start. Now, are you ready to talk?"

I took a deep breath. "No."

"Too bad. Get up."

He grabbed the rope that was tied around my wrists, dragged me along for a few steps, and then pushed me to the ground. My blindfold was pulled off. A thin, small man with short brown hair and a mustache stood over me, holding my blindfold in his hand. He was in his early forties and was wearing brown casual pants and a white shirt. The room was empty except for a bare wooden bed with a metal headboard. He untied my wrists.

"Rope won't do; we need something harder and stronger," he said. He took a pair of handcuffs out of one of his pockets and put them on my wrists.

Another man entered the room. He was about six feet one and two hundred pounds, had very short black hair and a trimmed black beard, and was in his late twenties.

"Hamehd, has she talked?" he asked.

"No, she's pretty stubborn, but don't worry; she'll talk soon."

"Marina, this is your last chance," the newcomer said. I recognized his voice. Ali. His nose was a little too large, his brown eyes were expressive, and his eyelashes were long and thick. "You're going to talk at the end anyway, so you'd better do it now. Will you give us the names?"

"No."

"What I really want you to tell me is where Shahrzad is."

"I don't know where she is."

"Ali, look; she has such small wrists! They'll slide out of the cuffs," said Hamehd. He forced both my wrists into one cuff and dragged me to the bed. The metal cuff dug into my bones. A scream escaped my throat, but I didn't struggle, knowing that my situation was hopeless and would only worsen if I put up a fight. He fastened the free cuff to the metal headboard. Then, after pulling off my shoes, he tied my ankles to the bed.

"I'm going to whip the soles of your feet with this cable," Hamehd said, waving a length of black cable, which was a little less than an inch thick, in front of my face.

"Ali, how many do you think it will take to make her talk?"

"Not many."

"I'm saying ten."

The sharp, threatening whistle of the cable cut the air, and it landed on the soles of my feet.

Pain. I had never experienced anything like it. I couldn't even have imagined it. It exploded inside me like a bolt of lightning.

Second strike: my breath stopped in my throat. How could anything hurt so much? I tried to think of a way to help myself bear it. I couldn't scream, because there wasn't enough air left in my lungs.

Third strike: the scream of the cable and the blinding agony that followed. The "Hail Mary" filled my head.

Blows came, one after the other, and I prayed, struggling against pain. I hoped to lose consciousness, but it didn't happen. Each strike kept me wide awake for the next.

Tenth strike: I begged God to ease the pain.

Eleventh strike: it hurt more than all the ones before it.

*God, please, don't leave me on my own. I can't take it.*

It went on and on. Endless agony.

*They'll stop if I give them a few names . . . No, they won't stop. They want to know about Shahrzad. I don't know anything about her anyway. The beating can't go on forever. I'll take it one at a time.*

After sixteen strikes of the lash, I gave up counting.

Pain.

"Where is Shahrzad?"

I would have told if I knew. I would have done anything to stop it.

Strike.

I had experienced different kinds of pain before. I had broken my arm once. But this was worse. Far worse.

"Where is Shahrzad?"

"I really don't know!"

Agony.

Voices.

When Hamehd stopped, I could just find enough energy to turn my head and see him leave the room. Ali removed the handcuffs and untied my ankles. My feet ached, but the agonizing pain was gone, replaced by a soothing emptiness that spread inside my veins. A moment later, I could hardly feel my body, and my eyelids began to feel heavy. Something cold splashed against my face. Water. I shook my head.

"You're passing out, Marina. Come on, sit up," said Ali.

He pulled on my arms, and I sat up. My feet were now stinging as if a hundred bees had stung them. I looked at them. They were red and blue and very swollen. I was surprised that my skin had not burst.

"Do you have anything to tell me now?" Ali asked.

"No."

"This isn't worth it!" He glared at me. "Do you want another beating? Your feet will look a lot worse if you don't talk."

"I don't know anything."

"This isn't bravery anymore! It's stupidity! You could easily be executed for not cooperating with the government. Don't do this to yourself."

"Don't do this to me," I corrected him.

He looked me straight in the eyes for the first time and told me that they had all the names from my school. Khanoom Mahmoodi had given them the list. He said that my cooperation would change nothing for any of my friends, but it would save me from torture. He said that my friends would be arrested whether I talked or not, but if I wrote down their names, I wouldn't have to suffer any longer.

"I believe that you're telling the truth about Shahrzad," he said. "Don't try to be a hero; you could lose your life for it. Hamehd is sure that you're a member of the Fadayian, but I don't think so. A Fadayee wouldn't pray to Mary under torture."

I hadn't realized I had prayed out loud.

I asked if I were allowed to go to the bathroom, and he took my arm and helped me up. I felt dizzy. He put a pair of rubber slippers on the floor in front of the bed. They were at least four sizes too big for me, but because of the swelling they were too small. It hurt to put them on. He helped me walk across the room. It was not easy to keep my balance. Once we got to the door, he let go of my arm, gave me my blindfold, and told me to put it on. I did. He put a length of rope in my hand and guided me to the bathroom door. I stepped in, turned on the tap, and washed my face with cold water. A sudden wave of nausea rushed through me, my stomach contracted, and I vomited. It felt like a knife had cut me in half. A loud ringing filled my ears, and darkness swallowed me.

When I opened my eyes, I didn't know where I was. As my mind gradually cleared, I realized I wasn't in the bathroom anymore but was lying on the wooden bed where I had been tortured. Ali sat on a chair, watching me. My head felt very sore, and when I touched it, I felt a big bump on the right side of my forehead. I

asked Ali what had happened, and he said I had fallen in the bathroom and had hit my head. He said that the doctor had seen me
and had said that my condition wasn't too serious. Then he helped
me sit in a wheelchair, put my blindfold back on, and pushed me
out of the room. When he took off the blindfold, we were in a very
small room with no windows and a toilet and a sink in the corner.
There were two gray military blankets on the floor. He helped me
lie down and spread one of them over me; it was rough and stiff
and smelled of mold, but I didn't care; I was freezing. He asked if I
was in pain, and I nodded, wondering why he was being nice to
me. He left but came back in a few minutes with a middle-aged
man wearing a military uniform whom he introduced as Doctor
Sheikh.

The doctor gave me some kind of injection in the arm, and he
and Ali left the cell. I closed my eyes and thought of home. I
wished I could crawl into my grandmother's bed as I used to when
I was a child, so she could tell me there was no reason to be scared,
that it had all been a nightmare.

# Three

As a young child, I loved the sleepy silence and dreamy colors of Tehran's early mornings: they made me feel light and free, almost invisible. This was the only time of day when I could wander inside my mother's beauty salon; I could walk between the styling chairs and hair dryers without making her angry. One morning in August 1972, when I was seven, I picked up her favorite crystal ashtray. It was almost the size of a dinner plate. She had told me a million times not to touch it, but it was beautiful, and I wanted to run my fingers over its delicate patterns. I could see why she liked it so much. In a way, it looked like a giant snowflake that never melted. As far back as I could remember, this ashtray had been in the middle of the glass table, and my mother's customers, women with long, red fingernails, sat in the waiting chairs, which were covered with a fuzzy white fabric, and flicked their cigarettes over it. Sometimes they missed, and the ashes landed on the table. My mother hated it when the table got dirty. Whenever I made a mess, she screamed at me and made me clean up. But what was the point of cleaning? Things got dirty all the time.

I held the ashtray up. A gauzy, golden light poured in through the room's only window, which covered more than half the southern wall. The light reflected off the white ceiling and spread inside the ashtray's sparkling, transparent body. As I tilted it to look at it from another angle, it slipped through my fingers. I tried to catch it, but I was too late: it hit the floor and shattered.

"Marina!" my mother called from my parents' bedroom, which was adjacent to the salon.

I ran to my left and through the door that led to the dark, narrow hallway, dashed to my bedroom, and crawled under my bed. The air smelled of dust and made my nose itch, so I held my breath to prevent a sneeze. Although I couldn't see my mother, I could hear the sound of her rubber slippers against the linoleum floor; their angry rhythm made me squeeze closer to the wall. She called my name again and again, but I remained as still as possible. When she entered my room and stood next to my bed, I heard my grandmother ask her what had happened. My mother told her that I had broken the ashtray, and Grandma said I had not broken it; she said she had dropped it while cleaning. I couldn't believe what I had heard. Grandma had told me that liars went to hell when they died.

"*You* broke it?" my mother asked.

"Yes. I was dusting the table. It was an accident. I'll clean up in a minute," Grandma answered.

After a little while, my bed creaked under someone's weight. I lifted my old beige bedspread a few inches from the floor and saw my grandmother's brown slippers and her slim ankles. I crawled out from under the bed and sat next to her. As always, her gray hair was gathered in a tight bun behind her head. She wore a black skirt and a perfectly ironed white blouse and stared straight ahead at the wall. She didn't look angry.

"Bahboo, you lied," I said.

"I lied."

"God won't get mad at you."

"Why not?" she raised an eyebrow.

"Because you saved me."

She smiled. My grandmother rarely smiled. She was a serious woman who knew how everything was supposed to be done. She always had the answer to the most difficult questions and had never failed to cure a stomachache.

Grandma was my father's mother and lived with us. She went grocery shopping at about eight o'clock every morning, and I usually went along with her. That day, like many others, she grabbed her purse, and I followed her down the stairs. As soon as she opened the pink wooden door at the bottom, the mixed sounds of cars, pedestrians, and vendors poured into the hallway. The first thing I saw was the toothless smile of Akbar Agha, who was at least eighty years old and sold bananas from a broken cart.

"Bananas today?" he asked.

My grandmother inspected the bananas; they were a healthy, spotless yellow. She nodded, brought up eight of her fingers, and Akbar Agha gave us eight bananas.

We turned left on Rahzi Avenue, a narrow, one-way street with dusty sidewalks. To the north, I could see the blue-gray Alborz Mountains resting against the sky. It was the end of summer, and the snowcaps of the mountains were long gone. Only Mount Damavand, the dormant volcano, had a touch of white on its peak. We crossed the road and walked through a cloud of steam saturated with the scent of clean, ironed linen flowing out of the open door of the dry cleaner's.

"Bahboo, why didn't you say eight in Persian? You know how."

"You know very well that I don't like to speak Persian. Russian is a much better language."

"I like Persian."

"We speak only Russian."

"In the fall when I go to school, I'll learn to read and write in Persian, and I'll teach you."

My grandmother sighed.

I skipped ahead. The street was quiet; there was hardly any traffic. Two women walked along, swinging their empty shopping bags beside them. When I entered the small general store, the owner, Agha-yeh Rostami, who had a thick black mustache that looked awkward on his thin, kind face, was talking to a woman with a black chador covering her from head to toe so that only her face remained visible. Another woman wearing a miniskirt and a tight T-shirt waited her turn. This was the time of the shah and women didn't have to dress according to Islamic rules. Although the store was small, its shelves were stocked with many different goods: long-grain rice, spices, dried herbs, butter, milk, Tabriz cheese, candy, skipping ropes, and plastic soccer balls. Giving me a carton of chocolate milk while handing the woman wearing the chador a brown paper bag, Agha-yeh Rostami smiled at me over the counter. As I drank my milk in large gulps, enjoying its silky coolness, Grandma came in and pointed at everything she needed. On our way back, we saw Agha Taghi, the old man who walked the streets at around this time every year and yelled out: "I card camel wool and cotton!" Women opened their windows and asked him to go inside their houses to prepare their duvets for winter by combing the wool or the cotton fibres inside them.

When we returned home from the store, I followed Grandma into the kitchen. Our two-burner oil stove was on the left, the white fridge on the right, and the dish cabinet stood against the wall opposite the door. With Grandma and me in the kitchen, there was hardly room to move. The kitchen's small window was close to the ceiling and beyond my reach and opened above the yard of an all-boys school. Grandma put the old stainless steel kettle on the stove to make tea and then opened the cabinet.

"Your mother has been in here again, and I can't find a thing! Where is the frying pan?"

From the other side of the cabinet, pots and pans spilled onto the floor. I rushed to help Grandma put them where they belonged. The kitchen was my grandmother's domain, and she was the one who took care of me and did all the housework. My mother spent about ten hours a day in her beauty salon and hated cooking.

"Don't worry, Bahboo; I'll help."

"And how many times have I told her to stay out of here?"

"A lot."

Soon, everything was back in place.

"Colya!" my grandmother called out to my father, who was probably in his dance studio. But there was no answer.

"Marina, go ask your father if he wants some tea," said Grandma, putting some of the groceries in the fridge.

I walked down the dark hallway opposite my mother's beauty salon and to my father's dance studio, which was a large L-shaped room with brown linoleum floors where pictures of elegantly dressed dancing couples hung on the walls. In the center of the waiting area—the smaller leg of the L—a round coffee table covered with magazines was surrounded by four black leather chairs. My father sat in one of them, reading the paper. He was five feet eight and fit, with gray hair, an always clean-shaven face, and amber eyes.

"Good morning, Papa. Bahboo wants to know if you would like a cup of tea."

"No," my father snapped without looking at me, and I turned around and retraced my steps.

Sometimes, when I woke up early in the morning and everyone else was still asleep, I went to my father's dance studio. I imagined the music, usually a waltz, because that was my favorite, and spun and danced around the room, imagining my father standing in a corner, clapping and saying, "Bravo, Marina! You really know how to dance!"

When I entered the kitchen, Grandma was chopping onions, tears rolling down her face. My eyes started to burn.

"I hate raw onions," I said.

"You'll appreciate them once you get older. Then, when you need to cry and don't want anyone to know you're crying, you can just chop onions."

"You're not really crying, are you?"

"No, of course not."

When my parents married, during the Second World War, they rented a modest apartment at the northwest corner of the intersection of Shah and Rahzi Avenues in downtown Tehran, the capital of Iran and its largest city. There, above a small furniture store and a small restaurant, my father, Gholamreza Nicolai Moradi-Bakht, opened his dance studio. Since many American and British soldiers passed through Iran during the war, Western culture became popular among the higher class, so my father found many faithful students who wished to learn to dance like Westerners.

My mother, Roghieh Natalia Fekri, gave birth to my brother in 1951. When he was about two years old, my mother went to Germany, even though she didn't speak German, to take a hairdressing course. When she returned six months later, she needed a place to open a beauty salon. There was another apartment identical to my parents' beside theirs, and they rented that one also and connected the two apartments.

I was born on April 22, 1965. Since 1941, the pro-Western and autocratic Mohammad Reza Shah-eh Pahlavi had been the king of Iran. Four months before my birth, Iranian premier, Hassan Ali-eh Mansur, was assassinated by reputed followers of Shia fundamentalist leader, Ayatollah Khomeini, who was pushing for a theocracy in

Iran. In 1971, Amir Abbas-eh Hoveida, who was the prime minister at the time, organized lavish festivities at the ancient ruins of Persepolis, commemorating the 2,500th anniversary of the founding of the Persian Empire. Twenty-five thousand guests from around the world, including kings and queens, presidents, prime ministers, and diplomats, attended this celebration, the expense of which reached $300 million. The shah announced that the purpose of this celebration was to show the world the progress Iran had made during recent years.

When I turned four, my brother left home to attend Pahlavi University in the city of Shiraz in central Iran. I was very proud of my tall, handsome brother, but he was rarely around and never stayed for too long. On those treasured occasions when he visited, he would fill my bedroom door frame, smiling at me and asking, "How is my little sister?" I loved the way the wonderful smell of his cologne saturated the air. He and Grandma were the only people who ever gave me gifts for Christmas. My parents thought Christmas was a complete waste of time and money.

Grandma took me to church every Sunday. The only Russian Orthodox Church in Tehran was a two-hour walk from our apartment. Our path to church took us through the streets of downtown Tehran, which were lined with stores, vendors, and ancient maple trees. The delicious aroma of roasted sunflower and pumpkin seeds floated in the air. Nahderi Avenue with its toy stores and bakeries was my favorite part of the trip. The scent of freshly baked pastries, vanilla, cinnamon, and chocolate was intoxicating. And there were many sounds, which became entangled and hung over the street: cars honking, vendors advertising their merchandise and haggling with their customers, and traditional music blaring. Grandma didn't believe in buying toys, but she always bought me a little treat.

One Sunday, we set out early enough to visit one of Grandma's friends who lived in a small apartment. She was an old, fussy Russian woman with short, curly blond hair, who always wore red lipstick and blue eye shadow and smelled like flowers. Her apartment was filled with old furniture and many knickknacks, and she had the most beautiful collection of china figurines. They were everywhere: on side tables, bookshelves, windowsills, and even on kitchen counters. I especially loved the angels with their delicate wings. She served her tea in the most beautiful china cups I had ever seen. They were white and shiny and had pink roses painted on them. She put tiny golden spoons next to each cup. I loved to drop sugar cubes in my tea and watch the bubbles rise as I stirred it.

I asked her why she had so many angels, and she told me that this was because they kept her company. She asked me if I knew that everyone had a guardian angel, and I said my grandma had told me this. Looking at me with her pale blue eyes, which seemed strangely large from behind her thick glasses, she explained that we all have seen our guardian angel but we have forgotten what our angel looks like.

"Now, tell me," she said, "has it ever happened to you that when you were about to do something kind of bad, you felt a whisper in your heart, telling you not to do it?"

"Yes . . . I think so." I thought of the ashtray.

"Well, that was your angel speaking to you. And the more you listen, the more you'll hear."

I wished I could remember my angel. My grandma's friend suggested that I should take a look at all her figurines, and she assured me that my angel looked like the one I liked the most. I examined the figurines for awhile and finally found my favorite: a handsome young man wearing a long white robe. I took it to Grandma to show it to her, and she said that it didn't exactly look like an angel because it didn't have any wings, but I told her that his wings were invisible.

"You can keep it, dear," Grandma's friend offered, and I was delighted.

\*   \*   \*

Grandma took me to the park every day. There was a big park, named Park-eh Valiahd, about a twenty-minute walk from home. We spent hours exploring it, admiring its ancient trees and fragrant flowers. To cool down on a hot summer day, we sat on a bench and licked ice cream cones. In the center of the park was a shallow pool with a fountain in the middle, which shot the water high into the air, and many small fountains gurgled around it. I always stood next to the pool and let the wind spray the water over me. Around the pool, there were bronze statues of young boys, each of them different from the other. One stood tall, looking toward the sky, another knelt next to the water, looking into it as if searching for a precious lost item, the next held a brass stick toward the water, and another had one leg poised in the air, as if he were ready to jump in. There was something terribly sad and lonely about these statues; they looked real but were perpetually frozen into a dark, solid state, unable to break free.

The greatest fun was being on a swing. Grandma knew I liked to go very high, and she always pushed me as hard as she could. I loved the way the wind brushed my hair and the world disappeared when I was up in the air. In my small seven-year-old world, this was how life was going to be forever.

One afternoon as I was running in the park, Grandma called me from a distance to say that it was time to go home, but she had called me by the wrong name; she had called me Tamara. Confused, I ran to her and asked her who Tamara was. She apologized to me and said it was better if we headed back home because it was too hot for her, so we started to walk. She looked tired, which was odd, because I had never seen her sick or tired before.

"Who's Tamara?" I asked again.

"Tamara is my daughter."

"But you don't have a daughter, only me, Bahboo, your grand-daughter."

She explained that she did have a daughter, Tamara, who was four years older than my father and I looked very much like her, as if we were twins. Tamara had married a Russian man at the age of sixteen and had returned to Russia with him. I asked why she had never visited us, and Grandma said that Tamara was not allowed to leave Russia: the Soviet government didn't allow its citizens to easily travel to other countries. My grandmother used to send Tamara nice clothes, soap, and toothpaste because those things are hard to find there, until she received a letter from SAVAK, the shah's secret police, saying that she was not allowed to communicate with anyone in the Soviet Union.

"Why?" I wanted to know.

"The police here believe that Russia is a bad country, so they told us that we weren't allowed to write to Tamara or to send anything for her."

As I was trying to understand this new information about an aunt I had never known, Grandma went on as if talking to herself. I couldn't make much sense of what she said. She mentioned names of people and places I had never heard of before and used words that were strange and unfamiliar to me, so I could only grasp bits and pieces of her sentences. She said that when she was eighteen years old, she had fallen in love with a young man who was later killed in the Russian revolution. She described a house with a green door on a narrow street, a wide river, and a large bridge, and she talked about soldiers on horses, shooting at a crowd.

". . . I turned around to see he had fallen," she said. "He had been shot. There was blood everywhere. I held him. He died in my arms . . ."

I didn't want to listen to her any longer, but she wouldn't stop. I couldn't cover my ears; it was rude and would upset her. Maybe I could walk faster and create some space between us, but something was wrong; she wasn't well, and I had to take care of her. Finally, I started humming, and my voice kept her words out of my head. She had always told me stories when I went to bed, but all those stories had happy endings, and no one was ever killed in them. I knew that good people went to heaven when they died, so death couldn't be too bad—but it still terrified me. It was like walking into absolute darkness where every terrible thing could happen to you. I didn't like darkness at all.

We had been walking toward home. She finally stopped talking and glanced around, looking lost and confused. Although we were almost there, I had to take her hand and lead her the rest of the way. The strong woman I had known all my life, the familiar companion I had relied on, the one who had always been there for me was suddenly vulnerable. She was just like a child, just like me. She, who had always listened and had rarely spoken more than a few words at a time, had told me her life story. Her words about blood, violence, and death had shocked me. My world had always been safe with her, but she had told me that nothing was here to stay. Somehow, I could feel that Grandma was dying. I had seen it in her eyes, as if it had been whispered to me in secret.

At home, I helped her to bed. She didn't join us for dinner, nor did she get out of bed the next morning. My parents took her to the doctor's office that day, and, when they returned, Grandma went straight to bed, and my parents didn't answer any of my questions about her illness.

I went to her room. She was asleep, so I sat on a chair next to her and waited for a long time until she finally moved. It was only then that I realized how thin and fragile she had become.

"What's wrong, Baliboo?" I asked.

"I'm dying, Marina," she said, as if this were a simple, everyday matter.

I asked her what happened to us when we died. She told me to look carefully at a painting that had been hanging on a wall in her bedroom since I could remember. She wanted me to tell her everything I saw in that painting. I said that it was the picture of an old lady with gray hair and a walking stick. She was walking on a path in a dark forest, and at the end of the path there was a bright light.

Grandma explained that she was like that old lady. She had walked through her life for many years and felt tired. She said her life had been dark and difficult, and she had faced many obstacles, but she had never given up.

"Now," she said, "it's simply my turn to go and finally see the face of God."

"But Bahboo," I protested, "why can't you see God's face here with me? I promise to let you rest, and you won't have to go anywhere."

She smiled. "Child, we can't see the face of God with these eyes," she said, touching my eyelashes with her trembling fingers, "but with our souls. You have to know that death is only a step we have to take to reach the other world and live, only in a different way."

"I don't want anything to change; I like things the way they are."

"You have to be brave, Marina."

I didn't want to be brave. I was afraid, and I was sad. Being brave sounded like being a liar, pretending that everything was okay. But nothing was okay.

She took a trembling breath and instructed me to go to her dresser and open the top left drawer. Inside it was a golden box. I brought it to her. Then she told me to crawl under her bed and bring out a pair of black shoes. Inside the left shoe was a small golden key.

With tears rolling down her face, she gave me the box and the key.

"Marina, I've written my life story, and I've put it in this box. It's yours now. I want you to have it and to remember me. Will you take care of it for Bahboo?"

I nodded.

"Put the box somewhere safe. Now go and don't worry. I need a little bit of rest."

I left her and took refuge in my room, which felt lonelier than ever before. I hid the box under my bed, opened the glass door that led to the balcony, and stepped outside. The air was warm and heavy, and the busy street was the same as always. Nothing had changed, but everything felt different.

Grandma never woke up. Liver cancer was killing her. My mother told me that she was in a coma. Grandma remained in a coma for almost two weeks, and my father walked up and down the hallway and cried. I sat next to Grandma for at least two hours a day to keep her company and not to feel so lonely myself. Her face was calm and peaceful, but very thin and pale. As days went by, I fought my tears, afraid that they would confirm her death and bring it closer.

One morning, I woke up very early and couldn't go back to sleep, so I went to Grandma's room. I turned on the light, and there she was. Her face had lost its color. I touched her hand; it felt cold. I stood in silence, knowing she was dead but not knowing what to do. I needed to say something to her, but I wasn't sure if she could hear me, if the barrier that death had created between us was penetrable at all.

"Good-bye, Bahboo. I hope you have a good life with God now, wherever He is."

I had an odd feeling that there was somebody else in the room with us. I ran back to my room, jumped in my bed, and said all the prayers I could remember.

The next day, Grandma's body was taken away. All day, I had listened to the sound of my father's crying. I covered my ears with my hands and looked around my room; there was nowhere to go. Grandma had been my refuge when bad things happened, and now she was gone. I finally grabbed my angel figurine from the top of my dresser and hid under my bed. I began to pray: "Hail Mary, full of grace, the Lord is with you. Blessed are thou amongst women, and blessed is the fruit of thy womb, Jesus. Holy Mary, Mother of God, pray for us sinners now and at the hour of our death."

*The covers were lifted from the side of my bed, and a wave of light poured into the darkness of my hiding spot. An unfamiliar face was looking at me. It was the face of a young man with black, curly hair and dark eyes, the darkest eyes I had ever seen. His face was extremely white against his hair and his smile was warm and kind. I wanted to ask him who he was, but I couldn't.*

*"Hello," he said.*

*His voice was gentle and soft, giving me the courage I needed. I crawled out from under the bed. He was wearing a long, white robe and was barefoot. I touched his toes. They felt warm. He bent down, lifted me, sat on my bed, and put me on his lap. A soft fragrance filled my nostrils; it was like the scent of daffodils on a rainy day.*

*"You were calling me and I came," he said and began to stroke my hair. I closed my eyes. His fingers moved along my hair, reminding me of the spring breeze braiding the warmth of the sun between the branches of waking trees. I leaned against his chest, feeling as if I knew him, as if we had met before, but where or when, I didn't know. I looked up, and he smiled a deep, warm smile.*

*"Why don't you have slippers on?" I asked.*

*"There's no need for slippers where I come from."*

*"Are you my guardian angel?"*

*"Who do you think I am?"*

*I looked at him for a moment. Only an angel could have eyes like his. "You are my guardian angel."*

*"You're right."*

*"What's your name?"*

*"I'm the Angel of Death."*

*My heart almost stopped.*

*"Death is sometimes difficult, but it's not bad or scary. It's like a journey to God, and because people usually die only once, they don't know the way, so I guide them and help them through."*

*"Are you here to take me with you?"*

*"No, not now."*

*"Did you help Bahboo?"*

*"Yes, I did."*

*"Is she happy?"*

*"She's very happy."*

*"Will you stay with me for a while?"*

*"I will."*

*I leaned against his chest again and closed my eyes. I had always wondered how birds felt as they glided on the wind, bathing in sunlight and blending with the sky. Now, I knew.*

When I woke the next morning, I was in my bed, and there were no angels.

# Four

I WOKE FROM A DREAMLESS SLEEP with a sharp pain in my right shoulder. Someone was calling my name. My vision was blurry. Hamehd stood over me, kicking my shoulder. I remembered that Ali had left me in a cell, but I had no idea how long I had been there.

"Yes, yes!" I said.

"Get up!"

My knees were shaky, and my feet were burning.

"You're coming with me to watch us arrest your friends," Hamehd said, "the ones you tried to protect. We had their names

39

and addresses all along. We just needed to know more about you, and you proved to us that you're an enemy of the revolution. You're a danger to Islamic society."

I was blindfolded once again. Hamehd tied my wrists with a length of rope and dragged me along. I was pushed into a car, and after a few minutes, someone removed my blindfold. We had left the prison. I wasn't sure what day or time it was, but it seemed like the early hours of the evening; the sky was cloudy and dim but not completely dark. We headed south on the narrow, winding street. There were hardly any cars or pedestrians. Old clay and brick walls stood on both sides of the road, encircling large properties, making the road seem like a dry riverbed. Bare trees reached toward the sky, trembling with the wind. Soon, we entered the Jordan Highway and continued south. This was a newer, upscale neighborhood. A high-rise condo building stood on one of the hills, surrounded by two-story houses and large bungalows. I looked at the driver. He had a thick black beard and was dressed in the green military-style uniform of revolutionary guards. Hamehd sat in the front passenger seat. They were both silent, looking ahead. At a set of traffic lights, from the backseat of a white car that had come to a stop next to us, a little girl, maybe three or four years old, smiled at me. A man and a woman sat in the front seats of that car, talking. I wondered what my parents were doing. Were they trying to help me, or had they given up hope? I knew very well that there was nothing they could do. How about Andre? Was he thinking of me?

We entered the downtown core. Traffic was quite heavy here, and sidewalks and stores were full of people. Every single wall was covered with the Islamic government's slogans and Khomeini's quotes. One of them caught my eye: "If one permits an infidel to continue in his role as a corrupter of the earth, the infidel's moral suffering will be all the worse. If one kills the infidel, and this stops him from perpetrating his misdeeds, his death will be a blessing to him." Yes, in Khomeini's world, murder could be considered a good deed, a "blessing." So Hamehd could put a gun to my head, pull the trigger, and believe that he had done me a favor and that he himself would go to heaven because of it.

Pedestrians wove between cars to cross the street. At an intersection, a young man looked inside our car and, noticing the guard behind the wheel, took a step back and stared at me. It had started to snow.

The car stopped. We were at Minoo's house; she was a school friend of mine. Another black Mercedes parked beside ours. Two guards stepped out of it, went to Minoo's door, and rang the doorbell. Someone opened the door. It was her mother. The guards went into the house. Hamehd turned around and handed me a sheet of paper. I looked at it. There were about thirty names on it. I knew them all; they were kids from my school. I recognized my principal's signature under it. The sheet of paper I held in my hands was my school's most-wanted list.

"We won't be able to arrest them all tonight, but we should have them in three days or so," Hamehd said with a smile.

The guards left the house in about half an hour. Minoo was with them. Hamehd stepped out of the car, opened one of the back doors, and told her to sit next to me. I could see her mother crying and speaking to one of the guards. Hamehd told Minoo that I had been arrested a couple of days earlier. He told me to tell Minoo to cooperate if I didn't want her to suffer.

Minoo stared at me, her eyes wide with terror.

"Tell them whatever they want to know," I said, pointing at my feet. "They—"

"That will do," Hamehd interrupted.

Minoo looked at my feet, covered her face with her hands, and started to cry.

"Why are you crying?" Hamehd asked her, but she didn't answer.

We were in the car for what seemed like hours. We went from house to house. Four of my schoolmates were arrested that night. I tried to whisper to Minoo that she should give the guards a few names during her interrogation. I tried to tell her that they had a list and knew everything, but, at the end, I wasn't sure if she had understood me.

We were blindfolded as soon as we arrived at the prison gates. When the car came to a stop, the door on my side opened and Hamehd instructed me to step out. I limped after him into a building, and he told me to sit on the floor in the hallway. I sat there for a long time, listening to the prisoners' cries and screams. My head was throbbing, and I felt sick to my stomach.

"Marina, get up." Hamehd's voice made me jump. I had dozed off.

I managed to find my balance, leaning against the wall for support. He told me to hang on to the chador of a girl who was standing in front of me. I held on, she started to walk, and I limped after her. My feet were burning as if I were walking on broken glass. Soon outside, we walked on, and the cold wind whipped against me. The girl in front of me started to cough. The snow on the ground filled my rubber slippers, numbed my feet, and helped with the pain, but I was slowly losing the feeling in my legs, and each step was more difficult than the one before. I stumbled over a rock and fell. Resting my head on the frozen earth, I licked the snow, desperate to relieve the bitter-tasting dryness of my mouth. I had never been so cold or thirsty. My body was shaking out of control, and the sound of my chattering teeth filled my head. Rough hands lifted me off the ground and forced me back on my feet.

*Where are they taking me?*

"Walk properly or I'll shoot you right here!" Hamehd barked.

I struggled on. We were finally told to stop, and someone removed my blindfold. An intense light shone into my face, blinded me, and created a sharp bolt of pain that exploded in my head. After a few seconds, I looked around. A spotlight cut the night like a white, sparkling river. Blending into ghostly shadows, black hills surrounded us. We seemed to be in the middle of nowhere; there were no buildings close by. The night sky was patched with clouds gliding against a lace of sparkling stars. A few snowflakes floated lightly in the air, trying to prolong their crystalline flight before facing an earthly death. There were four other prisoners with me: two girls and two young men. Four revolutionary guards were pointing their guns at us, their faces expressionless as if carved out of the darkness. "Move next to the poles!" Hamehd yelled out, his voice echoing against the hills. Twenty feet away, a few wooden poles, which were my height, reached out of the ground. We were about to be executed. The cold feeling inside my chest paralyzed me.

*This is the moment of my death. No one deserves to die like this.*

One of the two male prisoners began to recite in Arabic a part of the Koran that asked God for forgiveness. His voice was deep and strong. The other young man was staring at the poles. One of his eyes was swollen shut, and there were bloodstains on his white shirt. "Next to the poles right now!" Hamehd repeated, and we silently obeyed. Sorrow filled my heart and lungs like a thick suffocating liquid.

*Dear Jesus, help me. Don't let my soul be lost into darkness. "Even though I walk through the valley of the shadow of darkness, I do not fear; for you are with me."*

One of the girls started to run. Someone yelled, "Stop!" But she kept on going. A gunshot tore through the night, and she fell to the ground. I took a step forward, but my legs gave way. The girl moved onto her side, and her back curved in pain. "Please . . . please don't kill me," she moaned. The snow covering her chador glittered in the clean, white light. Pointing a gun to her head, Hamehd stood over her. She covered her head with her arms.

The girl standing next to me began to cry. Her deep screams seemed to rip her chest. She fell to her knees.

"Tie the others to the poles!" Hamehd yelled.

One of the guards lifted me off the ground and another tied me to the pole. The rope dug into my flesh.

I was so tired.

*Is dying going to hurt as much as being lashed?*

Hamehd was still pointing his gun at the injured girl.

"Guards! Ready!"

*Death is only a place I've never been. And the angel is going to help me find my way. He has to. There's light beyond this terrible darkness. Somewhere beyond the stars, the sun is rising.*

They aimed their guns at us, and I closed my eyes.

*I hope Andre knows I love him. Hail Mary, full of grace, the Lord is with you . . .*

I heard a car speeding toward us and opened my eyes. For a moment, I thought we were going to be run over. There was a loud screeching noise, and a black Mercedes came to a stop right in front of the guards. Ali stepped out of it. He went straight to Hamehd and gave him a piece of paper. They spoke for a moment. Hamehd nodded. His eyes focused on mine, Ali walked toward me. I wanted to run. I wanted Hamehd to shoot me and end my life. Ali untied me from the pole. I collapsed. He caught me, lifted me, and walked toward the car. I could feel his heartbeat against my body. I uselessly tried to struggle out of his arms.

"Where are you taking me?"

"It's okay; I won't hurt you," he whispered.

My eyes met the eyes of the girl tied to the pole next to mine.

"God . . ." she screamed and closed her eyes.

Ali dropped me in the front passenger seat of his car and slammed the door. I tried to open it, but it wouldn't open. He jumped in the driver's seat. Gathering all my strength, I began punching him, but he held me back with one hand. Guns fired as we sped away.

I opened my eyes to a lightbulb shining over me. There was a gray ceiling. I tried to move but couldn't feel my body. Ali sat in a corner, staring at me. We were in a small cell, and I was lying on the floor.

I closed my eyes and wished he would go away, but when I

opened my eyes a couple of minutes later, he was still sitting there. He shook his head and said that I had brought all this upon myself by being stubborn. He said he had gone to Ayatollah Khomeini, who was a close friend of his father's, to have my sentence reduced from death to life in prison. The ayatollah had given the order to spare my life.

I didn't want the ayatollah to save me. I didn't want anyone to save me. I wanted to die.

"I'm going to get you something to eat now. You haven't eaten for a long time," he said without taking his eyes off me. But he didn't move. Feeling the weight of his stare on my skin, I held the blanket covering me so tightly that my fingers began to hurt. He finally stood up. Every muscle in my body tightened.

"Are you afraid of me?" he asked.

"No." I swallowed.

"You don't need to be."

The longing in his eyes was deep and real. My stomach hurt. I could feel a scream forming in my throat, but he turned around and left the cell. My body shook with every tear that streamed down my face. I hated him.


Ali came back with a bowl of soup and sat next to me.

"Please, don't cry."

I couldn't stop.

"Do you want me to leave?"

I nodded.

"I'll leave only if you promise to finish the soup. Do you promise?"

I nodded again.

He paused at the door and turned around, saying, "I'll check on you later," with a tired, heavy voice.

What was going to happen to me? Why had he taken me away from the firing squad? I didn't know.

My last thought before I fell asleep was of Sarah. I hoped she was all right. All I could do was to pray for both of us and for Sirus and Gita and all my friends who had been arrested.

It wasn't too long ago when we were all in school, playing tag and hide-and-go-seek at recess. Now we were political prisoners.

# Five

I ATTENDED AN ELEMENTARY SCHOOL with vine-covered red brick walls. This was during the time of the shah. My school was a ten-minute walk from home, so I walked there and back by myself. The old school building was originally a two-story mansion, and my friends had told me that the principal, Khanoom Mortazavi, who had gone to university abroad, had turned it into a school once she had returned to Iran. Although every classroom had tall windows, because of a few ancient maple trees that grew in the yard, it was always dark inside, and we usually had to turn on the lights in order to be able to see the blackboard. Every day, after the final bell, Sarah and I would step out of school and cross the street together, but then she would turn left and I would turn right. I would continue south on Rahzi Avenue and walk past the tall brick walls surrounding the Vatican embassy, past Ashna restaurant, which filled the air with the smell of aromatic rice and barbecued beef, and past a small lingerie store with a window displaying lacy, delicate nightgowns. Without my mother dragging me along and telling me to walk properly, I sometimes pretended to be a little white cloud drifting across the blue sky, a ballerina dancing in front of a large crowd, or a boat traveling down a magical river.

As long as I wasn't too late in getting home, I didn't need to rush, but I always had to be careful not to upset my mother. If she had customers, I had to stay out of the beauty salon, and if she didn't, I had to be very quiet, because she usually had a headache. I was clumsy, and I had to be careful not to break anything and not to make a mess while fixing myself a sandwich, and when pouring iced tea or Pepsi in a cup, I had to be careful not to spill my drink. My mother was short-tempered and beautiful. She had brown eyes, a perfect nose, full lips, and long legs and loved to wear dresses with open necklines to show off her smooth white skin. Every strand of her short dark hair was always obediently in place. If I made her angry, she would lock me on the balcony that was connected to my bedroom. My balcony was enclosed by bamboo shades leaning against two horizontal and a few vertical metal poles. From here, I would watch cars and pedestrians filling the street, vendors advertising their merchandise, and beggars begging. The paved four-lane street seethed with traffic during rush hours and the air smelled of exhaust fumes. On the other side of the street, Hassan Agha, the vendor who had only one arm, sold sour green plums in spring, peaches and apricots in summer, cooked red beets in autumn, and offered different kinds of cookies in winter. I loved the cooked beets; they slowly simmered in a shallow, large pan over the flames of a portable burner, and their sticky juices bubbled and steamed, making the air sweet. At the other corner of the intersection, an old blind man wearing a torn, dirty suit held his bony hands to the passersby and cried "Help me, for the love of God" from morning till night. In front of our apartment stood a fifteen-story office building with large, mirrored windows sparkling in the sun, reflecting the movement of the clouds. At night, the bright neon lights above stores came on and colored the darkness.

One day, I decided that any punishment was better than being locked up on the balcony. I looked down; jumping was impossible. I could scream, but I didn't want to make a scene and let the whole neighborhood know how my mother locked me on the balcony. Looking around, I fixed on the small plastic bag in which my mother kept her wooden clothespins. I looked down at the busy sidewalk again. If I dropped the clothespins on passersby, they wouldn't get hurt, but they would want to find out what had fallen on their heads from the sky. Then I could tell them about the clothespins and beg them to ring the doorbell and ask my mother to let me inside. I knew that my mother would get angry, but I didn't care; I couldn't bear my solitary confinement any longer. It was winter and a cold wind had begun to blow. Soon, the sun disappeared behind the clouds, and snowflakes began landing on my face. Collecting all my courage, I grabbed one pin, and, leaning on the bamboo shades surrounding the balcony, held it over the sidewalk, took a deep breath, and dropped it. It didn't land on anyone, just on the pavement. I tried again and succeeded. A middle-aged woman with long brown hair, stopped, touched her head, and looked around. Then, she bent forward, picked up the pin, and examined it. Finally, looking up, she looked straight into my eyes.

"Little girl, what are you doing?" she asked, her face a deep red.

"I'm sorry. I didn't mean to hurt you, but my mother locked me up here on the balcony, and I want to go inside. It's cold. Will you please ring the doorbell and ask my mother to let me in?"

"I certainly will not! It's none of my business how your mother punishes you. By the looks of it, you probably deserve it," she said and walked away. But I wasn't going to give up.

Next time, the pin landed on the head of an older woman wearing a black chador, and she looked up right away.

"What are you doing?" she asked, and I told her my story.

She rang the doorbell. Soon my mother appeared on the other balcony, which was only a few feet away from mine, and looked down, asking, "Who is it?"

As the woman told my mother what I had done and why, I watched my mother's eyes darken with anger. After a minute, the door of my balcony opened. I hesitated.

"Get in now," my mother said between her teeth.

I stepped into my bedroom.

"You are a terrible child!" she said.

I shivered. I was expecting her to slap me, but instead, she turned around and walked away. "I'm leaving. I'm tired. I hate this life. I don't want to ever see you again!"

My stomach hurt. She couldn't possibly leave, or could she? She sounded serious. What would I do without a mother? I ran after her and grabbed her skirt. She didn't stop.

"Please don't leave! I'm sorry!" I begged, "I'll go back on the balcony, and I'll stay there without causing trouble. I promise."

Ignoring me, she walked to the kitchen, grabbed her purse, and walked toward the stairs. Panicked, I started crying, but she didn't stop. I grasped one of her legs, but she continued down the stairs, dragging me along. The stairs were hard and cold against my skin. I begged her to stay. She finally stopped at the door.

"If you want me to stay, go in your room, stay there, and don't make a sound."

I stared at her.

"Now!" she screamed, and I ran to my room.

For awhile after that, every time my mother stepped out of the house to go to the store or to run an errand, I sat by the window and shook with fear. What if she never returned?

\* \* \*

I decided to stay out of my mother's way, and the best way to achieve this was to stay in my room as long as possible. Every day, as soon as I arrived home from school, I tiptoed to the kitchen to see if my mother was there. If she wasn't, I fixed myself a bologna sandwich, and if she was, I said a quick hello and then went to my room and waited for her to leave the kitchen. After eating, I stayed in my room, did my homework, and read the books I had borrowed from my school library. Most of these books were translations: *Peter Pan, Alice in Wonderland, The Little Mermaid, The Snow Queen, The Steadfast Tin Soldier, Cinderella, The Sleeping Beauty, Hansel and Gretel,* and *Rapunzel.* My school library was small, and soon I had read all its books not only once, but three or four times. A couple of times every night, my mother opened the door of my bedroom to see what I was doing and smiled when she found me reading. In a way, books had saved us both.

One day, I gathered all my courage and asked my mother if she would buy me books, and she said she could buy me only one book a month because books were expensive and we couldn't spend all our money on them. But one book a month wasn't enough. A few days later, when my mother and I were walking home after visiting her father, I noticed a small bookstore. The sign read: Secondhand Books. I knew "secondhand" meant cheap, but I didn't dare ask my mother to check it out.

One week later, when my mother told me it was time for us to visit my grandfather, I told her I wasn't feeling well, and she agreed to let me stay home. My father was at work. Not too long after Grandma's death, he had closed down his dance studio and had found a job at a division of the Ministry of Arts and Culture, working with folklore dance groups. He liked his new job and sometimes traveled to different countries with the dancers, young men and women who represented Iran at different international events. As soon as my mother left the house, I ran to my parents' bedroom and took my mother's spare house keys from the drawer of her dresser. I had saved all my chocolate-milk money for a week and hoped it would be enough for a book.

I ran to the secondhand bookstore. All day, the late-spring sun had shone on the black asphalt, creating quivering waves of heat, which rose into the air and pushed against me. When I arrived at the bookstore, drops of sweat were dripping down my forehead and into my eyes, making them burn. I wiped my face with my T-shirt, pushed open the glass door of the store, and stepped in. Once my eyes adjusted to the low level of light, I couldn't believe what I saw. All around me, piles of books were stacked on bookshelves up to the ceiling, leaving only narrow tunnels that disappeared into darkness. I was surrounded by thousands of books. The air was heavy with the scent of paper, of stories and dreams that lived in written words.

"Hello?" I called.

There was no answer.

"Hello?" I called again, a little louder this time.

From the depths of one of the book tunnels, a man's voice called, "How can I help you?" in a thick Armenian accent.

I took a step back, calling, "Where are you?"

Right in front of me, a gray shadow came into focus. I gasped.

The shadow laughed.

"I'm sorry, little girl. I didn't mean to scare you. What do you want?"

I had to remind myself to breathe.

"I . . . I want to buy a book."

"What book?"

I took all my money out of my pocket and showed the coins to the thin, old man standing in front of me.

"I have this much money. Doesn't matter what book, as long as it's good."

He smiled and ran his fingers through his gray hair.

"Why don't you go to the bakery next door and buy yourself a few donuts instead?"

"But I want a book. Isn't this money enough?"

"Young lady, the problem is that all my books are written in English. Do you speak English?"

"I'm very good in English. In school, we study English for an hour every day. I'm in the third grade."

"Okay, let's see what I can find for you," he said with a sigh and disappeared behind the book mountains.

I waited, wondering how he could possibly find anything in that mess, but he miraculously emerged from the dark clutter with a book.

"Here you go," he said, handing it to me. "*The Lion, the Witch, and the Wardrobe*. It's a wonderful book and the first one of a series."

I examined it. It had a blue-gray cover in the center of which was the picture of a lion with a boy and a girl sitting on its back. The lion had leaped into the air. The book looked old but was in a reasonably good shape.

"How much does it cost?"

"Five tomans."

"But, I only have four!" I said, almost in tears.

"Four will do."

I thanked him, ecstatic, and ran home.

Three days later, I had read *The Lion, the Witch, and the Wardrobe* twice and had fallen in love with it. I wanted more. But only having two tomans saved, I wasn't sure if the man at the bookstore was going to be generous again, and I was afraid to ask my mother for money, so I decided to sell my pencil box to my friend Sarah. At the beginning of the school year, Sarah had asked me where I had bought the box, and I had told her that my mother had bought it at the big department store at the intersection of Shah and Pahlavi Avenues. But when Sarah's mother went to buy one like mine, they were sold out, and Sarah was very disappointed. It was a blue plastic box with a magnetic lock that clicked when you closed its lid. The next day, I caught up with Sarah on my way to school. She had large dark brown eyes, thick curly black hair that fell on her shoulders, and she owned a fancy watch, on the face of which was a picture of Cinderella with Prince Charming putting a glass slipper on her foot. Cinderella was sitting on a stool and had crossed one leg over the other, and her leg moved back and forth every second. Sarah's mother had bought the watch for her when they were vacationing in England. I asked her if she still wanted my pencil box, and she said she did. I told her I was willing to sell it to her. She wanted to know why, sounding rather suspicious. So I told her about the bookstore. She agreed to give me five tomans if I also gave her my scented eraser. I accepted her condition.

After school, it took Sarah and me less than five minutes to run to her house, which was on a narrow residential crescent where all houses had small yards and were surrounded by tall brick walls to provide privacy for the residents. I loved her street, because without cars, stores, vendors, and beggars, it was quiet. The air was filled with the mouthwatering fragrance of sautéed onions and garlic. One of the neighbors was probably making dinner. Sarah had a house key because both her parents worked and didn't return home until later in the day. She opened the door, and we stepped in her yard. On our right, a small flower bed overflowed with the reds, greens, and purples of geraniums and pansies.

I secretly wished to live in a house like Sarah's. Her mother, who worked at the bank and always wore elegant suits and very high-heeled shiny black shoes, was a small, round woman with short black hair. She hugged me whenever I went for a visit, telling me how wonderful it was to have me over. Sarah's father was an engineer and a big man, who always told funny jokes, laughed loudly, and recited beautiful old poems. Sarah's only brother, Sirus, was twelve, three years older than Sarah and me, and, unlike the rest of his family, was very shy. Sarah's house was always colored with noise and laughter.

I gave Sarah the pencil box, and she gave me the money. Then I called my mother and told her that I was at Sarah's to help her with homework. My mother didn't mind. I thanked Sarah and ran to the bookstore to find it as dark, dusty, and mysterious as my first visit. Again, the old man emerged from the darkness.

"Let me guess: you couldn't understand a word, and now you want your money back," he said, narrowing his eyes.

"No. I read it twice, and I loved it! I didn't understand a few words, but I used my father's dictionary. I'm here to buy the second book of the series. Do you have it? I sold my pencil box and my scented eraser to my friend, Sarah, so I have enough money this time."

The old man stared at me and didn't move. My heart sank. Maybe he didn't have the second book.

"So, do you have it?"

"Yes, I do. But . . . you don't have to pay for it; you can borrow it if you promise to take good care of it and return it when you have read it. Twice."

I thought of my angel. Maybe he was pretending to be an old man. I looked into the old man's eyes, and they seemed almost as dark, deep, and kind as the angel's eyes. I looked at the book; it was *Prince Caspian*.

"What's your name?" he asked.

"Marina. What's your name?"

"Albert," he answered.

Hmm. An angel named Albert.

From that day on, I went to visit Albert and to borrow books from him at least once a week.


I went to junior high at the age of eleven. At the time, the government funded all schools and universities in Iran, but some schools had proven themselves better than others, and Anooshiravan-eh Dadgar, which was a Zoroastrian junior high and high school for girls, was one of them. My parents didn't choose this school for me because it was one of the best but simply because it was close to our apartment.

Zoroastrians follow the teachings of their prophet Zarathushtra. Born in Persia almost three thousand years ago, he invited people to believe in the one and only God: Ahura Mazda. During my time at the school, the majority of students were either Zoroastrians or Muslims, but there were also Bahais, Jews, and only three or four Christians.

The high ceilings and many windows of the school's forty-year-old main building made it feel very spacious. The long hallways seemed endless, and two wide stairways connected the first floor to the second. Two-story pillars stood on both sides of the main entrance, above which, in large letters, it read: Good Thoughts, Good Words, Good Deeds—the main motto of the Zoroastrian faith. We had a separate gym building with basketball and volleyball courts, and tall brick walls surrounded the paved schoolyard.

For three years, my visits to Albert's bookstore were the highlight of my life. Albert had read all the hundreds of books that were piled up in his store, knew exactly where each one of them was located, and loved to talk about them. He had a wife and a son and told me that his son, who was married and had two boys, had moved to America two years earlier. The Christmas after we first met, Albert gave me a package wrapped in red paper. I opened it to find *The Narnia Collection* and a beautiful blue pencil box filled with colored pencils and erasers that smelled like bubblegum.

The last time I saw Albert was a few days after my twelfth birthday, a beautiful spring day filled with bird songs and warm sunshine. Smiling, I opened the heavy glass door to Albert's bookstore, holding *Little Women* close to my heart.

"Hi, Al—"

Dust particles floated in the stream of sunlight that poured onto the linoleum floor. The empty store stretched in front of me. It was as if I were standing at the edge of a desert. Feeling like a strong, fierce wind had just rushed against me, I gasped and tried to breathe. Albert sat on a large cardboard box in the middle of the terrible emptiness, looking at me with a sad smile.

"Where are the books?" I asked him.

He told me he had sold most of them to another bookstore but had saved all my favorites. They were in the box he was sitting on. He promised to bring them to my house later. He had wanted to tell me earlier, but he wasn't able to. He and his wife would soon leave Iran to join their son in America. Albert didn't want to go, but his wife was not well and wanted to spend the time she had left with their son and grandchildren. He couldn't refuse her. They had been married for fifty-one years, and this was her last wish.

He took a white handkerchief out of the pocket of his shirt and blew his nose. My arms and legs felt weak. He stood up, came to me, and put his hands on my shoulders.

"I watched you grow. You brought joy and happiness to my life. I'll miss you. You're like a daughter to me."

I wrapped my arms around him and held him tight. Moving to America felt as splitting and eternal as death.

# Six

I WOKE WITH THE TASTE of chicken soup in my mouth. I was sitting up. The world seemed to be covered with a thick fog and was spinning around me. There weren't any solid lines or shapes, only vague colors. Someone was calling my name. Chicken soup again. I coughed.

"Swallow it. It's good for you."

The warm liquid washed down my throat. It was good. I swallowed again. There was a bright, white square in front of me. I tried to focus. It was a small, barred window. I was achy and feverish.

"That's better," said the voice. It was coming from behind me. I tried to move.

"Don't move, swallow."

It hurt to move. I swallowed. Some of the soup was dripping down my chin.

The cell slowly came into focus.

"I'm going to let you lie down now," the voice said. It was Ali's.

He sat on the floor about two or three feet away from me and said he was going to send me to a women's dorm in Evin, named 246, where I would see a few of my friends and would feel better. He said he knew one of the guards in charge of 246 and would ask her to look after me. Her name was Sister Maryam.

"I'm going away for a while . . ." he said and then kept his eyes on me in silence, as if waiting for me to say something. I had no idea what kind of a place 246 was. Had he really told me that I had a life sentence or had I dreamt it?

"Do I really have a life sentence?" I asked.

He nodded, the shadow of a sad smile crossing his face.

I tried not to cry, but I couldn't help it. I wanted to ask him why he had saved me from execution. I wanted to tell him that death was better than a life sentence. I wanted him to know that he had no right to do what he had done—but I couldn't.

He stood and said, "May God protect you," and left.

I slept.

After a few hours, he came back and took me to the door of a small room where about twenty girls were sleeping side by side on the floor.

"You'll have to wait in this room until they come and take you to 246. Take care of yourself. Things will get better. Put on your blindfold after you sit down."

I spotted a small empty space in a far corner of the room. I was still dizzy, and my feet hurt, so it took me a great deal of effort to reach it without stepping on anyone. No one had reacted to my arrival. There wasn't enough space to lie down, so I sat, folded my knees to my chest, leaned against the wall, and cried.

After awhile, a man yelled out about ten names, including mine.

"All the people I've called pull their blindfolds up just a little so they can see where they're going and line up in front of the door here. Each of you has to hang on to the chador of the person ahead of you. Don't forget; raise the blindfold just a little. If I see anyone peeping around too much, they'll be sorry, and once you've found your place in the line, fix your blindfolds and make sure they're tight."

I grasped the chador of the girl in front of me, and the person behind me grabbed my shawl. We went through a couple of corridors and were soon outside. It was cold. I prayed for us to arrive at our destination soon because I was close to collapsing. All I could see were the gray pavement and the chador and the feet of the girl ahead of me. Her feet were not swollen, but she had rubber slippers on, which were similar to mine and at least two sizes too big for her. I wondered what had happened to my shoes. We entered a building, followed a hallway, and climbed a couple of flights of stairs. Then the guard told us to stop, called my name, and told me to step out of the line.

"Grab this rope and follow me," he said.

I took the rope and followed him through a doorway.

"*Salam aleikom*, Sister. Good morning. I have a new one for you: Marina Moradi-Bakht. Here're the papers."

"Good morning to you, too, Brother. Thank you," said a woman.

The door closed with a small click. The room was filled with the scent of freshly brewed tea. I realized I was starving.

"Marina, take off your blindfold," the woman said with a demanding voice, and I obeyed. She was about twenty-five years old and ten inches taller than I, with large dark eyes, a large nose, and narrow lips; features that had come together to create a very serious face. She was wearing a black chador. I wondered if she had ever smiled in her life.

The room we were in was an office of some sort. It was about fourteen by twelve feet with a desk, four metal chairs, and a plain metal desk covered with piles of paper. Through the barred window, the morning's yellow sunlight reached across the floor.

"Marina, I'm Sister Maryam," the woman said. "Brother Ali has told me about you." She explained that the building we were in, 246, had two floors, the first floor with six rooms and the second with seven. I was to stay in room 7 on the second floor. Then she called a name over the loudspeaker. Within a few minutes, a girl about my age entered the office. Sister Maryam introduced her as Soheila. She was a prisoner and the representative of room 7.

Soheila had short brown hair and was wearing a blue sweater and black pants, and her hair wasn't covered. I guessed that since 246 was a women's building, we didn't have to wear the *hejab* all the time. The office doors opened into an empty foyer, which was about twenty-five feet long and nine feet wide, and, as we crossed it, I noticed the stairs that led downstairs. I limped after Soheila and fell behind. She stopped, turned around, and stared at my feet.

"I'm sorry . . . I didn't realize . . . Here, put your arm around my shoulder. I'll help you."

We came to a barred metal door, Soheila pushed it open, and we stepped into a narrow hallway. There were girls everywhere. We passed by three doors and followed the hallway as it turned at a ninety-degree angle. Three more doors, and then we entered the one at the very end: room 7. I looked around. The room was about twenty-five by seventeen feet, and the floor was covered with a worn brown carpet. A little above my eye level, a metal shelf ran across the wall; plastic bags filled with clothes sat on top of it and smaller bags hung from hooks beneath it. The beige paint covering the walls and the metal doors was thin and dirty. In one corner, there was a bunk bed. Jars and containers of different shapes and sizes covered the first bunk, and plastic bags filled with clothes rested on the second. In another corner, next to a barred window, gray military blankets were stacked almost to the ceiling. The room was surprisingly clean and tidy. In small groups of three or four, about fifty girls sat on the floor, talking. They were all about my age and looked at me with curiosity when I entered the room. Unable to carry my weight any longer, I dropped to the floor.

"Girls, fix a spot for her so she can rest!" Soheila yelled as she knelt beside me. "I know how much your feet hurt, but you'll be fine. Don't worry."

I nodded, tears filling my eyes.

"Marina!" a familiar voice called.

I looked up and, for a moment, didn't recognize the girl standing over me.

"Sarah! Thank God! I've been so worried for you!"

Sarah had withered. Her once glowing white skin had become dull, and there were dark circles around her eyes. We embraced until we were exhausted.

"Are you okay?" Sarah asked, looking at my feet.

"I'm fine. It could have been worse."

I pulled off my shawl from my head and ran my fingers through my hair, the strands of which were stuck together. I had never been so dirty in my life.

"Why is your name written on your forehead?" asked Sarah.

"What?"

"Your name is written on your forehead with a black marker."

I touched my forehead and asked for a mirror, but Sarah said there were no mirrors here. She said since she had been in Evin, she had not seen anyone with their name written on their forehead. I couldn't remember how it had happened. Then she asked me about the bruise on my head, and I told her about fainting in the bathroom.

"Marina, how're my parents? When was the last time you saw them?" Sarah's eyes focused on me with an intensity I had never seen before, as if she had been wandering in a desert without water for days and I was a gurgling fountain.

I told her about how worried her parents had been and about their efforts to see her and Sirus. I asked her if she knew where Sirus was and if he was all right. She didn't know. Then I asked her if she had been lashed.

The night they had been arrested, the guards had made Sarah watch as they lashed Sirus. They had wanted him to give them the names of his friends, but he had refused. She closed her eyes not to witness what was being done to her brother, but they hit and kicked her and made her watch. Then, they untied him and strapped her to the bed. They told Sirus that if he gave them the names, they would not lash Sarah, but he didn't say a word, and Sarah was tortured as well. They asked her if she knew his friends, but she didn't know any of them. Then they asked her about her own friends.

"I gave them your name, Marina . . . I'm sorry . . . but I couldn't take it," she said.

I didn't blame her. I would have given Hamehd all the names he wanted if he had lashed me only a little while longer.

I told her about the list. It was hard for her to believe that the guards had tortured us for what they already knew. She asked me why I had not told her anything about the list earlier, and I explained that I didn't know who else was on it and I didn't want to worry anyone.

"Have you seen Gita?" I asked her.

"Before he tortured me, Brother Hamehd said that Gita had given him my name and address. I believed him and got mad at her. I thought it was her fault that I had been arrested. Then, Hamehd lashed me and I ended up telling him everything I knew. I hated myself for hating Gita."

Sarah covered her mouth to silence the pain that had to find its way out of her. I put my arms around her, and she screamed in my chest.

She finally looked up. "Just before he sent me here, Hamehd told me that Gita was executed the night before. He said if Sirus didn't cooperate, the same thing would happen to him. So I knew Hamehd had lied to me when he had said Gita had given him my name and address. If Gita had talked, she would have lived. She didn't talk and that was why they killed her. It wasn't her fault."

"Gita is dead?"

Sarah nodded.

It couldn't be true.

A voice in my head was saying, "You're alive, and you don't deserve it."

I clearly remembered the day Gita and I became friends. It had been three and a half years earlier. Summer of 1978, up north at my family's cottage, the summer I met Arash.

# Seven

THE YEAR I WAS BORN, my parents bought a cottage in the small town of Ghazian—across a bridge from Bandar-eh Pahlavi—by the Caspian Sea, where life was slow and green. Although owning a cottage by the Caspian was a sign of wealth at the time, my family was not rich. My father loved the peace and beauty of northern Iran so much that instead of buying a house in Tehran, he decided to buy a cottage. However, he didn't have enough money and bought it together with one of his friends, a loud and cheerful Russian-Armenian man named Partef who owned a stainless steel factory in Tehran. Uncle Partef, as I called him, was not married, was usually very busy, and rarely came to the cottage, so we had the place to ourselves most of the time.

The cottage was in the middle of a large piece of wooded land behind the harbor on a quiet street that led to the beach. Its first owner had been a Russian doctor, a close friend of my parents, who had built it himself with sturdy Russian lumber. There were four bedrooms, a living-dining room, a small kitchen, and a bathroom. The outside walls were painted a light green, and twelve stone steps led to the front door.

The trip from Tehran to the cottage took about five hours by car. Heading west from Tehran, we continued on the flatlands until we reached the city of Ghazvin. Here, the road turned north toward the Alborz Mountains, which seemed like an imposing sheer wall, separating the deserts of central Iran from the Caspian Sea. Through tunnels, steep climbs and descents, and wild bends and curves, the road stubbornly made its way across the mountain range. It followed the valley of the White River to where thick forests covered the hills and the wind carried the fragrance of rice fields.

A see-through metal fence, which was painted sky blue and was even taller than my brother, surrounded our property. When we arrived, my father would stop our blue Oldsmobile at the gates, and I would step out and open them to let the car through. The long, unpaved driveway stretched away toward the cottage, disappearing behind maple, pine, poplar, and mulberry trees. Under my feet, multicolored pebbles poked through the dirt and sparkled in the sunlight that had managed to penetrate the thick canopy of leaves. The driveway led to an opening that seemed too bright for a moment. The white stone stairway leading to the house suddenly appeared.

The building always greeted us with a familiar damp scent that had saturated the stale air during the months of our absence. A dark green carpet covered the floors. Before entering the house, my mother made us take off our shoes and clean our feet, so we wouldn't bring in any sand. My parents had furnished the small living room with a cast-iron patio set, which they had bought from a moving sale; it was painted white and had velvety purple cushions and a glass-top table. The bedrooms were very simple with plain beds and old wooden dressers, and the curtains hanging in the windows were made of bright floral fabrics. At night when I went to bed, I usually left the three windows of my room open to welcome the cry of the roosters in the morning. When it rained, ducks quacked and played in puddles, and the scent of wild lemon trees dripped from their thick leaves.

There was a special place on the property where, as my grandmother had taught me, I said the Our Father every morning. From a distance, it resembled a big moss-covered rock, but as you approached, you could see that it was made of many small stones. It was about four feet high and six feet wide, and a thick, rusty metal bar reached out of one of its corners. It belonged to ancient times when the sea covered most of the land. Once useful as a place where fishermen tied their boats, it looked strange and out of place when I discovered it in a forgotten corner of the property. I loved to stand on it, open my arms to the gentle breeze, close my eyes, and imagine the sea surrounding me, its glassy surface moving and living, transforming the sunlight into a golden liquid that glided toward the shore where sand hills were like blisters on the hot skin of the earth. I came to call this strange monument the Prayer Rock.

I would usually wake at sunrise and wander outside. A river of mist would float between the trees, rise over the tall grass, and cover my legs. When I reached the Prayer Rock it seemed as though the sun had breathed into the fog, making it pink with light. The top surface of the rock was an island resting on a glowing sea. I would lie down on the rock and let the sun cover my skin, making me feel weightless as if I were made of mist and light.

Every summer, my mother and I spent about two months at the cottage, but my father couldn't take such a long time off work and only stayed with us for a couple of weeks. Then, he came up every other weekend or so. For years, I spent my days at the cottage biking, building sand castles, swimming, chasing ducks, and playing with local kids. Free to do whatever I wished all day, I would only go home for dinner and to sleep. As years went by and I grew, my summer days remained the same with the exception that my daily adventures covered more ground and took me farther from home. At the age of twelve, I could explore the town on my bike in half a day. Following the old, narrow streets lined with small white houses, I would go to the market. The rice cookies and *koloochehs*—ground walnut- and sugar-filled cookies—I bought from the bakery sustained me on the many days I skipped lunch. The fish markets were filled with the loud voices of vendors, the strong smell of fish, and the fragrance of fresh herbs.

One of my favorite spots was a bridge that connected the two sides of the harbor. Standing on the bridge, I watched the boats and ships go by. The blue waters stretched to the horizon, heavy ships tore the surface of the sea into a white foam, and saltwater air filled my lungs. I especially loved the fog; it made the harbor seem dreamy and unreal. Not able to see much through the mist, I could hear the paddles of a boat slicing the water, and then the boat would emerge, appearing as if from another world.

When I was about ten years old, my mother's eldest sister, Zenia, bought a cottage about four miles outside of Ghazian in a recently developed subdivision complete with tennis and basketball courts, restaurants, and swimming pools. Here, expensive houses, which were surrounded by perfect lawns and waist-high white metal fencing, gleamed with fresh paint and kids rode their bikes on clean streets.

Aunt Zenia didn't look like the rest of the family. She was blond with blue eyes, and everything about her was big. She had a very big house in Tehran, a big car, and even a big chauffeur. Her husband, who had been killed in a car accident two years after Grandma's death, had owned a meat-processing factory in the city of Rasht about twenty-two miles from our cottage. After his death, my aunt had taken over the business and had done quite well. Her daughter, whose name was also Marina but whom everyone called Marie, was my mother's favorite. She was twenty years older than I, a petite woman who always seemed tense when her mother was around. They were both stubborn and strong-headed and argued constantly about everything.

In 1978, when I was thirteen, Marie and her husband spent all of the summer at my aunt's cottage, and my mother and I visited them almost every day. Aunt Zenia was rarely at her cottage and spent most of her time at her factory, where she had a small but comfortable apartment, or at her house in Tehran.

During my daily excursions on my bike, I noticed that teenagers were hanging out at one of the basketball courts. Each day, they showed up at about five in the evening. Boys played basketball, and girls sat in the shade, chatting and cheering them on. Finally one day, I decided to approach them. In small groups of two or three, about fifteen girls were sitting on the grass. I left my bike by a tree and walked to them. No one seemed to have noticed me. I spotted a girl sitting by herself on top of a picnic table and sat next to her. She looked at me and smiled. Her straight light brown hair reached her waist, and she was wearing white shorts and a white T-shirt. She looked familiar. I introduced myself, and her eyes widened with recognition. We realized we went to the same school, but she was a couple of years older than I, and we had never talked. Like me, her aunt owned a cottage nearby, and she and her family were staying with her aunt for awhile. Her name was Gita.

One of the boys scored, and the girls clapped and cheered. He turned around and called out to a girl who was sitting close to us, "Neda, will you get me a Coke? I'm dying of thirst."

He was about five feet nine with large dark eyes that sat above strong cheek bones. His straight black hair bounced as he ran. Neda reluctantly stood up and shook the grass clippings from her white shorts. Her shoulder-length brown hair was tucked behind her ears.

"Who's coming with me?" she called out to the girls, and a few joined her. They walked to the other side of the narrow street to a fast-food restaurant called Moby Dick.

Whispering to me, Gita pointed out a young man standing on the other side of the court. He was about six feet two, two hundred pounds, and looked at least twenty. The petite blond girl standing next to him didn't even come up to his shoulder. Gita said his name was Ramin and that he was the most handsome man she had ever seen.

"I'll get him one day; he's mine," she said.

My girlfriends had always been my age, and my experience with boys was quite limited. I had never considered "getting" a boy.

"Hello there," someone said from behind us. "Gita, who's your new friend?"

It was Neda. Gita introduced us. I discovered that Neda had a cousin who went to our school and whom I knew quite well. At the end of our conversation, Neda invited me to her birthday party the next day.


I had the perfect dress to wear to Neda's party. A few months earlier, my mother had decided to order some clothes for herself from a German catalogue, and she had offered to order something for me as well. I chose a white dress. It wasn't too expensive but was beautiful. It had an open neckline, and its fabric was lacy and light. For Neda's party, the plan was to go swimming first and then to her place for dinner and dancing. Gita had told me to wear my bathing suit under my regular clothes and to bring my dress along.

On the day of the party, I woke up even earlier than usual and spent hours in the bathroom. I tried on all my bathing suits and, each time, stared at my reflection in the mirror, devastated by every flaw I saw: my arms were too thin, my hips too big, and my chest too flat. Finally, I decided to wear the white bikini Marie had given me. She had recently taken a trip to Europe, had bought herself new bathing suits, and had given me her old ones. I wrapped my white sandals in a plastic bag, folded my dress, and put everything in a canvas beach bag. It was ten o'clock in the morning. On most days, we left for Marie's at around ten-thirty. My mother didn't drive, and we always took a cab when my father was not around. I could hear my mother rattling around in the kitchen, which was odd; she was never in the kitchen at this time of day.

"Maman, I'm ready," I said, beach bag in hand, standing in the kitchen doorway.

The air smelled of fish. She was washing a large cutting board and looked at me from the corner of her eye.

"Ready for what? We aren't going anywhere today."

The kitchen counters were covered with bowls of different sizes and pots and pans.

"But . . ."

"There are no 'buts'! Your Uncle Ismael and his wife are here from Tehran to visit Marie. Your Aunt Zenia is here, too. They're all coming over for lunch and dinner today, and we'll be playing cards. They'll probably sleep over tonight."

"But I'm invited to a birthday party tonight!"

"Well, you can't go."

"But—"

She turned around to face me. I could feel her anger fill the kitchen.

"Don't you understand the meaning of the word 'no?'"

I turned around, went to my room, and plopped down on my bed. I could take a cab myself; I had enough money. But my mother wouldn't let me. Maybe I could sneak out. But then I had to be home before dark, which was my curfew unless I had told my mother where I was going. I heard a car pull into our driveway, its tires scrunching against the wet sand. Looking out the window, I saw Aunt Zenia's chauffeur, Mortezah, a polite man in his late twenties, open the back door of her brand-new Chevrolet. My mother rushed out of the front door and down the steps and embraced her sister. Mortezah opened the trunk and took out a small suitcase. Then they all walked into the house. I remained by the window, my heart pounding with frustration.

"Roohi, get me a glass of cold water!" I heard Aunt Zenia call out to my mother with her sharp, demanding voice. "Marie has taken Ismael and Kahmi to town for something. They'll be here soon. Where's Marina? I have something for her."

"She's around. Probably sulking in her room."

The door of my bedroom burst open.

"What's going on, Marina? You don't even say hello to your aunt anymore?"

I stepped forward, embraced her, kissing her on the cheeks. Although her skin was damp and sweaty, she smelled of Chanel No. 5. She squeezed me, and I found myself drowning in her large bosom. She finally let go, took a delicate bracelet out of her purse, and put it on my wrist. It was lovely. Aunt Zenia always gave me beautiful things. I wiped my eyes with the back of my hand.

"You've been crying? What for?"

"I'm invited to a party tonight, and I can't go."

She laughed. "And why can't you go?"

"Well—"

"Because I'm here?"

"Yes." I looked down.

"I might be old now, but I used to be young, you know. Young and beautiful. And, believe it or not, I remember what it was like."

I held my breath.

"Mortezah will take you to this party and pick you up."

"Really?"

"Yes, Cinderella. You can go. But be home by midnight."


I thanked Mortezah when he dropped me off in front of Neda's house, promised to be waiting for him right there at midnight, and waved as he drove away. I followed the gray stepping-stones that poked through the grass in Neda's front yard. She was standing on the porch, which encircled the one-story cottage, chatting with two girls. The back of the building faced the sea, and I could hear the waves gurgling against the sandy shore. Soon everyone arrived. All the girls left their bags in Neda's bedroom and the boys in her brother's, and we ran to the beach. We played tag and water polo until everyone was starving, and then we headed back to the house. In Neda's room, when I opened my beach bag to get my dress, I realized I had forgotten to put in a bra or underwear. I had to keep my bathing suit on, which was okay; although a little wet, it was white and wasn't going to show.

After a dinner of cold cuts, fresh bread, and different kinds of salads, we pushed all the furniture in the living room aside and the sound of the Bee Gees filled the air. Neda danced with Aram, the handsome basketball player who had asked her to get him a Coke when I had first met her. Neda's perfectly tanned body looked beautiful against her white dress, and I noticed Aram whispering something in her ear that made her laugh. Most people were soon paired off, and I found myself standing alone in a corner, sipping a bottle of Coke. When it was finished, I busied myself by opening another bottle and filling a plate with potato chips. Song after song was played, and I ate so many chips my stomach hurt, but no one asked me to dance. Gita danced with Ramin, the big guy from the basketball court. His hands moved up and down her back. She was blushing. I glanced at my watch: ten o'clock. I had been standing there for an hour, and for all this time, no one had said a word to me. Feeling out of place, embarrassed, awkward, and sad all at once, I just wanted to get out of the room.

The door to the back porch was only a step away from me. I opened it and took another glance around the room—no one reacted. I stepped outside. The half moon had spread its silver light over the sea, and the air was calm. I had to do something. Maybe I could go for a swim. Swimming always made me feel better. I had swum at night many times before. In the moonlight, the sea became one with the sky and turned into a warm, silver body of darkness. I stepped down the few steps that connected the porch to the yard and started to unzip my dress, but as I let it slide to the ground, a voice startled me: "What are you doing?"

By a lawn chair in a corner of the yard, stood a young man with his hands covering his eyes.

"You scared me!" I said, and my heart struggled to regain its normal rhythm. "What're you doing hiding there?"

"I wasn't hiding! I was sitting here, on this chair, getting some fresh air. Then, along comes a girl who undresses right in front of me!" He seemed more scared than I was, which was amusing. He looked no more than sixteen and was still covering his eyes.

"Have you put your dress back on?"

"What's wrong with you? I'm not naked. I have my bathing suit on. I'm going for a swim."

"Are you crazy?" he said, taking his hands off his eyes. "You're going swimming in the middle of the night in those dark waters?"

"It isn't too dark; the moon is out."

"No, no! You're going to drown, and I'll never forgive myself!"

"I won't drown."

"I won't let you go."

He had stepped closer to me, now standing about two feet away.

"Okay, okay, I give up. I won't go," I said, pulling my dress back on.

His large dark eyes looked at me from above slightly raised cheekbones. His small, somehow childlike mouth contrasted with his otherwise strong-featured face. He was about two inches taller than I and had very short brown hair. What caught me by surprise was the look in his eyes, which made me feel unique, special, and beautiful. His name was Arash.

Now that I couldn't go for a swim, I decided to sit outside. I sank into a comfortable lawn chair but was too aware of Arash. I could hear him breathe. After about ten minutes, he stood up, and I jumped.

"Do you enjoy scaring me?"

"Sorry, I didn't mean to. Have to go. Don't go swimming, okay?"

"Okay."

I watched him walk away and enter the cottage. A minute later, Neda came out, called my name, and asked me to go inside; she was going to cut her cake.

A few days after the party, I was riding my bike to the beach to meet Gita. There was some sand on the road due to construction, and I turned too fast. My bike slid to one side, and I fell. I managed to get up, but one of my knees and one of my elbows were bleeding. It was about two o'clock in the afternoon and far too hot, so the street was deserted. At least no one had seen me fall like that. As I was trying to get my bike off the road, I felt someone standing behind me. I turned. It was Arash, and he looked as surprised as I was.

"Do you always appear out of thin air?" I asked.

"Are you a daredevil?" He laughed and examined my scratches. "We have to clean you up. That's my aunt's cottage," he said, pointing to the cottage at the corner.

He carried my bike, and I followed him. My scratches were stinging. I had tears in my eyes but took a deep breath and didn't complain. I didn't want him to think of me as a weak little girl.

"I was sitting on the porch, watching the street, and there you came at a hundred miles per hour and crash! You're lucky your neck isn't broken," he said.

Blue hydrangeas and pink roses had taken over the white walls of the cottage, and the silver-green branches of an enormous weeping willow brushed against the red shingles covering its roof.

Arash held the door open, and I stepped in. The scent of freshly baked cookies wafted in the air.

"Grandma, I have a guest!" he called.

A handsome old woman with silver-gray hair came into the

room from the kitchen. She was wearing a blue dress, wiping her wet hands on her white apron. She looked very much like my grandmother.

"What happened?" she asked in Russian as she looked at me and noticed the blood. I couldn't believe it; she spoke like my grandmother. Grasping my arm, she led me to the kitchen as Arash explained what had happened. She even fussed the way Grandma used to, and before I knew it, I was cleaned up, disinfected, and bandaged. Soon, a cup of tea and a homemade cookie appeared on the table in front of me.

"Please, help yourself," she said in Persian but with a strong Russian accent.

"Thank you," I answered in Russian.

Her eyes twinkled with surprise. "A Russian girl!" she said with a big smile. "How nice! Now you have a girlfriend! Not even an ordinary girlfriend, but a nice Russian one!"

Arash's face turned scarlet.

"Grandma, that's enough! She isn't my girlfriend!"

I laughed.

"You can say whatever you want, but it's so nice. Good for you. I'll leave you young people alone," his grandmother said and walked out of the kitchen calling "How wonderful," over and over again.

"You have to excuse my grandmother," said Arash. "She's very old and sometimes gets confused."

"Have you shown her your flute?" yelled his grandma from another room.

Arash changed color again.

"What flute?"

"It's not important. I play the flute for fun. It's not a big deal."

"I've never known anyone who could play the flute. Will you play for me?"

"Sure," he answered, not sounding very enthusiastic.

I followed him to his room, where he took a silver flute out of a

long, black box and ran his fingers along the body of the sleek in-
strument. Soon, a sad song filled the room. I sat on his bed and
leaned against the wall. He stood in front of me, his body moving
with the music as if it were a part of him, as if he had thought it
into existence. His eyes stared ahead as if dreaming, seeing what no
one else could see. The white cotton curtain danced in front of the
open window, catching swirls of sunlight and shade. I had never
known music to be so beautiful. His eyes searched mine when he
finished playing, but I was left speechless. I found out that he had
written the piece himself, but he was very modest about it. He
asked me if I played any musical instruments, and I said I didn't.
Then he asked me about my age and was shocked when I told him
I was thirteen; he thought I was at least sixteen. And I was surprised
to find out he was eighteen.

I liked the way he looked at me when I talked to him. He sat
back in his chair, rested an elbow on the armrest, put his hand
under his chin, and smiled, his eyes giving me all their attention.
The way he paused a few seconds before answering my questions
made me feel that our conversation mattered to him. I asked him if
he wanted to come for a walk with me the next morning, and he
said he did.

The next morning his grandmother waved to us from the porch of
the cottage.

"She's driving me crazy. She still thinks you're my girlfriend and
wants you to come over for lunch today."

"I'd love to come, if it's fine with you."

He looked at me with questioning eyes.

"I mean, if inviting me was only your grandma's idea, and you
don't want me to come, you can tell me."

"Of course I want you to come."

"That's good, because I want to hear you play your flute again."

We walked to a quiet, secluded part of the beach. In the distance, I could see a few people lying on the sand and a few swimming. Foamy white waves curved, folded, and broke against the shore. I took off my sandals and let the sea seep between my toes. The water was soft and cool. I asked him to tell me about his family. He told me his father was a businessman and his mother was a homemaker. His parents went to Europe every summer, and he, his brother, and his grandmother came to stay with his aunt at her cottage. He mentioned that his brother, who was two years younger than he was, was named Aram.

"You must be kidding me! Aram is your brother?" I said, surprised.

"Yeah, do you know him?"

"Well, I've met him. He seems to be very outgoing. He's always hanging out with the other kids, but I'd never seen you before Neda's party. Where were you hiding?"

He told me that he was not as outgoing as his brother and preferred to read a book or play his flute. He had come to Neda's party only because Neda was his neighbor in Tehran and was his brother's girlfriend.

Arash had been a top student in high school and had just finished his first year of studying medicine at the University of Tehran. I told him I was a good student, too, and, like him, wanted to study medicine. I invited him to come for a swim with me, but he said he'd rather sit on the beach and read.

His grandmother, Irena, had prepared a feast for lunch. It was a beautiful day, so she had set the table in the backyard under the weeping willow. The table was covered with a perfectly ironed white tablecloth. I watched her as she poured lemonade in my glass, strands of her silver hair dancing in the sea breeze. She filled my plate with long-grain rice, barbecued fish, and salad, dismissing my protests.

"You should eat more, Marina; you're too thin. Your mother is not feeding you properly."

Since Irena had discovered that I spoke Russian, she had not said

80

a word to me in Persian. Like my grandmother, she was a proud woman, and although she knew how to speak Persian, she refused to use it unless it was absolutely necessary. My Russian had become rusty. My parents spoke Russian at home, but since Grandma's death, I had refused to use it, because I believed it was something special my grandmother and I had shared and I didn't want to share it with anyone else. Arash's language skills weren't much better than mine, so I wasn't too embarrassed. It felt good to speak Russian again with Irena, who reminded me of my childhood days.

After lunch, Irena went to lie down, and Arash and I went to the kitchen to clean up. I filled the sink with dirty dishes while Arash put the leftovers in Tupperware containers and organized them in the fridge. He knew his way around the kitchen. When he was finished with the leftovers, he stood next to me with a dishcloth, and as I handed him the first rinsed plate, our eyes met, and I fought the overwhelming urge to reach out and touch his face.

"I have to say my prayers before sunset," Arash told me that evening as we sat in his backyard.

"Can I watch you?"

"You come up with strange ideas," he said. But he agreed, and I watched him without saying a word. He stood toward Mecca and went through the different stages of *namaz*. He closed his eyes, whispered prayers in Arabic, knelt, stood, and touched his prayer stone with his forehead.

"Why are you a Muslim?" I asked him after he was finished.

"You're the strangest person I've ever met," he said, laughing, but he explained to me that he was a Muslim because he believed Islam could save the world.

"What about your soul?" I asked.

My question had surprised him. "I'm sure it will save my soul, too. Are you a Christian?"

"Yes."

"Why? Because your parents are Christians?"

I explained that my parents were not practicing Christians.

"Then, why?" he insisted.

I realized I didn't exactly know the answer. I said that I had studied Islam and that it wasn't for me, and I didn't know why I felt that way. I probably knew more about Mohammad than I knew about Jesus. I had read the Koran more than I had read the Bible, but Jesus was somehow much closer to my heart; he felt like home. Arash was smiling at me. I guessed he had expected a strong argument, and I didn't have one to offer. For me it was a matter of the heart.

I asked him if his parents were religious, and he said that his father was from a Muslim family and believed in God, but he didn't believe in Mohammad, Jesus, or any other prophets. His grandmother, Irena, was from a Christian family, but she wasn't religious at all, and Irena's husband, his mother's father, who had passed away years earlier, had never believed in God. Arash's mother was a Christian, and although she never went to church, she always prayed at home. I wanted to know what his family thought about his religious beliefs, and he said he had never missed even one of his daily prayers since he had turned thirteen, and they still thought he was going through a phase that would pass.

At home the next evening, I sat outside on the stone steps leading to our cottage to watch the sunset. The clouds in the horizon had turned into a wild shade of red as the sun brushed past them. Then the red changed into a dreamy purple as the night drew closer. I couldn't stop thinking about Arash. I was simply happy when he was around; an exciting, warm happiness that rose above everything else, that made the rest of the world seem small and insignificant. I closed my eyes and listened to the night. I could hear the clapping sound of the wings of bats looking for their dinner and the horn of a ship from the harbor. Arash had read some poetry to me. His deep, gentle voice made the works of Hafez, Sadi, and Rumi sound even more magical than when I read them on my own. He read them with authority, as if they were his, as if he had composed every word like a perfect melody. Maybe this was love; maybe, I loved him.

I wanted Arash to see my Prayer Rock, so I invited him to our cottage one morning.

"Why do you call it the Prayer Rock?" he asked as we walked toward it from the gates.

"I prayed there once when I was a little kid, and it felt extra special, so I kept going back. It became my special place."

We soon reached it. I had not shared it with anyone before. For a moment, I wasn't sure if I had done the right thing. After all, it was only an odd collection of moss-covered rocks.

"Do you think I'm crazy?" I asked.

"No. I guess you're as desperate as I am to find a way to get closer to God. My way is my flute and yours is praying on this rock."

"Let's pray together," I offered, "and maybe you'll be able to feel it. It's like opening a window to heaven."

We both climbed on the rock, raised our hands toward the sky, and I recited a part of the Twenty-third Psalm of David: "The Lord is my shepherd, there is nothing I shall want. He makes me lie down in green pastures; he leads me beside quiet waters. He restores my soul; he guides me in the paths of righteousness for his name's sake. Even though I walk in the valley of the shadow of darkness, I fear no evil; for thou art with me; thy rod and thy staff, they comfort me."

"Beautiful!" he said when I finished. "What was it?"

I explained to him that the Psalms of David were a part of the Bible. He had never heard of them. I told him that my grandma used to read them for me, and that one was my favorite.

We both sat on the rock. He stared far ahead.

"Have you ever wondered about what happens to us after we die?" he asked.

I said I had. He said that death was a mystery that could never be solved; it was the one place that if we ever visited, we would not be able to tell the tale. And no one could escape it.

"I hate it when people you love die. You never stop hurting," I said.

"I've never really lost anyone. My grandfather passed away when I was little, but I don't remember anything about it."

"I remember my grandmother's death."

There were tears in his eyes. Once again, I wanted to touch his face, to trace every line with my fingers. I wanted to kiss him. Overwhelmed, I stood up. He jumped to his feet, facing me, and, for a brief moment, his lips touched mine. We moved away from each other as if struck by lightning.

"I'm sorry," he said.

"Why are you sorry?"

"It's against God's law for a man to touch a woman like that unless they're married."

"It's okay."

"No, it's not. I want you to know that I care about you, and I respect you. I shouldn't have done that. And you're so much younger than me. We have to wait."

"Are you saying that you love me?"

"Yes, I love you."

I couldn't exactly understand why he felt guilty about our kiss, but I knew it had something to do with his religious beliefs. That summer, I had spotted boys and girls kissing in quiet corners, and I had always wondered what it felt like. If it were up to me, I would have kissed him again, but I didn't want to do anything wrong or to upset him. He was older and knew better, and I trusted him.

That night, my mother and I slept over at Aunt Zenia's cottage. I woke up at six in the morning and tiptoed to the kitchen to make myself a cup of tea. With the cup in my hand, I walked into the living room and was startled to find my Aunt Zenia sitting at the dining table, almost completely concealed by piles of paper. I stepped a little closer. She wore a lacy pink cotton nightgown, which was more suitable for a young girl than for a very large woman in her sixties, and was busy writing something in a little notebook. I paused, wondering whether to say "good morning" or not, for she seemed so immersed in what she was doing.

"Why are you up so early, Marina? Are you in love or something?" she asked so loudly I almost spilled my tea.

"Good morning, Aunt Zenia," I mumbled.

"Maybe this seems like a good morning to *you.*"

She had not stopped writing.

"Are you going out?" she asked.

"Yes."

"Where?"

My mother rarely asked me where I was going.

"Around."

"Does your mother know that you go out so early?"

"I don't know."

She looked at me with her pale blue eyes.

"It's tough, but you're tougher."

She had lost me.

"You're not stupid. Don't look at me like that! You know what I mean. Your mother and my daughter are both made of the same clay. God wasn't paying much attention to his work when He created the two of them. Go and get me a cup of tea."

I turned around and did as I was told. With my hands slightly shaking, I put the tea on the table in front of her.

"Sit down," she ordered, her eyes examining me from head to toe. "How old are you now?"

"Thirteen."

"You haven't lost your virginity, have you?"

"Pardon me?" I whispered.

"Good," she said, smiling.

"I know you better than your mother does. I look and see, but she looks and refuses to see. I think today is the very first time ever I've seen you without a book. Do you want me to name them for you?"

"Name what?"

"The books you've read."

I was sweating.

"*Hamlet, Romeo and Juliet, Gone with the Wind, Little Women, Great Expectations, Doctor Zhivago, War and Peace,* and many more. So, what have you learned from all this reading?" she said.

"Many things."

"Don't do anything stupid. You aren't involved with this revolution, are you?"

"Aunt Zenia, what are you talking about? What revolution?"

"Are you trying to fool me?"

I shook my head. I didn't have any idea what she was talking about.

"I'm happy that you're hearing this from me, for I know a great deal about revolutions. Now listen carefully. Something terrible is happening in this country, I can smell it in the air, and it smells of blood and disaster. There have been protests and rallies against the shah. This ayatollah, I forget his name, has been opposing the government for years, and I'm telling you that he's up to no good. One dictatorship will go, and a worse one will take its place, the same as in Russia, only this time with a different name, and it will be more dangerous, because this revolution is hiding behind the name of God. Well-educated people are now following this ayatollah. Even Marie and her husband like him. My own family. He's in exile now, but this hasn't stopped them. Stay away from him. He says that the shah is too rich. The shah is the shah. He's not perfect, but who is? The ayatollah says that there are too many poor people in Iran. But there are poor people everywhere. Don't forget what happened in Russia. They killed the tsar, and do you think that they're better off now? Do you think that the people of Russia are all free, rich, and happy? Communism isn't the answer to social problems, and neither is religion. Do you understand me?"

I nodded, confused and shocked, and she began writing in her notebook again.

Later that morning as Arash and I set out for our walk, Aram called to us from the porch and asked where we were going.

"Why do you want to know?" asked Arash.

Aram said he was bored and wanted to come with us. Arash told him to go back to bed, but he insisted on coming, and we finally gave in. As we walked toward the beach, Aram asked what Arash and I had been doing together all day, every day. This upset Arash, causing an argument between the two of them, which made me laugh.

At the beach, Aram came for a swim with me, but Arash didn't like the water and always read while I swam. Watching him from the water, I could see that he wasn't paying much attention to his book. He was watching Aram and me.

Arash was quiet for the rest of the day. In the evening, we went to his room, and I listened as he played his flute. I had closed my eyes. He suddenly stopped in the middle of his favorite piece. I opened my eyes and looked at him, surprised.

"What happened?" I asked.

"Nothing."

He looked down, avoiding me.

"Arash, tell me. What is it?"

He sat on the bed next to me. "Do you really love me?"

"Yes, I do. Tell me, what's wrong?"

"You looked so happy with my brother today. You were enjoying yourself, and I thought that maybe . . . I don't know . . ."

"You thought I had feelings for him."

"Do you?"

"You should know me better by now. He's fun, but he isn't my type."

"And what do you mean by 'your type'?"

"You're my type, and he isn't. That's all. I don't love your brother; I love you."

"I'm sorry. I don't know what got into me. Aram has always been very popular. Girls like him. I don't want to lose you."

"You won't."

He still didn't look very happy. "You don't believe me?" I asked.

"I do."

He stood and went to the window. It was a rather windy day and the waves roared, muffling every other sound. He suddenly said that he had to tell me something very important. I had no idea what to expect. He told me that there was a big movement against the shah, that a revolution was in progress and that there had been many protests and many arrests. I told him that Aunt Zenia had told me about the revolution that very morning.

I asked him why there would be a revolution against the shah, and he explained that the shah, his family, and the government were all corrupt. They had been becoming wealthier by the day when most of the Iranian people had been struggling against poverty. I told him that Aunt Zenia believed that the same thing that had happened in Russia would happen in Iran.

"The revolution in Russia didn't have the right foundation; communism was the wrong answer to their problems. Their leaders didn't believe in God and soon became corrupt themselves," said Arash.

"So, how can you be sure that whoever replaces the shah will be better?"

He asked me if I had heard of Ayatollah Khomeini.

"My aunt told me about some ayatollah, but she couldn't remember his name. Who's Khomeini?"

He told me that Khomeini was a man of God and had been exiled by the shah. The ayatollah wanted the people of Iran to live according to the laws of Islam. He wanted the riches of the country to be shared by everyone and not only by a small group.

He had been leading the movement against the shah for many years.

I told Arash that I had a bad feeling about this revolution. As far as I knew, neither my family nor his were rich. Our parents didn't hold important positions in the government, but we led comfortable lives. We received a good education for free, and he was going to university to become a doctor. Why did we need a revolution?

"It isn't only about us, Marina," he said excitedly. "It's about those who live in poverty. The government makes tons of money from selling oil, which belongs to the people of Iran, and a big part of this money ends up in the personal accounts of the shah and his government officials. And did you know that for years, people who have criticized the shah and his government have been arrested by SAVAK, the secret police, and have been tortured and even executed?"

"No."

"Well, this is the truth."

"How do you know all this?"

"I've met a few of these political prisoners. They do terrible things to them in prison, things that just hearing them makes you sick."

"This is terrible! I had no idea."

"Well, now you do."

I wanted to know if his parents knew he supported the revolution, and he said he couldn't tell them because they wouldn't understand.

"Many people die in revolutions," I said.

"I'll be fine. You have to be brave, Marina."

I was worried; I didn't want anything bad to happen to him. A cold feeling had just swept over me. He held my hands.

"Marina, please don't worry. I'll be fine. I promise."

I tried to believe him. I tried to be brave. After all, I was thirteen years old.

\* \* \*

I didn't get into any more political discussions with Arash for the rest of the summer. I wanted to forget the revolution; maybe it would go away. Arash played his flute for me every day, and we went for long walks and bike rides on the beach and read poetry sitting on the swing in his backyard.

Arash had to leave for Tehran two weeks before I did. My mother and I usually returned to Tehran in early September. This gave me enough time to get everything ready for school, which started on September 21, the first day of autumn. I watched Arash drive his father's white Paykan away from his aunt's cottage with his grandma sitting in the front passenger seat and his brother in the backseat. They all waved good-bye to me, and I waved back until they were out of sight.

I arrived in Tehran on Thursday, September 7, and called Arash right away. We decided to meet in a bookstore on the ninth at ten in the morning.

On the ninth, I woke before dawn. Feeling anxious, I stepped onto my balcony. At that early hour, the usually busy street was deserted, and the gentle breeze rustled the dusty leaves of maple trees. I wanted to call Arash and ask him to come earlier, but this was crazy. I had to wait. Then, I heard a strange noise, a hissing sound. I stared into the darkness. On the other side of the street something moved. I looked more carefully. A dark figure stepped into the glow of a streetlight and began writing something on the brick wall of a store with a can of spray paint. Someone yelled, "Stop!" but I didn't know from where, for the word echoed between buildings. The dark figure started running. I heard a loud thunderlike sound. The figure disappeared around the corner, and the shadows of two armed soldiers appeared. I ran inside.

After the sun came up, I went back on the balcony. The gray brick wall on the other side of the street was covered with large, red words: DOWN WITH THE SHAH.

I arrived at the bookstore a few minutes early and started brows-
ing through the shelves. At a quarter past ten, I looked around;
Arash was never late. I checked my watch constantly. Every time
the door opened and someone came in, a flash of hope brightened
my heart—but he never came. I waited until eleven o'clock and kept
on telling myself that it was okay, that he was fine and was probably stuck in traffic, or maybe his car had broken down.

I walked home, went straight to the phone, and called Arash's
house. Aram answered the phone, and from the way he said hello, I
knew something was wrong. I told him that Arash was supposed to
meet me at a bookstore but had not shown up.

"Aram, where is he?" I asked as calmly as I could.

Aram said he didn't know. Arash had gone out the previous
morning and was supposed to be back the same day for dinner but
had never returned. His parents had called everyone, but no one
knew where he was. There had been a big protest rally against the
shah that day. It had been held at Jaleh Square and had been organized by Khomeini's supporters. The army had opened fire on the
crowd and many had been hurt. One of Arash's friends had just
told Arash's father that he and Arash had gone to Jaleh Square together but had been separated. Arash's parents had called every
hospital in Tehran. His father had even gone to Evin, but they had
not been able to find him.

*"They do terrible things to political prisoners, things that just hearing
them makes you sick."* I pushed the thought away and made Aram
promise to call me as soon as he heard anything.

An empty, cold distance squeezed between me and the room I
was in, as if life itself had pushed me away. The muffled hum of the
cars moving along the street became strange and unfamiliar. I knew
this pain. This was grief.

The next morning, I rang the doorbell of Arash's house and waited.
Aram opened the door. We hugged and neither one of us could let

go of the other. I opened my eyes to see Irena staring at us. I had to be strong. I let go of Aram and embraced Irena. Then I helped her walk to the living room and sit on the couch. Arash's father came into the room, and Aram introduced us. Arash looked very much like his father.

"Thank you for coming," Arash's father said. "Arash has told me all about you. I wish we could meet under better circumstances."

I sat next to Irena and held her hand. She was crying. Arash's mother came in, and I stood up and kissed her cheeks. Her face felt cold and her eyes were swollen. There were family pictures everywhere. I didn't have any pictures of Arash and me together.

I asked Aram to show me his brother's room. It was very simple. There were no pictures or posters on the walls. His black flute box was on his desk, and there was a small white jewelry box sitting next to it. Aram picked it up and gave it to me.

"He bought this for you a few days ago," he said.

I opened the box. There was a beautiful gold necklace in it. I closed it and put it back on the desk.

"I found a letter in one of his desk drawers. I didn't mean to get into his personal things, but I had to look around to see if there were any clues about where he was," Aram said, giving me a sheet of paper. I recognized Arash's handwriting. The letter was addressed to his parents, grandmother, brother, and me. He had written that he believed he had to stand up for what he knew was right. He had to do something against all that was evil. He explained that he had been supporting the Islamic movement against the shah to the best of his abilities, and he was well aware that what he was involved with was dangerous. He wrote that he had never been very courageous, but now he felt he had to put fear aside, and he understood that he could lose his life for his beliefs. At the end, he mentioned that if we were reading his letter, it meant that he was probably dead, and he asked for our forgiveness and apologized for causing us pain.

I looked at Aram.

"My parents didn't know how involved he was with this stupid revolution, but I knew. I tried to stop him. But you know him; he never listens to me. I'm the little brother who doesn't know anything."

I sat on Arash's bed and handed the letter back to Aram. There was a blue T-shirt on Arash's pillow. I picked it up. It was one of his favorites that he had worn many times during that summer. I smelled it; it still carried his scent. I expected him to enter his room, smile his warm smile, and say my name in his kind, gentle voice.

I had watched the news the night before and there had not been any mention of the Jaleh rally at all. However, all TV channels were state-controlled and had ignored most of the recent events and the casualties. I couldn't understand why the shah would order the army to shoot people. Why didn't he listen to what the protesters wanted and why didn't he talk to them?

I went to the window, looked outside, and wondered if Arash had ever thought of me as he stood by his window and watched the quiet street. Aram stood next to me, staring outside, and my heart ached for him. He and his brother were very different and yet very close.

In the living room, a picture of the two of them had caught my eye: two little boys, seven and nine years old maybe, with their arms around each other's necks, laughing.

# Eight

"It's our building's turn to have warm water tonight," Sarah told me. It was my first night at 246. She explained that we got warm water only once every two or three weeks, and each time for only two to three hours. Our room's turn to use the showers would be at around two in the morning. "Each person has ten minutes in the shower. I'll wake you up," she said.

It was time to go to sleep. The lights in the rooms were turned off at eleven every night, but the lights in the hallway remained on at all times. Sarah introduced me to the girl who was in charge of "beds." Each of us received three blankets. Everyone slept on the floor side by side, each person with a designated spot that was rotated occasionally. There were so many girls that even the hallways were used for sleeping. I got a spot next to Sarah in the room. I triple-folded one of my blankets and used it as a mattress, the second one was my pillow, and the third was my cover. When everyone had settled down, there was no room to spare. Going to the bathroom in the middle of the night proved to be a challenge; it was almost impossible to reach the bathroom without stepping on someone. During the time of the shah, 246, upstairs and downstairs combined, had fifty or so prisoners in total. Now, the number was close to six hundred and fifty.

Sarah woke me as she had promised. At first, I was disoriented and didn't know where I was. I realized I wasn't in my bed at home. This was Evin. The sound of water from the showers mixed with the voices of the girls. Sarah helped me up, and I hobbled along. The shower room had cement walls and floors, which had all been painted a dark green, and thick plastic sheets divided it into six separate stalls. Two girls were to share each stall for ten minutes. The air was saturated with steam and smelled of cheap soap. I scrubbed my skin and cried.

The moment I took off my blindfold on the night of the executions, my life had changed completely. I'd had many profound experiences before that night, but they had left the essence of my life intact. I had lost loved ones, and I had been arrested and tortured, but on that night, I had traveled too far. My time in this world had ended, but I was still alive. Maybe this was the line that separated life and death. And I didn't belong to either side.

We went to our sleeping spots after showering. Space was so tight that if I lay on my back, I would disturb my neighbors, so I faced Sarah and kept my knees as straight as possible. Sarah opened her eyes and smiled.

"Marina, I don't say this in a mean way, and I know it might sound stupid, but I'm glad you're here with me. I was so lonely before you came."

"I'm glad we're not lonely, too."

She closed her eyes, and I closed mine. I wanted to tell her about the night of the executions, but I couldn't. There were no words to describe it. And I didn't want to tell her about my life sentence, because it would only distress her. Were they really going to keep me in Evin forever? This meant that I would never embrace my mother, see Andre, go to church, or see the Caspian again. No, they just wanted to scare me, to make me feel desperate. I had to pray long and hard. I had to beg God to save me. Not only me, but Sarah as well. We were going home soon. Both Sarah and I were going home soon.

It seemed as if we had only been lying down for minutes when the sound of the *moazzen* filled the room through the loudspeakers: *"Allaho akbar. Allaho akbar. . . ."* It was time for the morning *namaz*, which had to be said before dawn. Sarah and most of the girls got up and headed toward the bathroom for the ritual of *vozoo*, the washing of hands, arms, and feet, which has to be done before every *namaz*. I could finally lie on my back. Someone touched my shoulder, and I opened my eyes. It was Soheila.

"Don't you want to get up for *namaz*?" she asked.

"I'm a Christian." I smiled.

"You're the first Christian I've seen here! We had . . . I mean have Christian neighbors. They live right next door to us. Their last name is Jalalian. I'm friends with their daughter, Nancy. They once invited us to their house to have Turkish coffee with them. Do you know the Jalalians?"

I said I didn't.

She apologized for waking me and asked if Christians prayed. I explained that we did but that unlike Muslims, we didn't have to say our prayers at specific times.

We had to tidy up the room at seven in the morning. I was surprised at how quickly this was done and at how rapidly the tower of folded blankets went up in a corner. The two girls who had meal-time duties spread thin sheets of plastic called *sofreh,* which were about a foot and a half wide, on the floor and distributed metal spoons and plastic plates and cups. We didn't have any forks or knives. Then, the two girls went to the foyer and came back with a large, cylinder-shaped metal flask containing tea. The flask was very heavy, and they each held one of its handles, panting as they carried it into the room. They also brought our ration of bread and feta cheese. We lined up, received our food, sat around the *sofreh,* and ate. I was starving and swallowed my food in seconds. The bread was rather fresh. I was told that the prison had its own bakery. The tea was hot but had a very strange smell, and Sarah told me this was because the guards always added camphor to it. She had heard that camphor stopped female prisoners from menstruating; most girls didn't get their periods at all. But camphor had side effects, including swelling of the body and depression. I asked her why the guards would want to stop us from menstruating, and she said it was because sanitary pads were expensive. After the meal, the two girls who had dishwashing duties put the dirty dishes in plastic bins, took them to the shower room, and washed them with cold water.

I soon learned all the many rules. We weren't allowed to go past the barred doors at the end of the hallway unless the sisters called us over the loudspeaker. This usually only happened if we had to go for further interrogation or for visitations. Visitations were once a month, and the next one was in two weeks. Sarah hadn't had any visitors yet but was hoping that her parents would be allowed to see her soon. I also learned that only close family members were permitted to visit and that they could bring us clothes. There was a television set in each room, but the programs were strictly religious. We had books, but they were all about Islam.

Lunch was usually a little bit of rice or soup, and for dinner, we had bread and dates. There was supposed to be some chicken mixed in with the rice and the soup, but whoever found even the smallest piece of meat in their food was considered very lucky and showed it off to her friends. The representative of each room, who was sometimes chosen by the girls and sometimes appointed by the guards, organized the food distribution and cleaning duties and reported any serious illness or problem to the office.

One day, about ten days after my arrest, I sat in a corner of the room and watched the girls say their midday prayers. They stood in rows, facing Mecca. The first time I had closely seen a Muslim pray had been when I had watched Arash say his *namaz* at his aunt's cottage. I loved to watch him bow and kneel and whisper all the things he so passionately believed in. Would he have approved of this new government and all the terrible things it was doing in the name of God? No. Arash was good and kind; he would never have accepted such injustice. Maybe, we would both have ended up in Evin.

One of my roommates spoke to me, and I jumped. It was Taraneh, a twenty-year-old thin, fragile girl with large amber eyes and short amber hair. She sat in a corner most of the time, reading the Koran. Every time she stood for prayer, she pulled her chador over her face. Then, when she took off her chador, her eyes were red and swollen, but she always smiled.

"You looked like a statue for the longest time. You weren't even blinking," she said.

"I was thinking."

"About what?"

"About a friend."

I asked her why she had been arrested, and her answer was "long story."

"Well, it seems like we have a lot of time on our hands," I said.

"I don't," she responded.

A feeling of dread filled me. Sarah had told me that two girls from our room were sentenced to be executed, but Taraneh was not one of them.

"But Sarah told me—"

"No one knows," she whispered.

"Why haven't you told anyone?"

"What's the point? Then people fuss over you and feel sorry for you. I hate that. Please don't tell anyone."

"Why did you tell me?"

"You were supposed to be executed, weren't you?"

My heart sank. I couldn't lie to her. I collected all my strength and told her about the night of the executions and how Ali had taken me away at the last moment. She asked me why Ali had saved me, and I said I didn't know. Then, she found her way to what she really wanted to ask.

"Did he ever touch you?"

"No, what do you mean?"

"You know what I mean. Men are not supposed to touch women unless they're married."

"No!"

"This is strange."

"What?"

"I've heard things."

"What things?"

"A couple of girls told me they were raped, and they were threatened that if they told anyone about it, they would be executed."

I only had a vague idea of what being raped meant. I knew it was something terrible, something that a man could do to a woman, something that no one should ever talk about. And although I wanted to know more, I didn't dare ask.

"How about before they took you for execution? They didn't touch you then?" Taraneh asked.

"No!"

She apologized for upsetting me. I tried not to cry. I told her how painful it was to have survived when the others had died. She said it wouldn't have changed anything for them if I had died, too.

"How did you know about my death sentence?" I asked.

"When you came in, you had your name written on your forehead."

I didn't understand.

"After I was arrested, they beat me on and off for two days, but I didn't cooperate," she said. "Then my interrogator dragged me outside one night and took off my blindfold . . . There were bodies . . . covered in blood. They had been executed . . . ten or twelve people. I threw up. He told me that the same thing would happen to me if I didn't talk. He had a flashlight and aimed it at the face of one of the dead. A young man. His name was written on his forehead. Mehran Kabiri."

Although I knew all that had happened on the night of the executions was very real, I had dealt with my memories as if they were a nightmare. I had pushed them as far away as I possibly could. However, now they had come back to life. My breathing became heavy. What I had witnessed that night could happen to Taraneh. And there was nothing I could do.

Taraneh told me she had heard that before executing girls, guards raped them, because they believed virgins went to heaven when they died.

"Marina, they can kill me if they want," she said, "but I don't want to be raped."

We had a pregnant woman named Sheida in our room. She was about twenty years old and had been sentenced to death, but her execution had been postponed, because it was against the laws of Islam to execute a pregnant or breast-feeding woman. She had long light brown hair and brown eyes. Her husband was also awaiting execution. We never left her alone to have a chance to worry too much. At least two girls kept her company most of the time. But although she was always calm, every once in a while, tears silently fell down her face. I could only imagine how difficult it was for her not only to worry about herself, but also about her husband and her unborn child.

\* \* \*

One night, we woke to the sound of firing guns. All the girls sat up in their beds and stared at the window. Each bullet was a lost life, a last breath, a loved one torn apart while a family waited and hoped for him or her to come home. They would be buried in unmarked graves, and their names would not be carved in stone.

"Sirus . . ." whispered Sarah.

"Sirus is fine. I know he's fine," I lied.

Sarah's dark eyes were like a mirage in darkness. She began to sob, and her sobs became louder and louder. I put my arms around her and held her. She pushed me away and began to scream.

"Shhh . . . Sarah! Take deep breaths," a few of the girls said and came closer, trying to calm her.

Sarah began to punch herself in the head. I tried to hold her wrists, but she was surprisingly strong. It took four of us to stop her, but she was still struggling. The lights came on, and, a minute later, Sister Maryam and another one of the guards, Sister Masoomeh, stormed into our room.

"What's going on?" Sister Maryam asked.

"It's Sarah," said Soheila. "She was crying and screaming and then she began punching herself really hard."

"Get the nurse!" Sister Maryam said to Sister Masoomeh, who ran out of the room.

The nurse arrived in less than ten minutes and gave Sarah an injection in the arm. Soon, Sarah stopped struggling and passed out. Sister Maryam said that Sarah had to be taken to the prison hospital so she wouldn't hurt herself. The sisters and the nurse put Sarah on a blanket and carried her away. Her small hand dangled from the side of the blanket. I begged God not to let her die. Her family expected her to come home the same way Arash's family had awaited his return.

# Nine

W<small>E ALL WAITED</small> for Arash to come home although we knew he wouldn't.

The shah replaced one prime minister with another, trying to gain control of the country; he gave speeches and told the people that he had heard their cry for justice and was going to make changes. But this was all useless. There were more and more anti-shah gatherings and protests every day, and as the school year of 1978–79 continued, everyone felt worried and uncertain about the future. The world in which I had grown up and the rules by which I had lived and which I had believed to be set in stone were falling apart. I hated the revolution. It had caused violence and bloodshed, and I was sure that this was just the beginning. Soon came the military curfew, and soldiers and military trucks appeared at every corner. I was a stranger in my own life.

One day, our apartment trembled with a deep roaring sound that became louder and louder, penetrating my bones. I looked out the window and saw a tank moving down the street. It terrified me; I never knew that tanks were so loud and monstrous: When it was gone, I noticed that its wheels had left deep marks on the pavement.

Weeks passed and fear grew. Many of those who held important government or military positions left the country. Finally, schools were shut down in late fall of 1978. It was a cold winter, and due to strikes at oil refineries and political and economic uncertainty, there was a shortage of fuel for cars and for heating, so we were only able to keep one room warm. At gas stations, lines continued for miles, and people had to spend the night in their cars, waiting their turn to fill up. I was left at home with nothing to do all day but to shiver, stare out the window, and worry. Our street, Shah Avenue, which was usually congested with traffic, was now deserted most of the time. Sidewalks, which used to be full of people strolling, window-shopping, or bargaining with vendors, were empty. Even the beggars were gone. Every once in a while, groups of ten to twenty men appeared, set tires on fire, and wrote "Death to the Shah" and "Long Live Khomeini" on walls, leaving the air thick with smoke and the stench of burning rubber. A few times, the street filled with angry demonstrators; men led the way and women wearing black chadors followed them. With their fists in the air, they screamed slogans against the shah and the United States and carried banners with pictures of Ayatollah Khomeini.

Once a week, I went to visit Aram and his family. Keeping close to buildings for safety—stray bullets had injured and killed many people—I walked along the street as fast as I could, careful not to run into any protesters or soldiers. Once on the bus, I tried to sit in a safe corner. Aram was paranoid about my being on the streets; he hardly ever stepped out of his house and had begged me to stay home, but I had explained to him that the boredom of confinement would probably kill me before anything else. He asked me to at least call him right before I left my house.

"What's the point of my calling you before leaving?" I asked him.

"So that if you don't show up on time, I can do something."

"Do what?"

He stared at me with a bewildered look on his face.

"Then I'll come and look for you."

"Where?"

His eyes filled with hurt, and I realized how cruel I had been. He was worried for me and didn't want history to repeat itself.

I took his hand in mine.

"Aram, I'm sorry! Forgive me! I don't know what's wrong with me. I'm so stupid! I don't know what I was thinking. I'll call; I promise."

He smiled an uncertain smile.

Just to keep her busy, I asked Irena to teach me how to knit. When I visited, we all sat in the living room, drank tea, and, since the domestic TV and radio stations were censored, listened to BBC Radio to find out what was happening to our country. Sometimes, we heard guns fire in the distance, and the thundering sound made us pause and listen. Irena was very fragile, and Aram's mother seemed thinner every week. His father, who was forty-six, looked years older. His hair had turned gray, and there were deep wrinkles on his forehead.

Sarah and I talked on the phone almost every day, and I sometimes went to her house or she came to mine. Unlike my parents, hers were in favor of the revolution and had attended a few rallies but had never taken Sarah and Sirus along. Sarah said her mother wore a black chador when she went to demonstrations. It was very difficult for me to imagine her mother in a chador; she was one of the best-dressed women I had ever known. Sarah told me that Sirus was planning to sneak out of the house one day to go to a rally, and she had asked him to take her along, but he had refused, saying she was too young and that it was dangerous. I begged Sarah not to go, reminding her of Arash's disappearance, but she said people had to stop being afraid, and they had to fight the shah who had used our country's oil money to increase his personal wealth, building palaces, giving lavish parties, and putting enormous amounts of money into his personal accounts in foreign countries. And he had imprisoned and tortured the ones who had criticized him.

"You have to come, too," Sarah told me. "For Arash. The shah is a thief and a murderer, and we have to get rid of him."

One day, a group of people screaming "Down with the shah" broke into the small restaurant below our apartment. They smashed all its windows, took all the beer cans and other alcoholic beverages they could find, put them in the middle of the intersection, and set them on fire. The beer cans exploded, rattling our windows. I knew the owners of the restaurant very well; they were an Armenian family, and we had been neighbors for years. They weren't hurt during the incident but they were very scared.

Gradually, the presence of the military became less visible on the streets. Everyone said this was because the shah had finally realized that the use of extreme force would only fuel the revolution. People also believed that many soldiers had begun to refuse orders to open fire on protestors. Now, although military trucks sometimes went by, I never saw soldiers pointing their guns at demonstrating crowds.

My parents didn't seem to be too concerned about what was happening in the country. They had not taken the Islamic movement too seriously and believed that this was only a period of unrest and not a revolution and that the shah was too powerful to be overcome by a bunch of mullahs and clergymen. So, although my mother always warned me to be careful when I left the house, she said the dark clouds would soon pass.

The shah was forced into exile and left Iran on January 16, 1979. Political prisoners were released. There were celebrations on every street. I watched from my window as people danced and cars honked. Then, after his own long exile in Turkey, Iraq, and France, Khomeini returned to the country on February 1. As his plane neared Tehran, a reporter asked him how he felt about his return. His answer was that he felt nothing. His words repelled me. Many had lost their lives to pave the way for his return in the hope of making Iran a better place, and he felt nothing? It seemed as if instead of warm blood, cold water flowed in his veins.

Just after Khomeini's return, I heard that the army was still loyal to the shah. There were still tanks and military trucks on the streets. For about a month, the future of the country was completely uncertain. Emergency military governments had taken over most cities and military curfews were still in effect. Ayatollah Khomeini asked the people to go to their rooftops at nine o'clock every night and yell *Allaho akbar* continuously for half an hour to show their support of the revolution. My parents and I never took part in the *Allaho akbar* sessions, but most people did, even the ones who had not strongly supported the revolution. The sentiment of solidarity had overtaken the country. People had hopes for a better future and for democracy.

On February 10, 1979, the army surrendered to the will of the people of Iran, and on February 11, Ayatollah Khomeini declared a provisional government with Mehdi Bazargan as its prime minister.

Soon armed revolutionary guards and members of Islamic committees were everywhere, looking suspiciously at everyone, and hundreds of people were arrested, accused of having been members of SAVAK, the shah's secret police. They were imprisoned and their belongings were seized; some were executed, beginning with the top-ranking officials of the old regime who had not left the country. Horrendous pictures of their battered, bloody bodies were published in newspapers. During those days, I learned to look down as I walked by newspaper stands.

Not too long after the revolution, dancing was declared evil and illegal, and my father lost his job at the Ministry of Arts and Culture. Later, he began working as a translator and an office clerk at Uncle Partef's stainless steel factory. My father worked long hours and came home tired and unhappy. As usual, I rarely saw him, maybe even less now, and when he was home, with a serious, do-not-disturb-me expression on his face, he read the paper and watched television. We hardly ever spoke.

Schools reopened, and we returned to class. Our principal, an accomplished woman who had been very close to the last minister of education during the time of the shah, was gone. We heard she had been executed. She had skillfully managed the school for many years, and her absence was felt in every way. There were rumors that most of our teachers were soon going to be replaced by supporters of the government. To make matters worse, our new principal, Khanoom Mahmoodi, was a nineteen-year-old revolutionary guard, a fanatic young woman wearing the complete Islamic *hejab*. Wearing the *hejab* wasn't yet mandatory, but it seemed as if rules were about to change. *Hejab* is an Arabic word that means the proper cover for a woman's body. It can have different forms, one of which is the chador. After the *hejab* became mandatory, in big cities, especially Tehran, instead of wearing the chador, most women wore loose, long robes called the Islamic manteau and covered their hair with large scarves; if worn properly, this was also an acceptable form of *hejab*.

For a few months after the revolution, there was still some freedom of speech. At school, various political groups sold their news-

108

papers freely and during recess political discussions could be heard throughout the schoolyard. I had never met any Marxists before, and now they were everywhere. There was also the Mojahedin-e Khalgh Organization, which means "God's Fighters for the People." All these political groups had been illegal at the time of the shah but had existed underground for many years. I didn't know anything about the Mojahedin, and there seemed to be a great deal to learn about them. A Marxist friend of mine told me that the Mojahedin were Marxists who had gone astray and believed in God and Islam. They were Muslim socialists who believed Islam could lead Iran to social justice and free it from Westernization. They had become organized and armed in the sixties and had fought to overthrow the shah. However, they were not Khomeini's followers; years before Ayatollah Khomeini became well known, they had already led many protests against the shah, and their members, who were mostly university students, were tortured and executed in Evin. The fact that they were an Islamic group was reason enough for me to decide I could not belong with them.

Aram attended an all-boys high school named Alborz, which was next to my school. One afternoon, about a week after school resumed, I was on my way home when I heard him call my name. My heart almost stopped; I thought he had news from his brother, but he said he just wanted to see me and offered to walk me home. I sighed with relief. Although I was sure Arash was dead, I dreaded hearing it.

He asked me about my school, and I told him that our new principal was a revolutionary guard and that I wouldn't have been surprised to hear she carried a gun in her pocket.

"You aren't getting involved with any political groups, are you?" he asked. Since his brother's disappearance, Aram had matured in a sad, depressing way. Before the revolution, he only thought of basketball and partying, but now he worried about everything and gave me advice all the time. "My father says these are dangerous times," he said. "He thinks the new government is allowing all political groups to do and say whatever they want, so that the revolutionary guards can see who their friends and enemies are. Then, sooner or later, they'll arrest anyone who's done anything against the government."

Aunt Zenia had called me a few days earlier and told me the exact same thing. She had warned me to be careful. But I was very curious about different ideologies. Every day during recess, I attended reading and discussion meetings organized by eleventh- or twelfth-grade students who worked with different political groups.

Aside from the fact that they didn't believe in God, Marx's and Lenin's ideas were very attractive. They wanted justice for everyone and a society where riches were divided equally, but their ways had proven flawed in the real world. I knew very well what had happened in the Soviet Union and other communist countries. Communism didn't work. On the other hand, I was now looking at what an Islamic society was like. I believed that the mixture of religion and politics was dangerous. Anyone who criticized the Islamic government was said to be criticizing Islam and therefore taking a stand against God. In Islam, as I understood it, people like that didn't deserve to live if they didn't change their ways.

Before the revolution, at least in my lifetime, people's beliefs and faith had never been an issue. We had girls of different religions in my school, but we had been expected to concentrate on our education, to be polite and respectful of one another and our teachers, and to behave in a ladylike manner. But now the world seemed to have divided itself into four raging streams: fundamentalist Islam, communism, leftist Islam, and monarchism, and I didn't agree with any of them. Almost everyone belonged to a group, and I didn't, and this left me feeling lost and lonely.

Gita was now in the eleventh grade and a member of a communist party known as the Fadayian-eh Khalgh. Sarah's brother, Sirus, was a member of the Mojahedin, and Sarah supported their views and ideas.

\* \* \*

One night in May 1979, about three months after the success of the Islamic revolution, I was home alone. My parents had gone to a friend's house while I stayed to finish my homework. At about eight o'clock, I turned on the television. We had only two channels at the time. Since the revolution, there was rarely anything good on, but a documentary attracted my attention. It was about the Jaleh Square rally against the shah on September 8. Although I knew very well that Arash was dead, I still couldn't think of that day as the day of his death; it was the day of his disappearance. With tears in my eyes, I moved closer to the television screen. The film was of poor quality; the person shooting it was running most of the time and making sudden movements, so the picture was difficult to follow. Soldiers pointed their guns at the crowd and fired. People ran, and I saw a few fall to the ground. Soldiers threw bodies onto a military truck, and then, for an instant, I saw him. One of the bodies was Arash. I stood up, feeling sick and horrified. I couldn't speak, and I couldn't cry. I went to my room, sat on my bed, and tried to think. Maybe I just imagined it, I told myself. What could I do? I had to know the truth. I went straight to the phone and called Aram. He heard the panic in my voice. I didn't know how to tell him.

"Marina, what is it?"

Silence.

"Say something. Do you want me to come to your house?"

"No," I heard myself say.

"Please tell me, what's wrong?"

"They were showing a documentary about the September 8 demonstration. Soldiers were throwing bodies onto a truck. I think one of them was Arash." There, I had said it.

Silence, awful silence.

"Are you sure?"

"No, how can I be sure? It was a split second, but how can we find out?"

Aram suggested that we should go to the television station the next day after school. I wanted to go in the morning, but he said if we skipped school, our parents would get worried, and he didn't want to say anything to his parents until we were sure I was right.

The next day, we took the bus to the television station, and neither one of us said a word on the way. We first went to a receptionist, a middle-aged woman, and explained our situation. She was very sympathetic and told us she had lost a cousin at the September 8 demonstration. After making a few phone calls, she led us to a bearded young man in a small office. He wore thick glasses and never looked straight at me as we talked but nodded constantly. He took us to a large room filled with different kinds of equipment where we told our story to a man in his late forties named Agha-yeh Rezaii, who promised us to find the tape. And he did.

Aram and I both stared at the screen, and there it was. We asked Agha-yeh Rezaii to freeze the frame. There was no doubt that it was Arash. His eyes were closed and his mouth was slightly open. His white T-shirt was covered in blood.

I felt like a rock had crushed my chest. I wished I could have been with him when he had died, when he was lonely and scared.

We couldn't take our eyes off the screen for a long time. I finally looked at Aram. His eyes were blank and absent, as he, like me, tried to understand the devastating, lonely gap that death had left behind, the terrible falling from the known into the unknown and the terrifying wait to hit the solid ground and shatter into small, insignificant pieces. I touched his hand. He turned his head and looked at me. I embraced him. Agha-yeh Rezaii was crying with us.

"I have to call my parents. They have to know right away," Aram said.

They were both there within the hour, devastated and broken. After eight months of suffering, we had to face the reality of his death. They thanked me for finding him. Yes, they thanked me. My brain had shut down. I couldn't think. They wanted to drive me home, but I refused. I wanted to be alone.

I got on the bus, found a quiet seat in a corner, and prayed. Was there anything else to do? I was going to say the Hail Mary over and over again. I was going to say it until it was enough, until I could make up for the way he had died, for not being with him at that moment. But was it ever going to be enough? The sorrow that had invaded my soul was growing rapidly without any sense of forgiveness. I had to accept it and let it swell, overflow, and go wherever it needed to go or it was going to destroy my soul and turn it into nothingness.

At our front door, with my shaking hands, I struggled to put my key in the keyhole, but it wouldn't go in. I rang the doorbell. No answer. The thick, hot air mixed with the sound of traffic and weighed down on me. I took a deep breath and tried my key again. The door opened. I closed it behind me and leaned against it. The air in the hallway was dark, cool, and silent. Feeling exhausted, I took heavy steps toward the stairs and began climbing but collapsed after the first flight. For some time, the coolness of the stone against my skin was all I was aware of. Then, I heard a voice calling my name. Something warm touched my face. I looked up. My mother's eyes were staring at me, and she began to shake me.

"Marina, get up!"

She pulled on my arms, and I finally managed to stand on my feet, leaning against her. She led me to my room. She was talking to me, but I couldn't understand her. Her words were like fog, like smoke rising in the air, disappearing in the sunlight that crept into my room through the window. She helped me sit down on my bed. I needed to understand what had happened. I needed to understand why Arash had died. I stared out the window into the blue sky.

When I finally became aware of my surroundings, my mother was standing with a plate of my favorite dish—beef and celery stew and rice—in her hands. It had turned dark outside, and the light in my bedroom had been turned on. I glanced at my watch. It was past nine o'clock. Two hours had passed, and I was still sitting on my bed. I had somehow slipped through time as if my sorrow had cut me out of the world, like scissors snipping a simple shape out of a piece of paper.

"He's dead," I said out loud, hoping that saying it would help me understand why it had happened.

"Who?"

My mother sat on the edge of my bed.

"Arash."

She looked away from me.

"He was killed during the September 8 demonstration. He was shot. He's dead."

"This is terrible." She sighed, shaking her head. "I know you liked him. It's hard, very hard, but you'll get over it. You'll feel better tomorrow. I'll make you a cup of tea."

She left the room. Every once in a while, my mother gave me brief moments of affection. But they never lingered, flashing brightly like shooting stars and disappearing into darkness.

I fell asleep after a cup of chamomile tea but woke in the middle of the night with my chest burning. I had been dreaming of Arash. I ran to my dresser, grabbed my angel figurine, and crawled under my bed. Deep cries tore from my throat, and the harder I tried to silence myself, the worse they became. I pulled down my pillow from my bed and covered my face with it. I wanted the angel to come and tell me why people died. I needed him to come and tell me why God was taking the ones I loved. But, although I called him, he didn't come.

On September 6, 1979, Irena passed away from a heart attack. I had lost two loved ones before her, but I had never been to a funeral. Irena's was my first. On September 9, I put on a black skirt and a black blouse and looked at my reflection in the mirror. I hated how I looked in black: thin, pale, and overwhelmed. I tried to stand strong and tall. I took off the black and put on my favorite brown skirt and a cream-colored blouse. Irena would have liked this outfit better.

On my way to the bus stop, I went into the flower shop and bought a bouquet of pink roses. On the bus, I sat by the window and watched the streets go by. All color and happiness had been drained from the city. People only wore dark-colored clothes and looked down as they walked, as if to avoid each other as well as the scenery. Almost every wall was covered with harsh slogans that promoted hatred.

The Russian Orthodox Church in Tehran had no priests, so the funeral mass was held at the Greek Church with the burial in the Russian Cemetery. I was grateful to be able to be there for Irena's funeral. I had come to appreciate the gift of having a chance to say good-bye.

After the funeral, I asked Aram to help me look for my grandma's grave. I didn't know exactly where it was. My parents had not taken me to her funeral, and they had never taken me to visit her grave. I wanted to find it and say a little prayer. The cemetery wasn't too big and was encircled by clay brick walls. Graves were very close to one another, and weeds grew everywhere. There were many tombstones; finding my grandma's was going to be difficult. We tiptoed between tombstones, and the fifth or sixth one we looked at was hers. It seemed as if she had found me. I had saved a pink rose for her.

I looked around. Each tombstone was like the cover of a book that had been sealed forever. I went from one to the other and tried to read the names and the dates of birth and death. Some people had been old and some had been young when they died. I wanted to know them all. There were many stories never to be told. Did the angel know all these people? Had he been able to help them and listen to their hearts when they were dying? What were their last thoughts before they left their bodies? What were their greatest regrets? Was it possible not to have any regrets at the moment of death? What would I regret the most if I died at that very moment?

Aram's friends and family were beginning to leave the cemetery, and I noticed his parents looking in our direction and knew they were thinking of Arash. They deserved to know where he was buried—and he deserved to have a proper grave. I wanted to plant roses for him around the small piece of earth that held his body. Roses of every color. And I would never let weeds take over his tombstone. A year had passed since his death. Four seasons of loss and grief.

On November 1, 1979, Ayatollah Khomeini asked the people of Iran to demonstrate against the United States, which he called the "Great Satan." He said that the United States was to blame for all corruption on earth and that it was Islam's greatest enemy together with Israel. Thousands of people took to the streets and surrounded the American embassy. I watched the news coverage of the demonstrations on television and wondered where this angry mob had come from. No one I knew had participated. A sea of people had engulfed the streets around the embassy grounds, which were surrounded by brick walls.

On November 4, 1979, we heard that a group of university students who called themselves the Muslim Students Following the Line of the Imam had seized the embassy's main building and had taken fifty-two Americans hostage. They wanted the United States to return the shah, who was in the States for cancer treatment, to stand trial in Iran. This sounded like absolute madness to me and to everyone I talked to. People knew that the shah was very ill. The hostage-taking didn't make any sense. But nothing had really made sense since the revolution.

# Ten

O N VISITATION DAY, everyone was excited, and for the first time since I was arrested, I heard the girls laugh out loud. The sisters called prisoners' names alphabetically, usually fifteen names at a time, over the loudspeaker. The ones called put on their chadors and went to the office. Not knowing whether our parents were allowed to see us or not, Taraneh and I paced up and down the hallway. Taraneh had been arrested more than two months earlier but had not had any visitations yet. Her last name began with B, so her turn was to come before mine.

". . . Taraneh Behzadi . . ."

We both jumped and screamed. She was so excited that I had to run and grab her chador and blindfold. She disappeared behind the barred doors, and I continued pacing. Most of the girls returning from their visitations were crying. Taraneh came back in about half an hour, composed and calm.

"You saw your parents?" I asked her.

"Yes."

"How were they?"

"Okay, I guess. There's a thick glass barrier in the visitation room, and there are no phones. You can't talk. But we used some kind of a sign language."

I was finally called. In the office, we were told to put on our blindfolds. I followed the line of girls downstairs and outside. We walked to the visitation building and, before entering it, were told to take off our blindfolds. Armed guards stood in every corner. A thick glass barrier divided the room in half. There were men and women standing on the other side of it, a few of them crying, their hands on the glass, searching every face, trying to find their loved one. I soon saw my parents. They ran toward me and began to cry. My mother wore a black manteau, which came down to her ankles, and a very large black scarf covered her hair and shoulders. She must have bought the outfit for the sole purpose of coming to Evin. All the manteaus she had owned before I was arrested were shorter—about an inch below her knees—and her scarves were smaller.

"Are you okay?" I managed to read my mother's lips.

I nodded, holding back my tears.

She clenched her hands together, as if in prayer, and said something.

"What?" I frowned, desperate to understand her every word.

"Everyone is praying for you," she said more slowly, exaggerating the movement of her lips.

"Thank you." I bowed slightly.

"When will they let you come home?" she asked, but I pretended not to understand. I could never tell my parents I had a life sentence. This would kill them. They were terrified and devastated, but at least they had some hope that I might go home one day. I didn't know what to tell them. I wanted to embrace my mother and never let go.

"Sarah is okay," I finally said after staring at them for a minute.

"What?"

I wrote "Sarah" on the glass with my finger, and my mother followed my finger with hers.

"Sarah?" she asked.

"Yes."

"She's okay?"

"Yes."

"Time is up!" a guard yelled.

"Be brave, Marina!" my mother said.

The prison was always very quiet after visitation days. Sitting in our lonely corners, we tried not to think of how our lives used to be before Evin, but it was hopeless, because memories were all we had. We missed our families and our lives, the way we once were. We had no future, only the past.

The day after visitations, we received small packages of clothing from home. I opened mine. Shirts, pants, brand-new underwear, and a sweater. Everything in the package smelled like home, like hope. Taraneh was running her fingers over a faded red wool sweater and told me that it was her lucky sweater. "This will bring me luck," she said and explained that her mother had made that sweater years earlier when she had just learned to knit. Taraneh and her sisters all wanted it. When her mother decided to give it to Taraneh, her sisters were upset, but her mother explained to them that she had to give it to one of them and that it was fair to give it to the youngest. She had promised to make each of Taraneh's three sisters a sweater exactly like it, but she had not kept her promise. Taraneh believed that whenever she wore that sweater, good things happened to her, and she wondered if it still had its magic.

"Taraneh, we'll go home one day," I said.

"I know."

"We'll do all the things we love to do."

"We'll go for long walks, right?"

"Yeah, and we'll go to my cottage."

"We'll go shopping."

"We'll cook, bake, and eat everything!"

We laughed.

That night I couldn't sleep. I thought about how Ali had managed to reduce my sentence, and maybe, he could do the same thing for Taraneh; maybe he could help Sarah as well. But he had told me that he was going away, and the truth was that I didn't want to face him ever again. He terrified me. In a way, it was easier for me to deal with Hamehd, because with Hamehd, I knew what to expect. With Ali, things were different. He had never hurt me—but yet, I felt a raw, deep fear when he was close to me. I thought of the night of the executions. I had avoided thinking about it. My brain refused to recall the terrifying images. But I knew they were there, untouched and clear. And when Ali took me to the cell, I remembered the look in his eyes. The longing. It made me feel as if I were trapped in the bottom of a frozen ocean. But for Taraneh's sake, I had to talk to him.

I went to the office in the morning and knocked on the door. Sister Maryam sat behind her desk, reading something. She looked at me with questioning eyes.

"Is there any way for me to see Brother Ali?" I asked.

Her eyes dug into mine. "Why do you want to see him?"

I explained how he had saved my life and that now I wanted to ask him to save a friend of mine.

"Who?" Sister Maryam asked.

I hcsitated.

"Taraneh?"

"Yes."

"Brother Ali isn't here. He's at the front, fighting the Iraqis." Iran had been in war with Iraq since September 1980.

"When is he coming back?"

"Only God knows. But even if he was here, he couldn't do anything. You got very lucky. When an Islamic court condemns someone to death, the only thing that can save that person is Imam's pardon. But the imam doesn't usually interfere with these things. He trusts the courts and their decisions. The only person who might be able to do something for her is her own interrogator."

"Is there anything we can do for her?"

"Pray."

I tried not to think of happiness, of the way things used to be before the revolution, before terrible things happened, as if recalling the bright memories would make them fade like old pictures that are handled too many times. But sometimes, in the middle of the night, I would breathe in the fragrance of wild lemon trees and hear the rustling of their thick leaves in the clean, salty sea breeze. I would feel the warm waves of the Caspian swirling around my feet and the sticky, wet sand covering my toes. In my dreams, I would lie down on my bed at the cottage, watching the full moon rise. Then, I would step on the floor, but it wouldn't creak, I would walk around, but there would be nobody there, and I would try to call Arash, but no sound would come from my throat.

I thought of Andre all the time. Before my arrest, my love for him had been young and fragile. I was afraid to give in to my love for him because I was afraid of losing him—and I didn't want to betray Arash. Now, in the face of my own mortality, I knew I was in love with Andre. There was nothing I wished for more in the world than to be with him. But did he love me? I believed he did. He was my hope. I had to survive for him. He was the one I wanted to go back to.

One night in mid-March, Sheida went into labor and was taken to the prison hospital. The next day, she returned with a beautiful, healthy baby boy, whom she had named Kaveh, her husband's name. We all gathered around her and the baby. We were proud to have a mother in our room and called her Mother Sheida from then on. The baby was spoiled very soon; he had many eager aunts to look after him. And although it never completely went away, the dark shadow of worry on Sheida's face lightened a little; the baby gave hope not only to his mother, but to everyone around him.

When Kaveh was two or three weeks old, about seventy prisoners from 246 were transferred to Ghezel Hessar, a prison in the city of Karaj, about fifteen miles from Tehran. Most of the girls said the living conditions in Ghezel Hessar were slightly better than Evin, so the ones leaving were rather happy. I was glad that none of my close friends had been called. After the transfer, the rooms were a little less crowded, but this didn't last long. Every day, a few new girls joined us, and before long, sleeping spots were tighter than ever before.

As frequently as once a week, military marches played through the loudspeakers, and it was announced that the army had won major battles and our troops were about to gloriously end the war with Iraq, but none of us really cared much about the war; not only because it had not touched Tehran directly, but because Evin felt like another planet, a strange world with incomprehensible rules that could condemn any of us to torture or death without any reason.

One evening, as we were having our dinner of bread and dates, Sarah walked into the room, and, without taking off her chador, saying anything, or looking at anyone, went to a corner and sat down. I went to her and put my hand on her shoulder.

"Sarah?"

She didn't look up.

"Sarah, where were you? We were so worried."

"Sirus is dead," she said in a calm voice.

I tried to find the right words to say, but there were none.

"I have two pens," she whispered.

"What?"

"I stole them. They don't know."

She took a black pen out of her pocket, pulled up her left sleeve, and began writing on her wrist: "Sirus is dead. We went to the Caspian one summer and played on the beach with a beach ball. So many colors. The waves splashed . . ." I noticed there was more written on her arm. The words were small but legible. They were memories. Her memories of Sirus, her family, and her life.

"Do you have any paper or anything?" she asked.

"I'll find you some paper. Sarah, where were you?"

"I'm running out of room. Please, find me some paper."

I found her a piece of paper, but it wasn't enough for her. She began writing on walls. She wrote the same things over and over about our elementary and high schools, the games we played, the books we read, our favorite teachers, new year celebrations, summer vacations, her house, our neighborhood, her parents, and all the things Sirus liked to do.

When we finally had warm water one night, she refused to take a shower.

"Sarah, you have to wash up. Whether you shower or not, the words will fade. If you wash up, then you can write again. You'll smell really bad if you don't."

"My pens are running out of ink."

"I'll find you new pens if you shower."

"You promise?" she asked.

I didn't want to make a promise unless I was sure I could keep it, so I went to the office and explained the situation to Sister Maryam. I told her that Sarah didn't write anything political; she only wrote her memories of her family.

Sister Maryam gave me two pens, and I ran to Sarah, feeling like I had just found the world's greatest treasure.

When Sarah took off her clothes in the shower room, I couldn't believe what I saw. Her legs, her arms, and her stomach were covered with tiny words.

"I couldn't reach my back. I'll take a shower only if you promise to write on my back," she said.

"I promise."

And she washed the words off her skin. The Book of Sarah. Alive, breathing, feeling, hurting, remembering.


About three months after my arrival at 246, my name was announced over the loudspeaker. My friends looked at me nervously. I put my shawl over my head with trembling hands.

"I'm sure it's good news," Taraneh said, her eyes filling with hope.

I took a deep breath and opened the door leading to the foyer. Sister Maryam was waiting for me in the office. I sensed she was worried.

"Where am I going?" I asked.

"Brother Hamehd has sent for you."

"Do you know why?"

"No, but don't worry. I'm sure he just wants to see how you're doing."

I put on my blindfold and followed another one of the sisters to the other building. I waited in the hallway until Hamehd called me. I followed him into a room. He closed the door behind us and told me to remove my blindfold. He hadn't changed at all. His eyes were cold, dark caves. There was a torture bed in the corner, a desk, and two chairs. A lash made of black cable was hanging from the headboard of the bed. My breathing became rushed and shallow.

"Marina, how nice to see you," he said, smiling. "Sit down and tell me, how is *life?*"

His words were like bee stings.

"Life is fine," I said, smiling back.

"So, you took off on me in a hurry that night, remember? Did you ever wonder about what happened to the others who were with you?"

My heart was beating so fast I felt like my head was going to explode. "I didn't take off. Ali took me away, and I know exactly what happened to the others. You killed them."

There were bloodstains on the torture bed, and I couldn't take my eyes off them.

"I have to tell you that although I don't like you, you do amuse me. Have you ever wished you had died with them that night?"

"I have."

He was still smiling.

"You know that your sentence is life in prison, don't you?"

"Yes, I do."

*If he lashes me, he won't stop until I'm dead.*

"Doesn't this bother you? I mean, you haven't exactly had fun for the last couple of months, have you? Imagine it going on forever."

"God will help me through," I said.

He stood up and walked around the room for a minute and then came toward me and slapped my right cheek with the back of his hand so hard I felt my neck had cracked. My right ear was ringing.

"Ali isn't here to protect you anymore."

I covered my face with my hands.

"Don't ever say 'God' again! You're unclean and unworthy of His name. I have to go and wash my hands because I've touched you. I'm starting to believe that a life sentence might be better for you after all. You'll suffer for a long time without any hope."

There was a knock on the door. Hamehd opened it and stepped out. I was unable to think clearly. What could he possibly want from me?

A man whom I had never met before came into the room.

"Hello, Marina. My name is Mohammad. I'm taking you back to 246."

I looked at him, puzzled. I couldn't believe that Hamehd was letting me go so easily.

"Are you okay?" Mohammad asked me.

"I'm fine."

"Put on your blindfold and let's go."

He left me at the office of 246, where Sister Maryam told me to take off my blindfold as soon as I arrived. Sister Masoomeh sat behind the desk, reading something.

"Why is your face so red?" Sister Maryam asked.

Sister Masoomeh looked up.

I told them what had happened.

"Thank God I was able to find Brother Mohammad! He and Brother Ali are very close friends. They worked in the same building. I called and told him Hamehd had taken you. He promised he'd find you and bring you back," said Sister Maryam.

"You were lucky, Marina. Hamehd doesn't need a good reason to seriously hurt people if he feels like it," Sister Masoomeh whispered.

"As you can see," Sister Maryam turned to me, "Sister Masoomeh is not Hamehd's best friend, but she has learned to bite her tongue. Even though she was one of the Muslim Students Following the Line of the Imam, one of the hostage-takers at the American embassy, and she personally knows the imam, she's had problems with Hamehd. The only people I know around here who can really stand up to Hamehd are Brother Ali and Brother Mohammad."

"Don't worry, Marina. Now that Hamehd knows Brother Mohammad is watching your back, he won't bother you again," said Sister Masoomeh.

Everyone at room 7 was happy to see me and wanted to know where I had been. But once they saw the swollen red mark on my cheek, they knew I only had bad news. I had no hope of parole, but I was not going to give up. This was what Hamehd wanted me to do. He had tried to crush my spirits and had almost succeeded. Almost.

I thought about what Sister Maryam had told me about Sister

Masoomeh. It was hard to believe that she was one of the hostage-takers at the U.S. embassy in Tehran. I remembered watching the news about the hostage-taking on television when it happened. I had been worried for the hostages. They had families back home; people who loved them, needed them, and wanted them back. Their captivity lasted 444 days, and they were released on January 20, 1981. Now, my situation was much worse than theirs had been. They were U.S. citizens, and this meant that they were somebody. At least their government had tried to save them, and the world knew about the horrible thing that had happened to them. Did the world know about us? Was anyone trying to save us? Deep in my heart I knew that the answer to both these questions was no.

I thought of the church constantly. I could smell the candles burning in front of the image of the Virgin, their lights flickering with the hope of being heard. Had she forgotten me? I remembered that Jesus had said that with the tiniest amount of faith we could throw a mountain into the sea. I didn't want to move anything as big as a mountain; I just wanted to go home.

On my birthday, I woke up very early. It wasn't even time for the morning *namaz* yet. I was seventeen years old. When I was younger, maybe ten or eleven, I had dreamt of being this age. Back then, I believed that a seventeen-year-old could do anything. Instead, I was a political prisoner with a life sentence. Taraneh touched my shoulder, and I turned around. Her sleeping spot was next to mine.

"Happy birthday," she whispered.

"Thanks. How did you know I was awake?"

"By the way you were breathing. After all this time sleeping next to someone, you can tell if they're really asleep or just pretending."

She asked me if my family celebrated birthdays, and I said my parents usually bought me a cake and a little gift. She said birthdays were very important in her family. They had big parties and showered each other with gifts. She and her sisters had a competition between them: they sewed garments for each other, and every year, the garments got fancier.

"Marina, I miss them," she said.

I put my arms around her. "You'll go home, and everything will be the same."

After lunch, Taraneh, Sarah, and a few of my other friends surrounded me. Sarah handed me a folded piece of fabric. I opened it. It was a quilted pillowcase. I gasped. It was beautiful. Each of my friends had donated a small piece of their clothes or scarves to make it. I recognized every single square. It was a prison custom to make small, sewn bags, which we hung from a hook under the shelf in our room to store our little personal items. I was the first one to receive a pillowcase.

After dinner, we had a prison-style birthday cake made of bread and dates. I pretended to blow out imaginary candles.

"You forgot to make a wish!" Taraneh said.

"I'll make it now: I wish for all of us to spend our next birthdays at home."

Everyone clapped and cheered.

Two or three days later, it was announced over the loudspeaker that all the prisoners of the second floor of 246 were to put on their *hejab* and gather in the yard. Although we could go outside at specific times of day, this had never been mandatory. Everyone was worried. Once in the yard, we were told to stay clear of a marked area in the middle. Four armed, male revolutionary guards walked out of the building, escorting two girls. One of them was a friend of mine from our room, who was nineteen years old, and the other was from room 5. They had their chadors on and were told to lie down on the ground in the middle of the yard. One of the guards tied their wrists and ankles with rope. It was announced that they had had a homosexual relationship and therefore were going to be punished according to the laws of Islam. Everybody was horrified. We watched as two of the guards lashed the girls' backs. Many didn't look, covering their faces and praying, but I couldn't close my eyes. I watched the lashes rising in the air, turning into a blur, slicing the air with their sharp, piercing cries. Then, a second of silence when one's heart seems to stop, when lungs refuse to breathe. The two girls weren't screaming, but I wished they were. Their small bodies shook with every blow. I remembered the terrifying pain I had experienced when I had been lashed myself. After thirty lashes, they were untied, managed to stand up, and were taken away. We were left behind to think about what had happened to our friends. Suffering is supposed to make us stronger, but we first have to pay the price.

One day, it was my turn to help Sheida with her laundry. Washing cloth diapers in cold water was not an easy task. We had washed the diapers in the morning and had hung them to dry in the yard. Although everyone had to wait until the next day to collect their laundry from the clotheslines, Sheida was allowed to go outside in the evening. She walked a few steps ahead of me. It was spring and birds were chirping in the distance. The sun had just set, and the sky was a glowing pink. The five clotheslines were at the end of the yard, each tied to the bars of the first-floor windows, stretching all the way from one side of the yard to the other, covered with colorful clothes. Sheida disappeared behind the walls of fabric, and I followed her, using my arms to push dresses, pants, skirts, shirts, and chadors out of my way. Then I heard her scream.

"Marina! Run! Get scissors! Hurry! Now!"

I caught a glimpse of Sheida holding someone who was hanging from the bars of one of the windows. I ran to the office and banged on the door. Sister Maryam opened it.

"Scissors! Now! In the yard!"

She grabbed a pair of scissors from her desk, and we ran to where I had left Sheida. She was still holding someone. I realized it was Sarah. She had hanged herself with a short rope made of scarves. The rope was tied above the top horizontal bar of a first-floor window. If Sarah, who was short and small, had been even a little taller, she wouldn't have been able to do this. Her body was shaking. Sister Maryam cut the rope. Sarah was breathing, but her face had turned blue. We stayed with her while Sister Maryam went to get the nurse. Sarah was unconscious. We talked to her and touched her face, but she didn't react.

Sarah was taken away again.

I lost a little bit of hope with every passing moment. It was spring, and the air was light and carried the fragrance of blossoms. Life was going on outside the walls of Evin. Was I only a distant memory for Andre? Maybe he had forgotten me. Phones had been installed at the visitation area, and I had asked my parents about him. My mother had told me that he visited them all the time and was always thinking about me, but maybe they had said this not to upset me.

Every day was almost the same as the one before, which made our loneliness and desperation even more difficult to bear. Each day started with the morning prayer before sunrise. Breakfast came in at about eight o'clock, and after that we had to watch the religious education programs on the television. We were allowed to read the available books, which were all about Islam, or walk up and down the narrow hallways. We hardly ever spoke about politics or our political involvements and activities before Evin. Some girls were known as informants. There weren't many of them, maybe one or two in each room, so we didn't risk saying things we didn't want our interrogators to know.

For about an hour a day, we could use the small courtyard that was surrounded by the building. We had to wear our *hejab* while out there, because male guards walked on the roof all the time and watched us closely, but it wasn't mandatory to wear chadors in the yard; we could wear manteaus and head scarves. While outside, all we could do was to walk around in circles or sit by the walls and watch the slice of sky above us. That small patch of blue was the only part of the outside world we could see. It reminded us of the other place where we once used to live, where our homes were, and where we belonged. I usually sat by the wall with Taraneh. We leaned against its rough surface and watched the clouds as they disappeared out of our view and traveled to that other land. Imagining that we sat on a cloud and could steer it in any direction, we told each other about all the familiar places we could see from up there: the streets of our neighborhoods, our schools, and our homes, where our mothers looked out the windows and wondered about their daughters who had been taken away.

"How did you get in trouble and end up here?" Taraneh asked me one day as we soaked in the warmth of the spring sun, daydreaming about home. We had never talked about the events that had led to our arrests. The yard was filled with girls. Most of them walked around rather fast and in a purposeful manner, as if they had a destination. Black, navy, brown, and gray manteaus brushed against each other, and rubber slippers moved swiftly against the paved ground. I realized that what I saw sitting there was similar to the view of a beggar sitting on the side of a busy street, but my view was much more limited and more modest than a beggar's view. At that moment, my world was like a roofless square building with two levels of barred windows that looked inside dark rooms, a world of young women walking in circles. It was like a very strange science fiction story: "The Planet of Imprisoned Girls." I laughed.

"What?" asked Taraneh.

"It almost feels like we're beggars sitting on a sidewalk on another planet."

Taraneh smiled.

"Compared to us, a beggar is a king," she said.

"My trouble started the day I walked out of calculus class . . ."

# Eleven

IN EARLY 1980, Abolhassan Banisadr became the first elected president of Iran. Before the success of the revolution, he had participated in the anti-shah movement for many years, had been imprisoned twice, and had then managed to flee to France and join Ayatollah Khomeini. There were hopes that he would lead Iran to democracy. However, as the school year of 1979–80 inched forward, I felt like I was sinking into darkness. Everything gradually changed for the worse. One by one, inexperienced, fanatic young women replaced most of our teachers. The *hejab* became mandatory, and women had to wear either long, dark-colored robes and cover their hair with large scarves, or they had to wear chadors. Political groups that had opposed or even criticized the Islamic government became illegal. Wearing ties, cologne, perfume, makeup, or nail polish was declared "satanic" and therefore subject to severe punishment. Every day before going to class, students were forced to line up and yell hateful slogans like "Death to America" and "Death to Israel."

Every morning, our principal Khanoom Mahmoodi, and our vice principal, Khanoom Kheirkhah, stood at the school entrance with a bucket of water and a washcloth and inspected every student entering the school. If they saw one of the girls wearing makeup, they scrubbed her face until it hurt. One morning, during her inspection, Khanoom Mahmoodi pulled aside a good friend of mine, Nasim, and claimed that her eyebrows were too perfect—she must have trimmed them. Nasim cried and said she had never done anything to them, and the principal called her a whore. Nasim was naturally beautiful, and many of us defended her and testified that her eyebrows had always been like that. She never received an apology.

Day by day, anger and frustration built up within me. I suffered during most of my classes, especially during calculus. The new calculus teacher was a young woman from the revolutionary guards who wasn't qualified to teach the subject. She spent most of the class time spreading the Islamic government's propaganda, talking about Islam and the perfect Islamic society that resisted the influence of the West and moral corruption. One day as she was going on and on about the great things Khomeini had done for the country, I raised my hand.

"Yes?" she said.

"I don't mean to be rude, miss, but can we please get back to our main subject?"

She raised an eyebrow and said in a challenging tone, "If you don't like what I'm teaching, you can leave the classroom."

Everyone was looking at me. I collected my books and left the room. As I walked down the hallway, I heard the sound of many footsteps coming from behind me. Turning around, I saw that most of my classmates had followed me out. There were about thirty of us standing in the hallway.

By lunch recess, the school was in chaos. Everyone was saying that I had started a strike. Most afternoon classes were canceled because about 90 percent of the students were in the yard, refusing to go back to class. Khanoom Mahmoodi came outside with a loudspeaker and told us to go back, but no one listened. She said she would call our parents, but no one moved. Then she threatened to have us all expelled, but we said she could go right ahead and do that. Finally, the students chose me and two others as representatives to speak to the principal. We informed her that we were only going back to class if our teachers promised to stick to their subjects and put politics aside.

That day when I got home, my mother called my name. This was unusual. She hardly ever talked to me before dinnertime. She was in the kitchen, chopping parsley.

I stood in the doorway. "Yes, Maman?"

"Your principal called." She didn't look at me but kept her eyes on the cutting board. Her knife moved smoothly and precisely. Diced parsley covered her hands, making them green.

"What do you think you're doing?" she asked, throwing me a quick glance as sharp as her knife.

I told her what had happened.

"You'd better fix this problem," she said. "I don't want her to call me again. Just get along with them. This government isn't going to last long. Now go do your homework."

I went to my room and closed the door behind me, surprised to have escaped her anger so easily. Probably my mother disliked the new government as much as I did, and this was why her reaction had not been as severe as I had anticipated.

The strike continued for two days. We still went to school, but not to class. We passed the hours by walking around the yard or sitting in small groups, talking. Our conversations were mostly about all we had witnessed during the recent months. It was hard for us to believe that life had changed so dramatically. Just a year earlier, we would never have believed that our clothes would put our lives in danger, or that we would go on strike in order to learn calculus. On the third day of the strike, Khanoom Mahmoodi called the student representatives to her office.

Her face red with anger, she said she was giving us a final warning. She told us if we didn't go back to class, she'd have no other choice but to ask the revolutionary guards to come to our school and take the matter into their hands. She said she had no doubt we knew that the guards wouldn't be very patient with us, that this was a serious matter and people could get hurt. She warned us that we were acting against the Islamic government and that the penalty for this could be death. We had an hour to go back to class.

She had made her point. The revolutionary guards had a bad reputation. During the previous months they had arrested hundreds of people, many of whom were never heard from again. Their crime had been being anti-revolution, anti-Islam, or anti-Khomeini.

The strike ended.

The guards were not the only ones to worry about; there was also the Hezbollah, groups of fanatical civilians armed with knives and clubs, who attacked any kind of public protest. They were everywhere and could become organized in a matter of minutes. They were especially violent toward women who didn't wear the *hejab* properly. Many women had been attacked and beaten for wearing lipstick or because a few strands of their hair had been showing from under their scarves.

It was about a month or two after the strike that my chemistry teacher, Khanoom Bahman, asked me to stay behind after class and told me about the list of names she had spotted on Khanoom Mahmoodi's desk. Khanoom Bahman was one of only a few teachers who had been teaching at our school since before the revolution, and she knew me very well. As she spoke her eyes remained on the door to make sure no one walked in on us. Her voice was almost a whisper, and I had to bend down to hear her properly.

Somehow, I expected something like this could happen. I knew I would be in trouble after all I had said and done. The fact that I didn't like the new Islamic rules was not a secret, and during these times one couldn't exactly speak freely without repercussions. But even though I knew all this, the dangers I could face seemed vague and distant. Somehow, I thought bad things only happened to other people.

I thanked Khanoom Bahman for telling me about the list. She told me I had to leave the country. She asked me if I had any relatives abroad, and I explained to her that my family was not rich and could not afford to send me anywhere. She interrupted me, raising her voice.

"Marina, I don't think you understand. This is a matter of life and death. If I were your mother, I'd get you out of here, even if I had to go hungry," she said with tears in her eyes.

I liked her, and I didn't want to upset her, so I told her I would talk to my parents, but I had no intention of doing so. What would I tell them? That I was going to be arrested soon?

My brother and his wife had left the country shortly after the revolution and had migrated to Canada. They had realized that there was no future for them in the Islamic Republic. Not too long after their departure, the government of Iran denied Iranians the right to migrate to other countries. I liked the name "Canada"; it sounded far away and very cold but peaceful. My brother and his wife were lucky to be there. They could live a normal life and worry about normal things. My parents had thought of sending me to stay with my brother, but it couldn't be worked out. I had to stay and take my chances.

At home that afternoon, I watched the street from my balcony. The new regime had brought nothing but destruction and violence. School, which used to be the best part of my life, had turned into a kind of hell, and I had heard that the government was planning to close down all universities for restructuring, calling it the Islamic Cultural Revolution. And Arash was dead. There was nothing left.

Most of the summer of 1980 was quiet, and I was relieved to be out of school and to be going to our cottage. In July, Aram and his parents spent about two weeks at his aunt's cottage. I had been very lonely and had looked forward to their arrival, but when they came, I found myself thinking of Arash and missing him even more. Aram and I spent most of our time inside, playing cards or his favorite game, Mastermind. We sometimes went for walks on the beach but couldn't go swimming together because now women were not allowed to wear bathing suits in public. Most of our friends, including Neda, whose families had owned cottages in the area had left the country. We met a few old friends, but all of us were afraid of the revolutionary guards and the members of Islamic committees, who were everywhere and disliked it when boys and girls were seen together; according to the new laws governing the country, this was immoral.

The Iran-Iraq war began in September 1980. I was back in the city. I had gone to a friend's house, and we were sitting in her kitchen, having tea and rice cookies. She was showing me her new pair of Puma running shoes, which were white with red stripes on either side. Suddenly two deep booms interrupted our talk. They sounded like explosions. We were home alone.

More booms.

We looked out the window but saw nothing. My friend lived on the fifth floor of a five-story apartment building close to Jaleh Square. We decided to run up to the roof. In the hallway, we bumped into a few neighbors who were also on their way up. Once on the roof, we had a good view of the city. It was a cloudless, sunny day, and Tehran was wrapped in a thin haze. We heard planes.

"Over there!" someone yelled.

A few miles to the south, two fighter jets zoomed eastward. On the western horizon, columns of smoke rose into the sky. One of the neighbors had brought a radio with him and turned it on. Soon, an excited reporter announced that Iraqi MIGs had bombed Tehran's airport. Different divisions of Iraq's army had crossed the border and entered Iran. We were at war.

I had read about the First and Second World Wars and the American Civil War. I had read about bombs that demolished cities and left nothing but rubble and dead bodies. But those wars were in books. Even if the stories were true, they had all happened years earlier. The world was now a different place. No one would be allowed to destroy cities and kill thousands of people.

"We'll show them!" the man with the radio waved his fist in the air. "We'll conquer Baghdad and stone Saddam! Those bastards!"

Everyone nodded.

Once I got home, I found my mother taping large Xs on windows with masking tape to prevent glass from shattering in case of bombings. She explained to me that the radio was urging people to take precautions while promising that this war was not going to last more than a few days or weeks at the most and that our army was going to defeat the Iraqis in no time. My mother had also bought pieces of black cardboard to cover the windows at night so the MIGs wouldn't spot our lights and use them to target us. I wasn't too worried. It couldn't be that bad.

Days went by. Air raid sirens screamed a couple of times a day, but we rarely heard explosions. Radio and television channels played military marches all day and announced that the air force had attacked Baghdad and other Iraqi cities and that we had pushed back the Iraqis. All men, young and old and even teenagers, were encouraged to join the army and to become martyrs; after all, the government announced, becoming a martyr was the fast, guaranteed way to go to heaven. This was the war of good against evil. The city of Khorramshahr, which was close to Iran's border with Iraq, had been almost entirely destroyed and then invaded.

All borders were soon closed, and no one was allowed to leave the country without a special permit. However, every day, people who had paid great sums of money to human smugglers left Iran to avoid military service or to escape arrest by the revolutionary guards. They risked their lives to cross into Pakistan or Turkey.

Sometime in late fall, I heard from friends at school about a protest rally and decided to go. Although I knew it was dangerous, it seemed the right thing to do. The rally was to start at four o'clock at Ferdosi Square, a ten-minute walk from school.

On the day of the rally, after the final bell rang, Gita, Sarah, and I stepped outside and saw hundreds of people, mostly young men and women, filling the street. We joined the throng walking toward Ferdosi Square. Everyone was alert, looking around, knowing that eventually the revolutionary guards or the Hezbollah or both were going to attack us. My heart began to race. The street was a seething, breathing river. I noticed shopkeepers closing down their stores and leaving. At Ferdosi Square, holding a loudspeaker in front of her mouth, a young woman told the crowd about the violent attacks of the Hezbollah on women: "How long are we going to allow criminals and murderers hiding behind the name of God to attack our mothers, sisters, and friends and get away with it?" she asked. An old woman stood next to us, holding a sheet of white bristol board in front of her. She had tied her white chador around her waist, exposing her thinning gray hair to the sun. In the middle of the bristol board, there was a picture of a young girl with a big smile on her face and under the picture it said: "Executed in Evin."

Suddenly, the street was filled with loud, thunderlike roars. People began to run.

"On rooftops!" someone yelled.

I looked up and saw revolutionary guards everywhere. A young man standing close to us fell to the ground and moaned. He pressed his hands to his stomach. A narrow red line emerged from between his fingers, moved down his hand, and dripped onto the pavement. I stared at him and couldn't move. People screamed and ran in different directions. There was smoke in the air, and my eyes were burning. I looked around; I had been separated from my friends. I couldn't leave the injured man like that. Kneeling beside him, I looked into his eyes and saw the stillness of death. Arash had died like him—as a stranger. Somewhere, someone loved this man and was waiting for him to come home.

"Marina!" a familiar voice called.

Gita grabbed my hand and pulled me along. The air was thick with tear gas. Bearded men wearing civilian clothing swung wooden clubs in the air, attacking the fleeing crowd. People screamed. We ran through the madness surrounding us.

When I got home, I locked myself in the bathroom. I wished I had been shot to death. I didn't want to live. What was the point of so much suffering? I went to my parents' bedroom and opened my mother's medicine drawer. It was overflowing with jars and boxes of different shapes and sizes: cold syrups, antacids, aspirin, and different kinds of painkillers. I rummaged through them, found an almost-full bottle of sleeping pills, and rushed back to the bathroom. Death in a jar. All I needed to do was to remove the lid and swallow the little pills. The angel would come for me, and I would tell him that I had watched enough people die. I filled a cup with water and opened the lid of the container. But deep inside me, I knew that swallowing those pills was wrong. What if everyone who believed in goodness decided to commit suicide because there was too much suffering in the world? I closed my eyes and saw the eyes of the angel. I wanted my grandma, Arash, and Irena to be proud of me; I wanted to do something with my life, something good and worthwhile. I had watched a young man's life pour into a swollen circle of blood on the pavement. I couldn't hide; death was not a hiding place. Closing the lid of the container, I returned it to my mother's medicine drawer. Maybe there was something I could do. I ran to the store, bought a white sheet of bristol board, and wrote about the attack of the revolutionary guards on the peaceful rally.

The next day, I went to school earlier than usual. The hallways were empty. I taped the bristol board to a wall in one of the hallways and stood in front of it, pretending to read it. In about half an hour, students gathered, and soon, a big crowd was trying to read the story. It didn't take Khanoom Mahmoodi long to show up. She stormed down the hallway with quick, angry steps, her face red with rage.

"Move aside!" she yelled.

We stepped aside. She read a few lines and demanded to know who had written it. When no one answered, she ripped the board from the wall, shouting, "These are lies!"

"They are not!" I protested. "I was there!"

"So, *you* wrote it."

I told her the revolutionary guards had opened fire on innocent people.

"What innocent people? Only antirevolutionaries and the enemies of God and Islam attend rallies like that. You are in big trouble!" she said, pointing her finger at me. Then, she turned and left. I was enraged. How dare she call me a liar!

A few days later, my friends and I started a small school newspaper. Every week, we wrote a few short articles about daily political issues that had affected us, copied them by hand, and circulated them in the school.

The government had shut down a few independent newspapers, accusing their staff of being enemies of the Islamic revolution. I felt as if the country were slowly being submerged in water: breathing became a little more difficult every day. But we remained optimistic, believing they couldn't possibly drown everyone.

Since the war with Iraq had started, the Islamic regime had blamed everything on it. Prices had soared. Meat, dairy products, baby formula, and cooking oil were rationed. My mother usually went to the store at five in the morning to line up for our share and returned around noon. It was possible to find almost everything on the black market, but it was so expensive that low-income and middle-class families couldn't afford it, and the rations were very small.

In Tehran, the war felt distant; now, the sirens hardly ever sounded, and even if they did, nothing happened. However, cities that were close to the Iran-Iraq border paid dearly. Casualties were mounting. Every day, newspapers displayed dozens of pictures of young men killed at the front. And the government did its best to take advantage of people's emotions to coerce them to seek revenge. At mosques, through loudspeakers, mullahs yelled and screamed that the war was not only about protecting Iran but it was about Islam; Saddam was not a true Muslim but he was a follower of the devil.

Slowly, almost everything I loved became illegal. Western novels, my escape and solace, were declared "satanic" and became difficult to find. Then, in early spring of 1981, Khanoom Mahmoodi told me I needed to earn religion marks. Religious minorities had always been exempt from attending Islamic or Zoroastrian religion classes. Now, I either had to attend the Islamic religion class or provide my school with religion marks from my church. Although I had voluntarily attended Islamic religion classes in school before, I resisted doing it again. I had received enough Islamic education. Getting religion marks from church sounded like a practical and fair idea, but not in my case. Tehran's Russian Orthodox church hadn't had a priest for a long time. My mother called a friend who attended church regularly, and she directed me to a Roman Catholic church. Although this church was only a couple of blocks away from our place, I had not noticed it before, because without colorful stained-glass windows facing the street, it looked as gray and dull as the government offices and foreign embassies around it. The priests offered to assist me with my studies and to mark my efforts.

Once a week, I went to church for my catechism class: I had to ring the doorbell at the metal door that connected the street to the backyard of the church and be buzzed through. I would close the door behind me and walk along a narrow walkway wedged between the church and the brick walls surrounding the yard. Asphalt covered the ground. The church office and the priests' residence were in a separate building adjacent to the church. The priest would welcome me warmly, and we would read the Bible and discuss it. After the lesson, I would open the heavy wooden door that connected the yard to the church building. The door always creaked, and its sound spread into the deep silence, bouncing off the tall, curving walls. I loved to sit on a pew and look at the framed image of Mary: her long pink dress, her blue cloak covering her hair, and the peaceful smile on her face. Candles flickered in front of her. She knew about loss. She had experienced this pain. Here, I somehow felt at home.

# Twelve

ARLY IN THE AFTERNOON of May 1, 1982, Taraneh and five other girls were called to the office over the loudspeaker. Silence fell upon the prison. Everyone knew that the other five girls from this group were sentenced to death, but I was the only one who knew about Taraneh. As usual, Taraneh was sitting in a corner reading the Koran. She was the only one who had been called from our room. Everyone froze and stared at her. She stood up as if she were going for a little walk to stretch her legs. I went toward her, but she looked at me and shook her head. She grabbed her small bag, which was hanging from a hook, and her larger bag, which was on top of the shelf, walked over to me, and pushed them in my arms.

"You know I don't have much stuff. This is it. Find a good way of getting them to my parents."

I nodded. She put on her chador and walked out the door. I knew that my friend was going to her death. If I screamed until my throat bled, if I hit my head against the wall until my skull cracked, it would not save her. With Taraneh's bags in my arms, I stood in the middle of the room for a long time until my legs gave out. All day, not a word was said. We preserved the silence as if it were capable of preserving life, of performing a miracle. We waited, prayed, and cried silently, our lips moving without a sound. But the day came to a silent end and the horizon filled with reds and purples and the night crawled into the air. We listened for gunshots, and soon they came, as if glass clouds were falling from the sky.

# Thirteen

ABOUT FOUR AND A HALF MONTHS after my arrest, my name was called over the loudspeaker.

"Marina Moradi-Bakht, put on your *hejab*, and come to the office.

I didn't know why they had called me. Maybe Hamehd had missed me again. I covered my hair with my shawl and went to the office.

Sister Maryam greeted me with a smile. "Brother Ali is back," she said. "He's asked for you."

I put on my blindfold and followed her to another building,

where I waited in the hallway. My breaths felt like stones in my throat.

"Marina, follow me," said Ali's voice, and I obeyed him. He closed the door behind us and told me to sit down and take off my blindfold. He seemed taller than I remembered, but maybe this was because he had lost some weight.

I looked around. We were in a windowless room, and there were no torture beds. On one of the walls hung a picture of Ayatollah Khomeini, who, as Ali had told me, had given the order to spare my life. The ayatollah's dark eyebrows were knotted in a deep frown and his eyes stared at me with intense anger. He looked like a very mean old man. Next to Khomeini's picture was a picture of the president, Ayatollah Khamenei, who, compared to the imam, had a rather kind expression.

Limping, Ali brought out a chair from behind a metal desk and searched my face with his eyes. I had almost forgotten what he looked like. There was a new scar on his right cheek.

"You look a lot better than the last time I saw you," he said, smiling. "How have you been?"

"Well enough. How about you?"

"Are you just being polite or do you really want to know?"

"I want to know," I said, not meaning it. I just wanted to get out of that room. I wanted to run back to 246.

He told me he had spent four months at the war front fighting the Iraqis but had to come back when he was shot in the leg. I said I was sorry to hear it, which was true. I would never have wanted him or anyone else to get hurt.

He was watching me carefully, his smile changing to a serious expression.

"Marina, I have to discuss something important with you, and I want you to listen to me and not to interrupt me until I'm done."

I nodded, puzzled. He told me that his main reason for leaving Evin had been to stay away from me. He had believed that not seeing me would change his feelings, but it had not. He said he had had feelings for me since the moment we first met. He had tried to ignore them, but they had only become stronger. The night he walked me to the bathroom, he felt he had to save me at any cost, and this terrified him. When I didn't come out of the bathroom, he called me, but I didn't answer, so he came in to see what was wrong and found me on the floor. For a moment, he thought I was dead, but he took my pulse and realized I was alive. He knew that my name was on the execution list and that Hamehd didn't like me. He tried to reason with Hamehd, but Hamehd wouldn't listen. He said there was only one way for him to save my life and that was to go to Ayatollah Khomeini. Ali's father had been a close friend of the ayatollah for years. So Ali went to the imam and begged him for my life, explaining that I was too young and that I needed a chance to change my ways. The ayatollah told him that the charges against me were serious enough to put me on death row, but he kept pleading with him. The ayatollah finally agreed to reduce my sentence to life in prison. Ali rushed back to Evin and asked the guards where I was, and they told him Hamehd had taken me for execution. He said he prayed as he rushed to the site.

I felt a sense of panic rise inside me.

He said that after speaking with the ayatollah, he decided to send me to 246 and to go away. Since I had the imam's pardon, Hamehd could no longer harm me. Ali had tried to forget me but had found himself thinking about me all the time, and he was glad when he was shot, because he had a reason to come back. He said his father had always told him to sleep on every important decision of his life and to think about it thoroughly. He said he had slept on his decision of marrying me, had thought about it for more than four months, and had made his decision.

"I want you to marry me, Marina, and I promise to be a good husband and to take good care of you. Don't answer me now. I want you to think about it," he said

I tried to understand all I had just heard, but I couldn't. It didn't make any sense. How could he even think of marrying me? I didn't want to marry him. I didn't even want to be in the same room with him.

"Ali, you have to understand that I can't marry you," I said, my voice shaking.

"Why not?"

"There are many reasons!"

"I'm ready to hear them. Don't forget that I've thought about this for months, but you never know, I might've forgotten something. Go ahead and tell me your reasons."

"I don't love you, and I wasn't destined for you."

"I don't expect you to love me. Love can come in time, after you've given me a chance. And you said you weren't destined for me. Who were you destined for then? For Andre?"

I gasped. How did he know about Andre?

He told me that once when I was sleeping, he had stayed by my side, and I had called Andre's name in my sleep. He said he had done some research and knew exactly who Andre was and where he lived. Although Andre didn't have a political record, Ali said, he could arrange one for him if he had to.

Even though I knew I sometimes talked in my sleep, it was hard for me to believe what he had said. Maybe they had been watching me before my arrest, and this was how they knew about Andre. I had dragged Andre into this. What could I do?

"Do you want to see him here?" Ali asked. "Maybe on a torture bed? Let him live his life. You have to accept the fact that your life completely changed when you were arrested. And don't forget about your parents. I'm sure you don't want to put them in danger. Why should they pay for you? I promise to make you happy. You'll learn to love me."

I told him he had no right to do this to me, and he said he did. He told me maybe I had forgotten that he had saved me from certain death. As an enemy of Islam, I had no rights. He believed he was doing me a favor. He said I didn't know what was best for me.

I desperately searched for an escape. My death would solve many problems.

"I know you too well," he said, his voice separating me from my thoughts. "I know exactly what you're thinking right now. You're thinking of suicide. I can see it in your eyes, but I also know you're not going to do it. You're not the kind to give up. It's against your nature. You're a fighter just like me. Let go of the past, and we can have a wonderful life together. And just to be on the safe side, I promise you that if you put yourself in harm's way on purpose, I'll have your Andre executed. He'll pay for you."

How could I possibly have a "wonderful" life with him? He was threatening to execute Andre and to arrest my parents.

"I give you three days to think about this, but remember not to do anything stupid. I'm very serious about everything I said."

I had put Andre and my parents in danger, and I had to do everything I could to protect them. I had to remember that I had a life sentence. For me, there was no escape. I almost wished I had never met Andre.

# Fourteen

I MET ANDRE the very first time I attended the Sunday mass at my new Catholic church. That day, after the service ended, I went to the small office to chat with the priests. As I waited, Andre, who was the organist, came in. During mass, although I had sat at the back of the church, I had noticed that he was quite handsome. Now, I realized I was looking at the clothed version of Michelangelo's David. His face was oval, with a long, aristocratic nose, curls of golden hair covered his wide forehead, and his eyes were the color of the Caspian on a calm day. He was beautiful. Blushing, I looked down, hoping my thoughts were not as transparent as I feared. We introduced ourselves.

The church served a very small community, so every newcomer attracted a great deal of attention and curiosity. He asked me if I was a university student and when I told him I was in the tenth grade, he turned scarlet. I told him about my Russian background, and he said he was an electrical engineering student at the University of Tehran, but since all universities had been shut down to undergo the Islamic Cultural Revolution, he had been teaching English, physics, and math at an Armenian school.

As our conversation progressed, I felt a wave of trembling excitement wash through me. He was poised and soft spoken. I told him I had enjoyed his music, and he told me he was a novice. After the revolution when the government took over the all-boys school that belonged to the church, many of the priests who had run the school were deported, accused of being spies. Andre had attended their school for twelve years. One of the priests awaiting deportation had been the organist for a long time. He gave Andre, who had never played any musical instruments, a few music lessons, and once he left, Andre took over his job.

"You should join our choir," Andre told me. "We're looking for new members right now."

I said I couldn't sing.

"Give it a try. It's fun. Our next practice is on Wednesday night at six. You don't have any special plans for that night, do you?"

"No."

"Okay, I'll see you on Wednesday night then."

He stood up and shook my hand.

Once he was gone, I had a chance to catch my breath.


Aram still walked home with me at least once a week. He was in the twelfth grade, his last year of high school.

"We're planning to leave Iran in a few months and hopefully go

154

to the United States," he told me on a warm, sunny spring afternoon. I knew this day would come. We had been good friends for more than two years. I didn't want to lose him, but I knew that the best thing for him was to leave and to start a new life away from all the painful memories we shared.

I told him I was happy for him. He stopped and looked at me; there were tears in his eyes. He said he wished I could go with him; he was concerned for my safety. Many kids from his school had been arrested and taken to Evin, and he had heard that no one got out of there alive. I told him he was being paranoid, but he argued that it had nothing to do with paranoia.

"Aram, there's no need to worry," I insisted.

"Arash used to say the same thing . . . Hey, wait a second; I just thought of something, but no, it can't be . . . but on the other hand . . ."

He stopped in the middle of the narrow sidewalk in front of a small produce store. Boxes and baskets filled with fruits and vegetables blocked part of the sidewalk. The strong scent of fresh parsley, dill weed, chives, and basil thickened the hot afternoon air.

"You're not trying to get yourself killed, are you?" he suddenly asked, almost in tears.

I told him I had no intention of committing suicide.

A large woman, who was trying to get past us to enter the store and tired of waiting for our conversation to end, said a frustrated "excuse me" and almost pushed both of us into a big box of onions. Regaining his balance, Aram looked at me. I stepped out of the way and onto the side of the road and again reassured him that I'd be fine. As we walked along, I reached for his hand. He shook me off.

"What're you doing? We'll get arrested!" he said, glancing around, his face a deep red.

"I . . . I'm sorry! I'm an idiot! I wasn't thinking." I swallowed my tears.

"I'm sorry, Marina. I didn't mean to be rude. But how will I be able to live with myself if you get lashed for holding my hand?"

"I'm sorry."

"See, this is another reason why you should leave. Holding hands is not a crime. You tell this to someone who lives in a normal country and they'll think it's a bad joke."

A few minutes later, I remembered I had meant to ask him if he knew anyone who could translate Russian into Persian. I explained to him that my grandmother had written her life story and that she had given it to me before her death. I needed someone to translate it into Persian. He asked me why I didn't ask my parents to do that and I told him that my grandmother had entrusted it to me. Maybe she didn't want them to have it. I wanted someone who didn't know me to help me with it. He told me that Irena had had a friend who was a little strange but spoke many languages and was fluent in both Persian and Russian. He promised to call her.

We were almost halfway home when I noticed that a storm was approaching. Dark clouds covered the sky. It was strange how a beautiful sunny day could change within a few minutes. We heard the first roll of thunder. It started to rain. We were still far from home, and there was no shelter. At first, it came slowly; I could see each drop of rain as it hit the ground. Maybe we could still make it home before the peak of the storm, but no, it was too late. Thunder roared and the perfect drops of rain mixed together. A strong wind bent the trees and transformed the rain into a fierce wave of water. We had to stop. The familiar street faded, and its warm colors disappeared. Unable to find our way, we stood confused, knowing we had to stand up to the storm. We had to close our eyes and believe that this was only a passing moment.

The next day, Aram phoned and told me he had spoken with Irena's friend, Anna, and Anna had agreed to meet with me. A couple of days later, Aram accompanied me to Anna's house, which was on a quiet street off Takht-eh Tavoos Avenue. We rang her doorbell, and a dog began to bark from behind the door that connected her front yard to the street. "Who is it?" a woman's voice called out in Persian. When we answered, Anna opened the door. She was in her seventies, tall and thin, with beautiful thick black hair, which fell on her shoulders. She had large gray eyes, wore a silk white blouse and a pair of blue jeans, and greeted us in Russian. A German shepherd followed her. Her small, two-story house was filled with large and small tropical plants. We had to push their leaves out of our way in order to be able to follow her into the living room, where a colorful parrot sat on a perch, a couple of canaries sang in a cage, and a black cat rubbed herself against my legs. The air smelled of wet soil, and every wall in the room was covered with bookcases overflowing with books.

"Where is the text?" she asked me as we were sitting down. I gave it to her, and she sifted through the pages.

"It will take me a few hours to translate this."

She stood up and motioned us toward the door. "Irena was very fond of you, Marina. You can come back for it tomorrow afternoon at four-thirty."

The next day, almost as soon as we rang Anna's doorbell, she opened the door and handed me my grandmother's writings and the translation.

"There you go, my dear. Your grandmother was a sad but strong woman," she said and closed the door on us.

"I told you she was a little strange," Aram said and burst into laughter.

I read the translation as soon as I got home. It was about forty pages, was written in beautiful handwriting, and was grammatically perfect. If I didn't already know, I would never have guessed that Persian was not its writer's first language.

At the age of eighteen, my grandmother, Xena Mooratova, had fallen in love with a handsome, twenty-three-year-old man named Andrei. He had golden blond hair and large blue eyes and was a communist. Xena had begged him not to go to demonstrations and protests against the tsar, but he didn't listen to her. He wanted Russia to become greater than it was and he wanted poverty to disappear. Xena wrote that he had beautiful but impossible ideas and was very naïve. She started going to protests with him to protect him. During one of the demonstrations, the soldiers warned the crowd to go away, but nobody listened, so the soldiers opened fire.

*"People started running,"* Xena wrote. *"I turned around. He lay on the ground, bleeding. I held him in my arms until he died. The soldiers took pity on me and let me take him to his mother. I dragged his body through the streets of Moscow. A few young men came to my aid; they carried him for me, and I walked behind them, watching his blood drip to the ground. I never slept peacefully after that day. I still wake to see his blood on my bed."*

Xena met her future husband—my grandfather, Esah—a few months later. He was a jeweler and a kind young man. She wasn't sure how or when she had fallen in love with him. Soon, he asked her to marry him, and she accepted. They got married, had a daughter, and named her Tamara. Soon, they were forced to leave Russia and come to Iran. It was an especially difficult journey for Xena, because she was pregnant with her second child, my father. Once in Iran, the family first went to the city of Mashad, where my father was born, and then to the city of Rasht, where Esah had a few relatives. They didn't stay in Rasht for long and came to Tehran. Tehran was very different from Moscow, and Xena felt homesick. She missed her friends and family, but it didn't matter too much to her because she was very happy with Esah. But her happiness didn't last long. Esah left the house one morning and never came back. Thieves murdered him for the jewelry he planned to sell in order to buy a house.

Life was very lonely and difficult for Xena after this. She longed to go back home to Russia, but everything had been lost; her home and her way of life were destroyed by a bloodthirsty revolution. She had nowhere to go and believed she was to be a stranger forever.

She started a boardinghouse and worked hard. Years went by, her children grew up, and Tamara married a Russian man and went back to Russia with him. Then, Xena met Peter, a Hungarian man who was staying at her boardinghouse. He helped her and kept her company. After the beginning of the Second World War, he asked her to marry him, and she accepted, but they never had a chance. Countries were divided, and Hungary took Hitler's side. All Hungarians who lived in Iran became prisoners of war and were sent to special camps in India. Peter died there from an infectious disease.

I was in tears when I finished reading the translation. I knew how sad, helpless, and lonely my grandmother must have felt. Revolutions had devastated both of us. The communist revolution and the Islamic revolution had both resulted in terrible dictatorships. My life seemed like a distorted copy of her life. I could only hope that the future had better things planned for me. I had to remember that she had survived, and so would I.

The following Wednesday night, I went to choir practice. Andre smiled at me from behind the organ. I stood next to a woman who had a wonderful voice. Andre came up to me after the practice. Wearing blue jeans and a plain T-shirt, I wished I had nicer clothes on. Although the *hejab* was mandatory and not wearing it could result in lashing and imprisonment, women could wear what they wanted underneath the *hejab*. When I went to church, to visit friends, or to relatives' houses, I could take off my *hejab* after arriving.

"You have a beautiful voice," Andre said to me.

"No. I was standing beside Mrs. Masoodi. She has a beautiful voice." I laughed.

I asked him where he was originally from, and he told me both his parents were from Hungary, but he and his sister were born in Tehran. His sister was twenty-one and had recently moved to Budapest to go to university. He was twenty-two.

It was such a strange coincidence that he was Hungarian. But when I thought about it a little, I realized it wasn't that strange. Christians were such a small minority in Iran that we were all somehow connected in one way or another.

"Would you like to learn to play the organ?" Andre asked me.

"Is it hard?"

"Not at all. I'll teach you."

"Okay. When do we start?"

"How about now?"

Despite the frightening events at the rally in Ferdosi Square, I attended many other protest rallies organized by different political groups from communists to the Mojahedin. This was the least I could do to show my disapproval of the government and its policies. I didn't say a word about this to my parents, to Aram, or to Andre. All the rallies were more or less the same: young people gathered on a main street, placards condemning the government went up in the air, the crowd began to move, slogans were yelled out, and, after only moments, tear gas thickened the air, making eyes water and throats burn. Then came the sound of bullets. The revolutionary guards had arrived. Everyone ran as fast as they possibly could, keeping their heads down. Everything became focused and clear. Colors became sharper. *Avoid military green. Stay away from bearded men.* It was a mistake to try to escape through narrow streets; the possibility of being arrested or beaten was much stronger there. The wider the street, the better the chance of survival. A few times, I had to hide behind smelly garbage cans or boxes of rotten produce to escape the guards. Except for the one time at Ferdosi Square, I never saw anyone shot, but someone would always tell me that he or she had seen people fall or had seen smeared blood on the pavement. Every time I arrived home safe after a rally, my heart beat with excitement. Again, I had made it. Maybe I was immune to the bullets and the swinging clubs.

About two weeks before the summer holidays, Gita, who had graduated from high school a year earlier and was waiting for universities to reopen after the Islamic Cultural Revolution, came to see me one night and told me that a friend of hers named

Shahrzad wanted to meet me. She explained that Shahrzad was a university student and had been a political prisoner for three years at the time of the shah. Shahrzad had heard about the strike I had started at school and knew I had read a few of her group's books. She had even read a couple of the articles I had written for my school newspaper. I asked Gita why Shahrzad wanted to meet me, and she said Shahrzad wanted me to join the Fadayian. I told Gita that I didn't want to join the Fadayian; I believed in God and went to church, so I didn't have much in common with their group.

"Do you support the government?" Gita asked me.

"No, I don't."

"You're either with them or against them."

"Even if I'm against them that doesn't make me a communist. I respect you and your beliefs, but I don't want to get involved with politics."

"I think you're already involved, even if you think you aren't. Give her a chance. She just wants to talk to you for a few minutes. We'll catch up with you on your way home from school tomorrow."

I didn't want to argue with Gita, so I agreed to meet with Shahrzad.


Shahrzad and Gita appeared next to me as soon as I stepped out of school the next day. Gita introduced us but left right away, saying she had to go somewhere. Shahrzad was different from any other girl I had ever met. She had very sad eyes and nervously looked around all the time.

"From what I've heard, you're a natural leader," she told me as we walked toward my place. "There aren't many people who can do this. Others listen to you. I've also read your articles in your school newspaper. They're good. You can make a difference. This Islamic government is going to destroy this country, and you can do something about it."

"Shahrzad, I respect your beliefs, but we don't have anything in common."

"I think we do. We have the same enemy, so we're friends."

I told her that I couldn't look at it that way. I simply had a habit of speaking out, and if we had a communist government instead of the Islamic one, I probably would have spoken against it as well.

She asked me if I wanted to make a difference, and I told her that the kind of difference I wanted to make was not the same as hers. She suddenly stopped and stared at a young man who had just passed us, said a quick good-bye to me, and disappeared around the corner. I never saw her again.

I wanted new clothes. No more faded jeans, worn sweaters, and running shoes. But there was a problem. The inflation rate had soared after the revolution, and I knew my parents didn't have extra money to spare. It was unusual for teenage girls to work, so I had to be creative and find a way to make money. Nice shoes were especially expensive.

My parents, my Aunt Zenia, and my Uncle Ismael and his wife met once every couple of weeks to play rummy. They played for money and took the game very seriously. I had watched them play many times and had learned the rules of the game. One night when my uncle's wife was ill and couldn't play, I offered to replace her. Aunt Zenia thought it was a great idea and made everyone give me some money so that I could enter the game. I was in. By the end of the night, I had turned a hundred tomans into two thousand. The next day, I went on a shopping spree and bought myself dress pants, blouses, and three pairs of high-heeled shoes, and the day after that, I went to church, wearing clothes I had bought with gambling money: black dress pants, a white silk blouse, and a pair of black shoes with pointy toes.

When my grandmother was alive and my parents played cards with friends and family at our house, she always shook her head and told me that gambling was wrong, that it could hurt families and friendships and this was why God didn't like it. It was a sin. I knew all this and felt guilty. But I was sure God understood the situation. And just to be on the safe side, I was going to confess to gambling when I went to confession.

I loved the way my new fashionable shoes made a delicate clicking sound as I walked down the aisle to get to the choir pews in the front, and I loved how, with whispering voices, the choir members told me how wonderful I looked. When Andre saw me, his gaze lingered, and, during mass, I noticed him watching me from the corner of his eye.

Andre was persistent about teaching me to play the organ, but the more he tried, the more I realized I didn't have the gift of music. He spent most of his free time at the church, fixing different things from the pipe organ to appliances and furniture, and he usually asked me to keep him company. I enjoyed spending time with him. He told me about his life, family, and friends. Before the Second World War, his father, Mihaly, who was a carpenter, had come to Iran as a young man to work on a new palace that was being built for the shah. Mihaly had left his fiancée, Juliana, in Budapest in the hope of returning home after the job was done, but the war prevented that. While the war raged on in Europe and Hungary stood by Germany, the Allies entered Iran to deliver supplies to Russia from the south. And like my grandmother's fiancé, Peter, Mihaly was deported to a camp in India. But unlike Peter, he survived. After the war, he returned to Iran instead of his native Hungary because Hungary had become communist. The people of Hungary weren't allowed to leave their country at that time, and Juliana was unable to join Mihaly. She was forced to remain in Hungary until the anticommunist revolution of 1956, which opened the Hungarian borders, allowing her to enter Austria as a refugee and, later, to join her long-lost love in Iran after eighteen years of separation. They married immediately and had two children: Andre, and fifteen months later, his sister. Juliana passed away when Andre was only four and his sister two and a half. After her death, one of Mihaly's sisters, a spinster of about sixty years of age, came to Iran to help her brother raise his children. In time, she proved to be a wonderful substitute for the mother they had lost.

One day as we sat on the organ bench in the empty church, I told Andre about my troubles in school: the strike, the list Khanoom Bahman had seen in my principal's office, the school newspaper, and the fact that Khanoom Mahmoodi hated me. His large blue eyes were wide with shock.

"You did all those things?" He shook his head in disbelief.

"Yes. My problem is I can't keep my mouth shut."

"I'm surprised you haven't been arrested yet."

"I know. I'm surprised too."

He touched my hand, and my heart skipped a beat. His hand was ice cold.

"You have to leave the country," he said.

"Andre, be realistic. With all the trouble I'm in, there's no way they'd let me get a passport, and crossing the border illegally is not only dangerous, it needs a lot of money. My parents won't be able to afford it."

"Do your parents know about all this?"

"They know some things, but they don't know everything."

"So you're telling me that you're waiting to be arrested?"

"Do I have any other choice?"

"Hide."

"They'll find me. And where can I hide? Is it fair for me to put others in danger?"

I realized I had raised my voice: it bounced off the ceiling. We sat in silence for a moment, and then, he put his arm around my shoulder. I leaned against him, feeling the welcoming warmth of his body. When I was with him, I felt a strong sense of belonging, of being home, of having arrived after a treacherous journey. I was falling in love again, and this made me feel guilty; I didn't want to betray Arash. But love had its way of doing things; it was like spring crawling into the skin of the earth at the end of winter. Each day the temperature rose just a little, tree branches swelled with new buds, the sun remained in the sky moments longer than the previous day, and before you knew it, the world was filled with warmth and color.

In late June 1981, a couple of days after my mother and I arrived at the cottage to spend the summer there, Aram phoned and asked me if I had heard that under the influence of Ayatollah Khomeini, the parliament had impeached President Banisadr because he had opposed the execution of political prisoners and had written letters to Khomeini, warning against dictatorship. I had not heard this. At the cottage, we only had an old, not-quite-functional radio and couldn't listen to BBC News, and we usually didn't bother watching the local television stations. A few days later, Aram told me that Banisadr had managed to flee to France, but many of his friends had been arrested and executed.

On June 28, my mother happened to turn on the television set just before we sat down for dinner, and we found out that earlier that day, a bomb had exploded at the headquarters of the Islamic Republic's Party during a meeting. The bomb had killed more than seventy of the party's members, many of whom were government officials, including Ayatollah Mohammad Beheshti, who was the head of the judicial system and the party's secretary-general. The government announced that the bomb was planted by the Mojahedin.

In early August, the new president, Mohammad Ali Rajai, took office. He was well known as one of the leaders of the Islamic Cultural Revolution. His presidency lasted about two weeks: on August 30, a bomb went off at the prime minister's office, killing President Rajai, the prime minister, and the head of Tehran's police. This was also blamed on the Mojahedin, but I heard rumors that both bombings were the results of an internal war between different factions of the government.

The country seemed to have entered a perpetual state of mourning: at every street corner, loudspeakers broadcasted religious chants and music, and groups of men walked the streets, slapping their chests or hitting their backs with metal chains in the Shia tradition, while the women following them wailed and cried. I was shocked by recent events and sunk even deeper into my books, which usually offered a more reasonable, compassionate, and predictable world.

Before the end of summer, I decided not to go back to school. What was the point of going back? I was incapable of adjusting to the new rules and was only going to get in more trouble with Khanoom Mahmoodi and the teachers.

As soon as we returned to Tehran, I watched my mother's mood to find the best moment to tell her about my decision. I was sure she would not easily give in. She was very proud that my brother had a bachelor's degree, and she had always spoken highly of those who received a good education. But she couldn't make me go. I knew my situation would only worsen if I spent one more day in school.

We had bought a few pieces of furniture for the room that used to be my father's dance studio: four large chairs covered with a velvety olive-green fabric, two black coffee tables, a dining table with eight matching chairs, and a sideboard. But the waiting area had remained the same, with the round table in the center and four black leather chairs around it. There was a kerosene heater between two of the chairs to warm the room in winter. My mother had always loved to knit, and, especially since the success of the revolution, she spent most of her time sitting in the chair on the left side of the heater, knitting sweaters for us. She also crocheted tablecloths and bedspreads. When I stepped in the room that day, she was knitting, nestled in her favorite chair with her glasses sitting low on her nose. I sat on the chair opposite hers, remaining silent for a few minutes, trying to decide where to start.

"Maman?"

"Yes?"

She didn't look at me.

"I can't go back to school. At least not this year."

She dropped the sweater she was knitting on her lap and stared at me from above her glasses. Although she was about fifty-six years old and a few lines had appeared around her eyes and on her fore-head, she was still beautiful.

"What?"

"I can't go back to school."

"Are you out of your mind?"

I told her that they didn't teach us anything useful in school. If I stayed home, I wouldn't have to deal with the revolutionary guard teachers. I promised her I would study all the eleventh grade books at home and go for the exams.

"You know I can do it," I said. "I probably know more than the new teachers."

She sighed and looked down.

"Maman, don't make me go back." I was sobbing.

"I'll think about it," she said.

I ran to my room.

The next morning when my mother came into my room, my eyes were almost swollen shut from a night of crying. It was as if all my grief and frustration had broken loose. My mother stood next to the door of the balcony, watching the street.

"You can stay home," she said, "but only for a year." She had worked it out with my father.


Aram called me one night in early September to say good-bye; he was leaving the country the next day. I had a feeling he was crying.

"I'll miss you. Take care of yourself," I said in a controlled voice. I had not told him about Andre, and I decided it was time he knew. So I explained that I had met someone at my church whom I liked very much.

He was surprised and asked me how long it had been. I told him that Andre and I had met in the spring.

"Why didn't you tell me earlier? I thought we told each other everything," he said.

"I wasn't sure about it. I didn't want to become too close to anyone ever again."

He understood.

All males had to fulfill their military duty after finishing high school unless they managed to enter a university or if the government officially exempted them for medical or other reasons. Aram's father had obtained an exemption for him because his brother was considered a martyr and he was his parents' only living child. He didn't have to go to war because his family had already given a son. He found it ironic that his dead brother was saving his life. The government had issued Aram an official passport, and he was legally allowed to leave the country.

Sarah called me one day in November 1981 and told me she had to see me right away. Her voice was shaking, but she wouldn't tell me more on the phone. I ran to her house to find her waiting for me at the door. Her parents and brother were not home. We went to her room, and she dropped on her bed. Her eyes were red and swollen from crying.

She told me that two days earlier, revolutionary guards had gone to Gita's house to arrest her, but she had not been home, so they had arrested her mother and two sisters and had told her father that if Gita didn't give herself up in a week, one of her sisters would be executed. So Gita went to Evin and gave herself up, and they let her mother and sisters go. "Marina . . . you know how stubborn she is. They'll kill her. She doesn't know how to hold her tongue. And we're probably next. Well, Sirus is next for sure, but he says that anyone who has openly said anything against the government is in danger of arrest."

Sirus was right. I knew they would come for us sooner or later. They knew whom to look for. They knew where we lived. I had never told anyone about the list, because I didn't know who else was on it, and I didn't want to frighten anybody or to get Khanoom Bahman in trouble.

"Yes, we're probably next. It's only a matter of time, and there's nothing we can do. We can't run. They'll hurt our parents if we do," I said.

"We can't just sit here and wait."

"What do you want to do?"

"I could at least tell my parents," said Sarah.

"They'll panic. There's nothing anyone can do, unless you can all disappear together. If I tell my parents, they won't take me seriously. Don't worry too much. It can't be that bad. People exaggerate. We haven't done anything. Gita was really involved with her group. Why would they even bother with us?"

"I guess you're right. We shouldn't panic. We haven't done anything."

# Fifteen

AFTER HE PROPOSED TO ME, Ali walked me back to 246. My friends surrounded me as soon as I entered the room, wanting to know what had happened. I told them that Ali was back and that he just wanted to see how I was doing. I could tell from the look on their faces that they didn't believe me. They were worried, but there was nothing anyone could do to help.

I didn't want my roommates to know about Ali's proposal. I felt guilty and ashamed. I had put Andre and my parents in danger. Having no doubt that Ali's threats were serious, I had to do what he wanted me to do.

I remembered when Arash and I had kissed. It had been the best feeling in the world because I loved Arash. Was Ali going to kiss me? I wiped my mouth with my sleeve, and a cold sweat covered my body.

*"They can kill me if they want, but I don't want to be raped,"* Taraneh had said.

Even though I still didn't exactly know what rape meant, I told myself that this wasn't rape. Ali wanted me to marry him. This was okay . . . No, it wasn't . . . Why was I even thinking about it? I knew I had to do it.

Marriage was supposed to be forever. Could I live with Ali forever? Maybe Ali had a temporary marriage in mind. I had heard that there was something called *sigheh* in Islam, a temporary marriage that could last from minutes to years. I also knew that in a temporary marriage, the woman had no rights whatsoever. This didn't make any difference in my case, because I was a prisoner and had no rights to start with. Maybe he just wanted me to be his wife for a little while and then would let me go. If so, no one needed to know. I had to keep this marriage a secret for as long as I possibly could.

Hours went by, and I couldn't eat, think, or talk to anyone. I couldn't even cry. All I could do was pace up and down the hallway during the day and pass out from exhaustion at night.

Finally, on the third day, I went to talk to Sister Maryam. She knew about Ali's proposal, so I didn't need to worry about giving away my secret. I told her I didn't want to marry Ali. She said that every marriage in her family had been arranged, and the women never wanted to marry the man their parents had chosen for them. Her own mother hated the man she was supposed to marry, but she ended up being very happy with him. I said I didn't know how happiness would be possible under such circumstances. I explained to her that in my family, women chose their husbands themselves. She said that I didn't live with my family any longer and I had to remember that Ali had given me new life. In her opinion, I was being unreasonably difficult.

\* \* \*

My three days were over. At the beginning of the fourth day, I was called over the loudspeaker. Ali was waiting for me in the office.

"You don't need the blindfold," he said. "We'll talk in my car."

From the office, we entered a windowless hallway filled with fluorescent light. Until this moment, except for the 246 and the interrogation room, I had never seen the inside of Evin. It had been a black nightmare of angry voices, lashes, screams, firing guns, and the whisper of rubber slippers brushing against linoleum and stone floors. Yet, the hallway that now lay in front of me could have been any hallway, maybe in a regular government building or school. I followed Ali down the stairs, normal stairs like any other. A couple of revolutionary guards passed us on their way up and bowed slightly to Ali, saying *"salam aleikom,"* ignoring me completely. He bowed in return and greeted them. Once we reached the bottom of the stairs, Ali opened a gray metal door, and we stepped outside. The normalcy of what I saw shocked me. Evin reminded me of the campus of the University of Tehran on Enghelab Avenue. The main difference between the two was that Evin had more open spaces. The other difference was that a see-through metal fence encircled the University of Tehran, but Evin was surrounded by tall brick walls, lookout towers, and armed guards. Clusters of tall, ancient maple trees were visible here and there, and in the north, the Alborz Mountains towered over us.

Ali led me along a narrow, paved road and around the corner of a gray building to where a black Mercedes was parked in the shadow of a few trees. He opened the front passenger door, and I stepped in. The car smelled brand-new. Sweat dripped down my forehead. He sat in the driver seat and put his hands on the steering wheel. I noticed how long and slim his fingers were, and his nails were clean and carefully trimmed. He had the hands of a pianist, and yet he was an interrogator.

"What's your decision?" he asked, staring at a string of amber-colored prayer beads hanging from the rearview mirror.

A sparrow flew off a tree and disappeared in the blue vastness of the cloudless sky.

"Is this a temporary marriage you have in mind?" I asked.

He looked at me, surprised.

"This isn't a passing physical attraction I feel toward you. I want you for good."

"Ali, please—"

"Is your answer yes or no? And don't forget about the consequences. I'm very serious about this."

". . . I'll marry you," I said, feeling like I was being buried alive.

He smiled. "You're a sensible girl. I knew you'd make the right choice. I promise that you won't regret your decision. I'll take good care of you. I have to make the necessary arrangements and speak to my parents. It will take a little time."

I wondered what his parents would think about his marrying a Christian prisoner. And how about my family? How would they react?

"Ali, I don't want my family to know anything about the marriage yet," I said. "I've never been close to my parents. I know they won't understand the situation and will just make it harder."

I couldn't hold back my tears any longer.

"Marina, please don't cry. You don't have to tell anyone, not until you're ready, and it doesn't matter how long it takes. I understand that this is hard on you. I'll do everything I can to make it easier."

As long as my friends and family didn't know about this marriage, the girl I had been before Evin had a chance of survival. She could exist, dream, hope, and love even though she had to hide inside the new me: the wife of an interrogator. I wasn't sure how long she would be able to live like this, but I was going to protect her. She was the real me, the one my parents and Andre loved and wanted back.

Ali returned me to 246, and I asked Sister Maryam if it were possible for her to send me to one of the rooms downstairs. I didn't want to explain anything to my friends. Upstairs and downstairs were completely separate, and the prisoners couldn't interact with one another. I wanted to be left alone where nobody knew me. She consented and called the representative of room 7 to bring my belongings to the office, and I moved to room 6 on the first floor, which like my old room on the second floor, was home to about fifty girls.

Soon after this, my health began to deteriorate. I threw up every time I ate, and migraine attacks paralyzed me. With a blanket pulled over my head, I lay in a corner most of the time, unable to sleep. My thoughts ran in circles and found their way to Taraneh. How I missed her. Since they took her away, I had avoided thinking about her, not wanting to imagine the details of the last hours of her life. Why did we turn our backs on reality when it became too much to bear? I should have told Sister Maryam that I wanted to die with Taraneh. I should have tried to stop her execution. I knew I wouldn't have succeeded, but I should have tried. Wasn't an innocent life worth a fight, even if this fight was condemned to failure? I was responsible for her death, because I had accepted her fate. But why had I remained silent? Was I afraid of dying? I didn't believe this was the case. Maybe the reason was hope; I hoped to go home one day. My parents and Andre were waiting for me. How could I possibly choose death if it hadn't called my name? Right and wrong became intertwined, and I didn't know which way to go.

*I stood in the middle of darkness. An open field with black hills surrounding it. Taraneh stood next to me, wearing her lucky red sweater, staring ahead. I touched her hand, and she looked at me with her amber eyes. Ali emerged from the night. He walked to us and pointed a gun to my head. I couldn't move. With her small hand, Taraneh grabbed Ali's wrist. "No," she said.*

*Ali put the gun to her head and pulled the trigger. Taraneh's blood covered my skin. I screamed.*

I woke with a scream trapped in my throat. My lungs refused to inhale. A face appeared over me, vague and blurry. Loud, incomprehensible voices had filled the room. But when there is no air, nothing matters except finding it. I tried to reach out and grab something, anything that might save me from suffocating. I tried to say I couldn't breathe. The face . . . it was Sister Maryam's. She was saying something, but her words seemed to come from far away. The room faded, as if someone had dimmed the light and turned it off.

I opened my eyes to see Ali talking to Doctor Sheikh, who was wearing a khaki military uniform. I could breathe now. We were surrounded by white curtains. I was lying on a clean, comfortable bed. A white scarf covered my hair and a thick white sheet covered my body. From a plastic bag hanging from a metal hook, a clear liquid dripped into a transparent tube connected to my hand. Doctor Sheikh was the first to notice I was awake.

"Hello, Marina. How do you feel?" he said.

I couldn't remember what had happened, and I didn't know where I was. The doctor told me I was extremely dehydrated and had been brought to the prison hospital. Then he disappeared through a small gap in the curtain. I looked at Ali, and he smiled.

"I'm going home to bring you some of my mother's food. It can cure anything. Now try to rest. I'll wake you as soon as I'm back. Do you want anything? Can I bring you anything from the outside?"

"No."

"Why didn't you tell anyone you were so ill?"

"I really don't know what happened."

"Your roommates told Sister Maryam you had been throwing up for a few days."

Tears filled my eyes. "I've always had stomach problems. It was nothing new. Just a little worse than usual. But I didn't think much of it. Really. I thought it would go away. The nightmares and the headaches. I tried . . ." My chest began to tighten.

Ali bent closer to me, putting his hands on the side of the bed.

"Don't worry. It's okay. Everything is fine. You were sick. That's all. Now, you can rest and get better. Take a deep breath. A very deep one."

I did.

"The doctor will give you something to help you sleep. You need rest. And there will be no headaches and no nightmares. Okay?"

Ali's voice woke me. He was calling my name, holding a bowl of homemade chicken noodle soup. It smelled of lemons. At home, I always put lemon juice in my chicken soup. He told me that the doctor believed fresh air and a change of scenery would be good for me, and he offered to take me for a drive. I asked him if he meant outside Evin, and he said he did and told me to finish my soup so we could go.

As soon as I was finished eating, he helped me into a wheelchair and then pulled aside the white curtain surrounding us. We were in a large room; many white curtains had divided it into enclosed sections. Two of these curtains had been pulled aside, revealing two beds, one of which was empty, and a girl about my age slept in the other. She wore a navy headscarf, and a thick white sheet covered her body. There were no windows. Ali pushed my wheelchair through a door, and we entered a narrow hallway. Again, he had not blindfolded me. He opened a door, and I squinted against the brightness of the outside world. He guided my wheelchair down a ramp.

The sky looked like an upside-down sea; foamy waves of clouds floated toward the horizon. We passed a few blindfolded women wearing dark-blue chadors. In single file, they followed a male revolutionary guard. Each woman hung on to the chador of the person in front of her. The revolutionary guard leading them held a length of rope in his hand, the end of which was tied to the handcuff of the woman in the front; he dragged her along and the rest followed. A few days earlier, I had been like them. Now, I had Ali's protection, and things had changed. I felt ashamed. I had betrayed them. I had betrayed everyone.

On our right, tall maple trees blocked my view, and on the left was a two-story brick building behind which Ali's Mercedes was parked. Once at the car, I realized I didn't want to be alone with him. Fear had crawled under my skin.

"Here, let me help you," he said and took my left arm and tried to pull me up. I shook him off.

"Marina, please don't be afraid of me. I won't hurt you. I've never hurt you."

He was right; he had never really hurt me.

"Trust me. Even when we're married, I'll be considerate and gentle. I'm not a monster."

I didn't have a choice but to trust him. My muscles were raw and weak, and I felt dizzy as I stood up but managed to get into the car without losing my balance. At the exit, he waved at the guards, they opened the gates, and we simply drove out of Evin. I was shocked to see how easy it had been for him to take me out; he was probably far more important than I had imagined.

The street was empty and lifeless, but as we moved farther from the prison, it came to life. There were people, houses, and stores. In an empty lot, a group of young boys ran after a plastic ball, their faces covered with a flour-like layer of dust. Women carried their groceries home, and men stood around and chatted here and there. All the simple things people did seemed like miracles to me.

"You're very quiet. What are you thinking about?" Ali asked after about half an hour.

"About life and how normal it seems out here."

"I promise you that although it will take some time, we'll eventually have a normal life. I'll go to work and provide for you. You'll take care of the house, go shopping, and visit friends and family. You'll be happy."

How could he speak about his job in such a casual way? He wasn't a teacher or a doctor or a mechanic.

"My friends are either dead or in prison, and I'm not sure if my family will ever want to see me," I said.

"You'll make new friends. And why do you think your family would so strongly disapprove of our marriage?"

"For one thing, because of your job."

"Marina, trust me; there's hope. They'll see how much I care for you. I've had to overcome many obstacles just to keep you alive, and there are many people who are against our marriage. There are many more obstacles for me to overcome, but I'll take care of every problem. Your family will see the good life I'll provide for you, and they'll change their minds. We'll face your family together, whenever you're ready."

Why had he chosen *me?* I was the embodiment of everything he stood against: I was a Christian, an antirevolutionary, and a prisoner. He had had to fight to save me from death and now he had to fight again to marry me. Why was he doing this?


For some time, we went out for rides every night. While in his car, I tried to pretend that I was a normal person. I tried to stop thinking about the past or the future; I tried to concentrate on the soothing hum of the engine, the softness of the leather seats, and the streets that seethed with careless life. Although the city had remained exactly as I had left it, every sight, smell, and sound felt alien. Ali's voice rose above everything as he told me about his family. He was an only son and had one sister who was twenty-five years old and was married. His mother had become pregnant twice after his sister's birth but had miscarried both times. According to Islamic law, men are allowed to have more than one wife, but Ali's father, Hossein-eh Moosavi, had devoted himself to his only wife and two children. Mr. Moosavi was a very religious man and had helped Ayatollah Khomeini for many years. He was proud of Ali for being a brave soldier in the jihad against the shah. Mr. Moosavi was a smart businessman who had made a great fortune but remembered to help those in need. For years, Ali's parents had wanted him to get married, but at the age of twenty-eight, he still had not made the commitment.

"I told my parents about you," he told me during one of our nightly drives.

"What did they say?" I asked.

"They were horrified," he said, laughing.

Maybe there was hope that I wouldn't have to marry him after all.

"But I told them you were the one," he continued. "I told them I wanted you more than anything else. I've always been a good son for them. I've always obeyed them, but this time, the decision is mine. I can't settle for any less. I'm twenty-eight, I've been through so much in my life, and I've made up my mind. I want you to be my wife, my companion, and the mother of my children."

"Ali, we're from different worlds. Your parents will never like me. They'll always criticize me for my different ways."

He told me that his parents were kind and generous and he had no doubt they would love me.

I closed my eyes and tried not to think.

After a few minutes, he told me that there was one more thing he had to discuss with me. He knew I wouldn't like it, but he insisted it was just a formality. "My father has told me that if you convert to Islam, he'll have nothing against our marriage. He'll even encourage it," he said. "Then, my parents will be proud to accept you as their daughter. They'll support and protect you as their own. Marina, this is what I want to happen. I want you to belong with me, and I want my family to love you. From the moment I saw you, I knew we had to be together."

I had lost my family, the man I loved, my freedom, my home, and all my hopes and dreams. Now, I had to betray my faith.

He didn't care if I remained a Christian in my heart. I pleaded with him to let me go, but he said it was not possible.

"What if I say no?" I asked.

"Don't make this difficult for yourself," he said. "This is for your own good. You don't want the ones you love to suffer because of your pride. You're only seventeen years old. There are so many things about this world you can't understand. I promise you that I'll make you happier than you've ever been."

How could I make him understand that I would never be happy with him?

He parked the car on a quiet street. I knew the area; it was close to my Aunt Zenia's house. I asked him if he understood that I had to forget all about my parents, my friends, and my church, that they would hate me forever. He told me that if they hated me because of my converting to Islam, this would mean that they had never truly loved me.

He stepped out of the car and opened my door.

"What are you doing?" I asked

"Come. I've bought a house for us."

We climbed the few steps that led to the front door of a large brick bungalow. He unlocked the door and went in. I hesitated.

"What are you waiting for? Don't you want to see it?" he said.

I followed him. There was a family room, a living-dining room combination, the biggest kitchen I had ever seen, four bedrooms, and three bathrooms. The walls were all freshly painted in neutral colors, but there was no furniture. In the master bedroom, I stood in front of a sliding door that opened to the backyard. The lawn was thick and green, and geraniums, pansies, and marigolds were growing in mounds. Reds, whites, purples, and yellows. A white butterfly flew from one flower to the next, struggling to keep its trembling balance on the wind. A tall brick wall separated the yard from the street. How could there be so much beauty in such a cruel world?

Ali opened the sliding door.

"Let's go outside. The flowers need water," he said.

Once in the yard, he pulled up his sleeves, turned on the tap, and grabbed the hose. The wind carried the cool mist and touched my face. He watered the plants, careful not to disturb the soil. Large droplets of water appeared on the foliage, holding the golden sunlight inside their pearly bodies. He picked the spent flowers, humming a tune and smiling. He looked normal, like any other man. Had he ever killed anyone, not at the war front, but in Evin? Had he ever pulled the trigger and ended someone's life?

"Do you like the house?" he asked.

"It's beautiful."

"I planted the flowers for you."

"Ali, I'm a prisoner with a life sentence. How would I be allowed to live here?"

"I've convinced all the key officials in Evin to let you stay here with me, like a house arrest of some sort, and they've agreed. Marina, this is our house; yours and mine."

*Our house. I don't even know who I am anymore. This house is an extension of Evin.*

"So I'll be a prisoner here," I said.

"We have to do this the right way. You know very well that some people like Hamehd are against our marriage, and they're watching us. We shouldn't make any mistakes. You were condemned to death by an Islamic court and—"

"But I never had a trial," I said.

On the night of the executions, Ali had told me that I had been sentenced to death, but I had assumed that Hamehd, and maybe a few others, had simply decided to execute me. To me, a trial was what I had read about in books and had seen in movies: a large room with a judge, a jury, a defense lawyer, and a prosecutor.

Ali said that I had had a trial, but I wasn't present when it took place. Then I received Imam's pardon, and my sentence was reduced to life in prison. He said it wouldn't be appropriate for him to go to the imam again, but he was allowed to request a retrial. He believed if I received a retrial after converting to Islam and marrying him, my sentence wouldn't be more than two or three years.

I asked him why Hamehd hated me so much. He explained that Hamehd and many others like him didn't care for those who are different and have different ways.

I sighed. I didn't understand this strange Islamic society.

"Everything will be fine," he continued. "I haven't bought any furniture, because I thought you might want to decorate the house yourself. We can start shopping for the house tomorrow, then it will probably be ready in time. I know you're still worried about your family's reaction, but trust me. Once they see the life I've provided for you, they'll be happy."

Maybe Ali had a point. We weren't rich, and this house was far beyond our reach. My father had never believed in God and had always laughed at my religious beliefs, but money was something he had always cared about. Big, expensive things had always impressed him. Maybe he was going to like Ali. My father loved luxury cars, and Ali drove a brand-new Mercedes. My mother never owned anything expensive and lived in a rental apartment since she had gotten married. She was going to love this house. Did I even have a small chance of ever being happy with Ali? It did depend on him, but also on me. He loved me in his own way. Although his ways were very different from mine, I could see the love in his eyes when he looked at me.

As we drove back to Evin, Ali said, "I don't think you should go back to 246. The cells of 209 will be a better idea for the time being. I'll be able to see you more frequently and bring you food from home. What do you think?"

I nodded.

On our way, we stopped at a small restaurant, and Ali bought us each an egg sandwich and a bottle of Coke. I loved eggs and had not had any for months. We ate in the car. The bread was fresh and buttered, and there were slices of tomatoes in between slices of hard-boiled eggs. When I finished my sandwich, Ali wasn't even halfway through his. He asked me if I wanted another one, and I said I did. He bought us each one more.

In Evin, Ali parked the car in front of a building, and we entered it. A long, dimly lit hallway stretched before us, patched with many metal doors on either side. A guard walked toward us.

"*Salam aleikom,* Brother Ali, how are you?"

"Very well, Brother Reza. Thanks be to God. And how are you?"

"Not bad. Thanks be to God."

"Is the cell I asked for ready?"

"Yes, it is. This way."

We followed him to a door with number 27 written on it. He put a key in its lock and opened it. A loud creak echoed in the hallway. Ali stepped in the cell and looked around. Then, he came out and motioned me to step in. I did. The cell was about ten by seven feet and had a toilet and a small sink both made of stainless steel. The floor was covered with a worn brown carpet, and the only window, which was about one foot by one foot, was barred and beyond my reach. Ali stood at the door.

"You'll be all right here. I'll be back with breakfast in the morning. Get some sleep."

I watched the door close and heard the key turn in the lock. The click it made almost sounded like "traitor."

A military march began to play through the loudspeakers. Another victory. If all these "victories" were true, Iran would have had conquered the world by now.

I took off my scarf, went to the sink, and washed my face. It felt good. I did it over and over, thirty times or so, until my face felt numb. There was something comforting about the sound of running water and its coolness. The water somehow connected me to the world. But this connection, even though I could feel it on my skin, was like a memory. The comfort it brought me didn't belong to the present; it was something from the past, nostalgic and sad.

I was exhausted. There were a couple of folded military blankets in a corner. I spread them on the floor and lay down. The walls of the cell had been painted light beige, but some of the paint had peeled off, exposing the plaster underneath. The remaining paint was covered with fingerprints, strange, greasy-looking marks of different shapes and sizes, and a few brownish-red stains, which I suspected were blood. Also, quite a few words and numbers were engraved on the walls, most of them illegible. I traced the engravings with my fingers, as if they were written in Braille. One of them read: "Shirin Hashemi, January 5, 1982. Can anyone hear me?"

I was home on January 5, and this girl, Shirin, was here. Where was she now? Maybe she was dead. How badly tortured was she when she wrote these words? "Can anyone hear me?" she had asked.

"No, Shirin, no one can hear us. We're here alone."

There were other names: Mahtab, Bahram, Katayoon, and Pirooz, and more dates: December 2, 1981, December 28, 1981, February 12, 1982, et cetera. I managed to read a sentence that said: "Firoozeh *jan*, I love you." Trapped and lost lives had left their imprints on the walls around me. I followed an invisible line, like a road on a map, connecting words, dates, and sentences that surrounded me like tombstones. Death was present here, its shadow sieving every word with finality. "Can anyone hear me?"

*I'm a traitor. And I deserve all this, this pain, this cell. The moment I stepped in Evin, I was condemned to betraying myself. Even death turned its back on me. They'll hate me: my parents, Andre, the priests, and my friends. How about you, God? Do you hate me, too? No, I don't think you do, although you might. This is useless. Who am I to decide what you think? But you put me here, didn't you? You could have let me die. But I lived. So this was more your decision than mine. What did you expect me to do? Please, I beg you, say something . . .*

God didn't say a word.

\* \* \*

As he had promised, Ali brought me breakfast in the morning: *bar-bari* bread with homemade sour-cherry jam. The tea was in a plastic cup and deliciously fragrant and didn't smell of camphor. I spent the morning thinking about what Andre and my parents were probably doing. I was almost sure my mother was sitting in her favorite chair, knitting or sipping a cup of tea. My father was at work, and Andre . . . well, I didn't know what *he* was doing. It was almost the end of spring and the schools were out, so he wasn't teaching. Was I somewhere at the back of their minds, a memory pushed aside? Or was I a vivid presence, forgiven and prayed for?

*Can anyone hear me?*

That night, Ali picked me up at about six o'clock and told me he was taking me to meet his parents. Their house wasn't too far from Evin. Once we arrived, he parked the car on the quiet street. Old clay brick walls stood on both sides of the road, and behind them, ancient maple, willow, and poplar trees reached toward the sky but seemed like weeds against the enormity of the Alborz Mountains in the background. My throat was terribly dry and my hands cold and clammy. Although Ali had reassured me that his parents were very kind, I didn't have any idea what to expect. I followed Ali to a green metal door, and he rang the doorbell. A small woman opened the door. She had a white chador on, and I guessed she was his mother, Fatemeh Khanoom. I had expected her to be bigger.

"*Salam, Madar joon,*" Ali said and kissed her forehead. "Madar, this is Marina."

"*Salam,* dear. It's nice to meet you." She smiled. Her tiny brown eyes searched my face with curiosity. She had a kind face.

We stepped through the door and into the front yard. A narrow walkway covered with gray pebbles curved to the right, disappearing between ancient walnut and maple trees. The large house was soon in sight, its walls engulfed by vines. Clay pots overflowing with geraniums and marigolds flanked the wide steps leading to the large porch.

In the house, beautiful, expensive Persian rugs covered the floors. Ali's sister, Akram, was there with her husband, Massood. She had a round face, large brown eyes, and rosy cheeks. I wasn't sure whether I should embrace her, shake hands with her, or neither; some fanatic Muslims considered Christians to be unclean, so I decided not to touch her in case she would get offended. Ali embraced his father and kissed him on both cheeks. He was a couple of inches taller than Ali and rather slim and had a trimmed gray beard. The family greeted me politely, but I could see their discomfort. A Christian girl and a political prisoner wasn't their idea of a suitable wife for Ali, and I didn't blame them for trying to figure out what he had seen in this pale and strange girl.

We moved into the living room, which was spacious and attractively decorated. There were fruits and sweets on silver and crystal platters on every coffee table. I sat on a couch next to Akram. Ali's mother offered us some Earl Grey tea. I noticed she was watching me most of the time, and I felt a hint of pity in her eyes. I sipped my tea, which was in a delicate golden-rimmed glass cup, and began to feel a little more comfortable. It was almost as if I had gone to the house of my own acquaintances for a casual visit. Akram offered me some rice cookies, and I took one. Mr. Moosavi started talking to Ali about his business. He owned a shop at the Bazaar of Tehran and imported and exported goods, including Persian rugs and pistachios. Dinner was soon served. There was long-grain rice topped with saffron, roasted chicken, beef and herb stew, and salad. Although everything smelled delicious, I didn't feel hungry. Maybe my parents were having dinner, too.

"This is a difficult situation, Marina," Mr. Moosavi said after we were finished eating. "And you have the right to know my opinion. You need to know where you stand, especially because you're so young."

As a religious Muslim, Mr. Moosavi followed the custom of never looking a *namahram*—not a close relative—woman in the eyes.

"Babah, we've discussed this matter a million times," Ali began to protest.

"Yes, we have, but I don't remember Marina being present at any of those discussions. So, please bear with me and let me talk to my future daughter-in-law."

"Yes, Babah."

"Dear girl, you have to know that I do understand your difficulties. I need to ask you a few questions, and I need you to answer me truthfully. Is this acceptable to you?"

"Yes, sir."

"Has my son treated you well?"

"Yes, sir," I answered, looking at Ali. He smiled at me.

"Do you wish to marry him?"

"I don't wish to marry him," I said, "but he wishes to marry me. He has gone through a lot of trouble to save my life. I understand my situation. He has promised to take good care of me."

I hoped I had not said anything wrong.

Mr. Moosavi said I was a smart girl and much more mature than my age. He told me that I had been an enemy of God and of the Islamic government, and I had deserved to die, but Ali had intervened because he believed I could learn from my mistakes and change. Mr. Moosavi hoped that I realized that the person I had been before Evin was dead. He said I would soon begin a new life as a Muslim, and my conversion would wash away my sins. He also said he held his son responsible to his promises to me. He had tried to talk Ali out of his decision to marry me, but Ali had refused to listen. Ali had always been a good son and had never done anything against his father's will. Ali had never insisted on anything so much, so Mr. Moosavi had agreed to allow the marriage to take place only if I agreed to convert to Islam. He understood that my family might reject me if I converted, and he promised that as long as I honored my new faith and behaved in a respectable Islamic manner and as

188

long as I was a faithful wife to his son, I was his daughter, and he would personally protect me and ensure my well-being.

"Do we all have an understanding on this matter?" he asked when he finished speaking.

"Yes," everyone said.

I was surprised by Ali's father's efforts to resolve a difficult situation. Even though our perspectives were completely opposite one another, I decided that I respected Mr. Moosavi. I could see that he loved Ali and wanted him to be happy. If my brother had wanted to marry a girl my father disapproved of, my father would never have called a family meeting but would have told my brother that if he married that girl, he would never see him again.

"So, Marina," said Mr. Moosavi. "I welcome you to this family. You're my daughter now. Because of the unusual circumstances, we'll have a private marriage ceremony here in this house, and you, my dear, are under no pressure to inform your family for now. We'll be your family and will provide you with everything you need. You, my son, have always been good to us, and we wish you happiness in your marriage. You have our blessing."

Ali stood up, kissed his father, and thanked him. His mother was crying as she embraced me.

"What do you think about my family? Did you like them?" Ali asked me on our way back to Evin.

"They're very good to you. My family is different."

"What do you mean by 'different'?"

I told him that I loved my parents and missed them but they had always been very distant to me; we had never had a real conversation about anything. He said he was sorry to hear this and told me his father had been very serious about my being a part of his family. "In about a week, we'll have a small ceremony in Evin for you to convert, and our wedding will be on the Friday about two weeks after that," he said.

Everything was happening so fast I couldn't keep up. He told me there was no reason to worry; all I needed to think about was decorating the house. He was planning to take me shopping the next day. I couldn't understand how I could possibly go shopping.

I had expected his family to be mean and cruel to me. But they had been very kind. They had been everything my family had never been. It had been difficult for me to see Ali as a son, but now I knew that he loved and was loved.

"By the way, anyone converting to Islam has to attend religion and Koran classes and has to choose a Muslim name. You've already studied Islam since you were arrested, so you just need a name. I want you to know that I think you have a beautiful name, I love it, and I'll refuse to call you anything else, but you have to choose something just for the record," he said.

I was even going to have a new name. It was as if he were taking me apart, piece by piece; I was being dissected alive. He could call me whatever he wanted.

"You can choose a name for me," I said.

"No. I want you to do it yourself."

The first name that came into my mind was Fatemeh, and I said it out loud.

"My mother's name! She'll be very glad!"

I was going to turn my back on Christ. There was no way out. I thought of Judas. He had also betrayed Jesus. Was I walking the same path? Only at the end did he realize the terrible thing he had done, so he took his own life. In despair, he lost all faith and hope and surrendered to darkness. Wasn't this his greatest mistake? Maybe if he had faced the truth, maybe if he had asked God for forgiveness, his soul could have been saved. When Jesus was arrested, St. Peter said three times that he didn't know Jesus, but St. Peter believed in His forgiveness and sought it. God was love. Jesus was tortured, and He died a painful, terrible death. I didn't need to explain anything to Him. He already knew.

I had to say good-bye to Andre, only a good-bye and nothing more. He didn't have to know everything. I also had to tell my parents, but I could start by telling them that I had converted to Islam and see their reaction. I also wanted to see my church for one last time. Maybe then, I could move on with my new life.

Ali brought me some fresh *barbari* bread and cheese for breakfast the next morning.

"Are you ready to go shopping?" he asked after we were done eating.

"Yes, but I have to ask you something before we go."

"What?"

"Do you really want to help me love you?"

"Yes, I do." He looked surprised.

"Then take me to my church, just once, to say good-bye."

"I'll take you. Anything else?"

I told him that there was one more thing, and I knew he wouldn't like it. I explained that I understood that we had an agreement. I was going to remain true to my word and do my very best to be a good wife, but I needed to say good-bye to Andre. If I didn't do this, my past would never leave me.

I could see in his eyes that he wasn't angry.

"Well, I guess I have to accept that your heart can't change overnight. I'm going to let you see him only once, but I want you to know that I'm doing this against my will and just to make you happy."

"Thank you."

"I'll make the arrangements. He'll be allowed to come and see you at visitation time, probably not this one, but the one after that."

I thanked him and said I was planning to tell my parents about my conversion at the next visitation.

"Are you going to tell them about our marriage, too?"

"No, not yet. I'm going to do it step by step."

"Whatever you think is best for you," he said.

* * *

I converted to Islam about a week later. The ceremony was held
after the Friday prayer, which was celebrated outdoors in a quiet,
wooded area of Evin. Carpets covered the grassy ground. Evin employees and guards sat in rows, first the men and then the women,
but the majority were men. Everyone faced a wooden platform
where Ayatollah Ghilani, who was the *imam-eh Jomeh*—the leader of
the Friday prayer—that day, was to give a speech and lead the
*namaz*. I followed Ali to the last couple of rows where women sat.
Everyone was seated except a tall woman who was standing, looking around. She was Sister Maryam. She smiled, took my hand, and
told me I could sit next to her. Soon, Ayatollah Ghilani arrived and
began his speech. He told the crowd about the evils of the United
States and praised all that the revolutionary guards and the employees of the Courts of Islamic Revolution were doing to protect
Islam. Then, after the *namaz*, Ayatollah Ghilani called my name
and asked me to go to the platform. Sister Maryam squeezed my
hand, and I stood up, feeling a little dizzy. Everyone was staring at
me. With shaky steps, I made my way to the ayatollah, and he
asked me to say a very simple sentence: "I testify that there is no
God except Allah, and that Mohammad is His prophet." To show
approval, the crowd yelled *"Allaho akbar"* three times. I wasn't a
Christian anymore.

Sparrows continued to chirp happily on the branches of the surrounding trees, and the mountain breeze ruffled the leaves, making
sunlight quiver on its way to the ground. The sky remained as blue
as before. I was waiting for God's anger. I wanted a bolt of lightning to come and strike me where I stood. Ali sat in the first row,
and the look of love on his face struck me harder than lightning
ever could. It made my heart ache with guilt. "Love one another,
the way I have loved you," Jesus had said. Did He expect me to
love Ali? How could He possibly expect such a thing?

Ali rose and gave me a folded black chador.

"My mother cried with joy and prayed for you as she sewed this. We're very proud of you."

I wished I could feel the same.

At the visitation, I told my parents about my conversion. I didn't expect them to ask me why I had converted, and they didn't. No one dared question what happened in Evin. They stared at me and cried. I guessed they knew that an Evin prisoner was nobody's son or daughter, husband or wife, mother or father; he or she was only a prisoner and nothing more.

Ali kept his promise and took me to the church a few days later. His friend Mohammad came with us, because, as Ali had told me, Mohammad had never been to a church and was curious to see one from the inside. Ali parked the car in front of the building. It hadn't changed at all, but I felt like a complete stranger. I stepped out of the car and walked to the main door. It was locked. I went to the side door and rang the doorbell.

"Who is it?" called the priest, Father Martini, through the intercom.

My heart sank. "Marina," I answered.

Rushed steps neared the door, and it opened. For a moment, Father Martini was frozen with shock and disbelief.

"Marina, I'm so happy to see you. Please . . . come in," he finally said.

I followed him across the yard to the small office. Ali and Mohammad were behind us.

"Can I call her mother and Andre, one of her friends, to come and see her here?" Father Martini asked Ali.

Ali and I exchanged a glance. My heart almost stopped.

"Yes, you can," he said and asked Mohammad to step outside with him.

Mohammad came back in after a moment, but I couldn't see Ali. He was probably waiting in the car. I guessed he didn't want to see Andre. Father Martini asked me how I was, and I told him I was fine. His eyes moved from me to Mohammad and vice versa. I realized how terrifying it was for him to have me there. I had never thought of the fear my presence would create. I knew I had not put the priests in danger, but they had no way of knowing this. I expected to feel happy and safe here, but now I could see that my happiness and safety had died the day I was arrested.

Both my mother and Andre arrived within minutes. How I wished I could tell them the whole story, but I knew I might never be able to do that. Was it even possible to put so much pain into words? I had come to say good-bye. That was the only right thing to do. I had to give them and myself a chance to heal and forget. I had to close the doors on the past.

My mother wore a large navy scarf, which covered her hair, a black Islamic manteau, and black pants. She embraced me and wouldn't let go. I could feel her ribs under my fingers; she had lost weight and, as always, smelled of cigarettes.

"You all right?" she whispered in my ear.

Her hands carefully moved around my back and arms; she was trying to make sure I was not missing any limbs. I finally stepped away from her, and her eyes examined me from head to toe, but because of my black chador, there wasn't much of me she could see; only my face was visible.

"Mom, I'm okay," I said, smiling.

She managed a forced smile.

"Where did you get the chador?" she asked.

I told her a friend had given it to me.

"You know that Marina has converted to Islam, right?" Mohammad's deep voice filled the room.

"Yes," my mother and Father Martini said together. My mother opened her purse, took out a tissue paper, and wiped her tears.

"Are you sure you're okay?" asked Andre, looking at me and then at Mohammad.

"I'm fine." I had so much to say but couldn't think.

Andre had seen the struggle in my eyes.

"What is it?" he asked.

Words were lost deep inside me. The last few months of my life had created a circle of pain and confusion around me, holding me captive, not only within the walls of Evin, but inside myself. I opened my mouth, but nothing came out.

"When are you coming home?" Andre asked.

"Never," I whispered.

"I'll wait for you," he said and smiled with conviction. The look in his eyes told me that regardless of everything, he loved me. I didn't need to say another word. I knew that even if I begged him to forget me, he wouldn't. When someone waits for you, it means there is hope. He was my life the way it had been before Evin, and I had to hang on to him to survive. Silent tears falling down my face, I turned around and walked out. Mohammad and I stepped in the car, and Ali drove away but pulled over after a few minutes.

"Why have you pulled over?" I asked.

"I've never seen you this pale."

"I'm fine. Thank you for bringing me. You didn't have to let them come and see me. I'm grateful. I know it wasn't easy for you."

"You've forgotten that I love you."

"I don't know how to thank you."

"Yes, you do," he said.

# Sixteen

O<small>N OUR WEDDING DAY</small>, July 23, 1982, after the morning *namaz*, Ali picked me up at my solitary cell at 209, where I had spent about a month without having any contact with other prisoners. I hadn't slept the night before. My fear was my savior; it paralyzed my thoughts and left me numb. I sat in a corner, staring at my small, barred window, at the way its gray metal lines cut the dark-blue vastness beyond them into small, flat rectangles. I had always loved early mornings when light slowly filled the darkness of the night. A deep blue creeping into the blackness of the sky, like rain seeping into the body of the desert. But from here, this beauty seemed unreal.

Ali softly knocked on the door. With trembling hands, I put on my chador and stood up. Looking straight into my eyes, he came in and closed the door behind him. I looked down.

"You won't regret this," he said, stepping closer to me. "Did you sleep last night?"

"No."

"Neither did I. Are you ready?"

I nodded.

We drove to his parents' in silence. As soon as we arrived, Ali and his father left the house. His mother hugged and kissed me, insisting that I should have a good breakfast. I wasn't hungry, but she wouldn't have any of that. I followed her to the kitchen. She made me sit down and broke a few eggs over a frying pan. Unlike my mother's kitchen, hers was spacious and bright. The large stainless-steel samovar hummed gently, filling the uncomfortable silence.

"Family and friends all wanted to come to the wedding," she said after a couple of minutes. "I have three sisters and two brothers, and they all have children. Most of them are married and have children of their own. Mr. Moosavi has three brothers and a sister, who also have children and so on. There are also aunts, uncles, cousins, and family friends. They were very disappointed to hear that no one was invited to Ali's wedding. But we explained, and most of them understood and sent you their best wishes. As soon as you and Ali are ready, I'll invite them here to meet you."

She had spoken slowly and had paused a few times, trying to choose her words carefully.

Uncomfortable silence again. The wooden spoon scraping against the frying pan.

"I know you're scared." Ali's mother sighed, still standing in front of the stove with her back to me. "I remember the day I married Mr. Moosavi. I was younger than you are now. It was an arranged marriage, and I was terrified. Ali has told me that you're very brave, and from what I've heard and seen, I know you are. But I also know that today, you're scared, and you have every right to be, especially without your family by your side. But let me tell you that Ali is a good man. He's very much like his father."

When she turned around, we were both crying. She came to me, held my head to her chest, and stroked my hair. I had not been comforted like this since my grandmother's death. Then we sat together and had some scrambled eggs. She explained that it was traditional for me—the bride-to-be—to take a long bath, and she also mentioned that she was expecting the *bandandaz,* who was a close friend of hers, to arrive in about two hours. I had not taken a bath in months, only quick showers. I remembered the bath I never had a chance to take on the night of my arrest.

Before showing me to the bathroom, she took me to one of the bedrooms that had been cleared for the *sofreh-yeh aghd,* which means "the cloth of marriage": A silky white tablecloth was spread on the floor, and in the middle of it was a large mirror in a silver frame, on either side of which stood a large crystal candleholder holding a white candle, and in front of the mirror, there was a copy of the Koran. Silver platters filled with sweets and fruits covered the rest of the tablecloth. I knew it was customary for the mullah to perform the marriage ceremony with the bride and groom sitting by the *sofreh-yeh aghd.*

In the bathroom, the expensive ceramic tiles gleamed. I filled the tub and soaked in the steaming water. Although it was summertime, I had felt cold all morning. As the intoxicating warmth surrounded me, my tightened muscles began to relax. I closed my eyes. God had given me a lifesaving ability: I could usually switch off my thoughts when they were too much to bear. I was not going to think about what was going to happen that night.

A while later, when the water had started to cool down, there was a gentle knock on the bathroom door, and Akram told me that the *bandandaz,* Shirin Khanoom, had arrived. "You don't need your *hejab.* The men are still out and won't be back until late afternoon," she added. I dressed and stepped out of the bathroom. In Akram's old bedroom, a large woman was spreading a white bed sheet on the floor. As soon as I entered the room, her eyes moved up and down my body.

"Beautiful girl," she said, nodding in approval. "Too thin, though. Fatemeh Khanoom, you'll have to feed her. She'll look even better with fuller curves." She came up to me, put a finger under my chin and examined my face. "Nice skin. Her eyebrows need a little bit of work, though."

"Akram and I will be in the kitchen if you need anything," Ali's mother said to Shirin Khanoom and smiled at me as she and Akram left the room.

Sitting down on the sheet, Shirin Khanoom said, "Well dear, I'm ready. Take off your clothes and come sit in front of me."

I didn't move.

"What are you waiting for? Come on," she laughed. "There's no need to be shy. This needs to get done. You want to look your best for your husband, don't you?"

No, I don't, I thought but didn't say anything.

Shivering, I slowly took off my clothes, sat on the sheet, and folded my knees to my chest. Shirin Khanoom told me to stretch out my legs. I obeyed. She took a long piece of string, spun one end of it around her fingers a few times, held the other end between her teeth, and bending over my legs, moved the string in a scissors-like manner and at an amazing speed to remove the hair. It was painful. Once finished, she told me to take a cold shower. After the shower, she braided my hair, which was almost to my waist, and gathered it in a bun behind my head.

At noon, the voice of the *moazzen* traveled through the neighborhood from the mosque, inviting the faithful to prepare for the second *namaz* of the day. We performed the ritual of *vozoo*, the washing of hands, arms, and feet, and when finished, I stepped out of the bathroom to find Ali's mother waiting for me, holding a white silky bundle in her hands. She handed it to me: a beautiful prayer rug she had made herself. I felt enveloped by her kindness.

Ali's parents had a *namaz* room. Except for the thick Persian rugs that covered its floor, the room was completely bare. There, facing Mecca, each of us unrolled our prayer rug and stood on it for prayer; mine was delicately embroidered with silver and gold threads and beads. Ali's mother must have spent hours making it.

After the prayer, Akram set the dining table with the best china, and we sat for a lunch of eggplant and beef stew with rice. I managed to swallow some. We had tea after lunch, and as I was sipping my tea, I noticed that Ali's mother was looking at me thoughtfully, as if she had something important to say but didn't know where to start. I looked down.

"Marina, there's something about Ali, I'm not sure if you know," she finally said. "Has he told you that he was a prisoner in Evin during the time of the shah?"

I was shocked. "No, he's never told me."

"SAVAK—the shah's secret police—arrested him about three years and three months before the revolution. I was devastated," she said. "I didn't think he'd survive. He was very dedicated to the imam and hated the shah and his corrupt government. I was expecting them to arrest Mr. Moosavi, too, but they didn't. But Ali was gone. I knew he was being tortured. We went to Evin and asked to see him, but for three months they didn't let us. When we were finally allowed a visit, he looked terribly thin and frail. My beautiful, strong son."

Tears slowly fell down Fatemeh Khanoom's face. "They released him about three months before the success of the revolution. They hadn't told us they were letting him go. That day, I was right here in the kitchen when I heard the doorbell. It was a cloudy fall day, and the yard was covered with leaves. I ran to the door and asked, Who is it? There was no answer. And I knew it was him. I don't know how, but I knew. I opened the door, and there he was. He smiled and embraced me and we couldn't let go. He felt so thin. I could feel his bones under my fingers. And his smile was different. It was weighed down and sad. I knew he'd seen terrible things. I knew the sadness in his eyes was there to stay. He went right back to his life, but he had changed. The pain he carried with him never completely went away. Sometimes, I heard him walk around the house all night. Then, a few months ago, he came home from work one day, packed a bag, and went to the front to fight the Iraqis. Just like that without any explanation. I was shocked. This wasn't like him. Don't get me wrong; his going to the front didn't surprise me; he'd been to the front before, but the timing was strange. I knew something had happened, but he didn't tell me what it was. And for the four months he was away, I hardly ever slept. Finally one day, they called and told us that he'd been shot in the leg and was in the hospital. I thanked God a million times. When I went to see him, he smiled at me like the old times, like the little boy he used to be, and told me that something wonderful had happened to him. I first thought he'd lost his mind."

So Ali had been a prisoner in Evin and had been tortured. Maybe this was one of the reasons why after I was lashed and he took me to the solitary cell, he asked me if I needed something to help with the pain and he arranged for the doctor to come and see me. Maybe he had done this because he had suffered just like me.

After the revolution, he wanted revenge, so he began working in Evin. During the first few months after the revolution, most Evin prisoners were former SAVAK agents, and he had his chance to get even with them. An eye for an eye. They weren't only enemies of Islam, they were his personal enemies. But things changed. Those who had fought alongside him during the time of the shah, the Mojahedin and the Fadayian, were now being arrested. I was sure that at the beginning it wasn't too difficult for him to justify their arrests; his former cell mates and their followers had become the enemies of the Islamic state, and as Khomeini had put it, they were the enemies of God and His prophet, Mohammad. Ali had been raised a devout Muslim, and he would follow his imam to the death, but he probably began to see that what was now being done in Evin in the name of Islam was wrong. However, because of his devotion to his religion, he had difficulty accepting this truth and didn't know how to deal with it. His faith had blinded him, but, maybe because of his personal experience, he would sometimes see the situation from the perspective of the prisoners. And his parents were proud of him for being in the front line of the battle against the enemies of Islam. For them, his being an interrogator was one of the most honorable things a Muslim could do. For them, all that happened in Evin after the revolution was completely justified; they were protecting their way of life and their values. After all, they believed this was a war between good and evil.

After we cleared the table, Ali's mother asked me if I knew how to cook.

"I do, but not as good as you and Akram. I've learned from cookbooks. My mother didn't like having me in the kitchen."

"Would you like to help us with dinner? We have to start right away. Agha—the mullah—will be here at five o'clock, and we'll eat after the wedding."

I helped them around the kitchen. Akram and I diced and sautéed onions, fresh parsley, chives, and other herbs. Ali's mother chopped the beef and boiled the long-grain rice. She had already marinated chicken pieces in a mixture of yogurt, egg yolks, and saffron. We made some *khoresh-eh ghormeh sabzi*—a beef and herb stew—and *tachin*—a mixture of chicken, rice, yogurt, egg yolks, and saffron.

Mr. Moosavi, Ali, and Akram's husband, Massood, came home at about four o'clock. Ali's mother pushed me into the bathroom, saying I had to take another shower because I smelled of onions.

After the shower, I put on the white Islamic manteau, large white scarf, white pants, and the white chador Ali's mother had left for me on the bed. Soon, there was a knock on the bedroom door.

"Marina, it's time," Akram called.

I opened the door and stepped out without giving myself time to think. Ali was already sitting by the *sofreh-yeh aghd*. I sat next to him, wondering if anyone had noticed how badly I was shaking. The mullah entered the room. He chanted a few sentences in Arabic, which I would have been able to understand if I could concentrate. Then, he asked me in Persian, "Fatemeh *khanoom-eh* Moradi-Bakht, are you ready to take Seyed Ali-eh Moosavi as your wedded husband?"

I knew it was customary for the bride not to answer this question the first time it was asked. The mullah was to wait for an answer and, not receiving one, repeat the question twice more. I said yes the very first time. I just wanted to get done with it.

After dinner, Ali and I drove to the house he had bought for us. He took my left hand, which had been resting on my lap, and held it tight until we arrived. This was the first time he had touched me like this.

As I stepped into my new house and my strange new life, I promised myself not to look back and not to think of the past, but this was a difficult promise to keep. Ali led me to our bedroom, where gifts had been piled on the bed.

"Open them," he said. "Some are from me, and the rest are from my family."

There were many pieces of jewelry, crystal bowls and glasses, dishes, and silver-plated platters. Ali was sitting on the bed beside me, watching me as I opened them.

"I'm your husband now, you don't need your *hejab* anymore," he said.

I wished I could hide somewhere. He pulled at the large scarf covering my hair. I reached back for it.

"I understand your discomfort, but you really don't need it. You'll get used to me."

He undid my braided hair and ran his fingers through it.

"You have beautiful hair. It's soft as silk."

He put a necklace around my neck and a bracelet around my wrist. I looked at my wedding ring. It had a large diamond shining on it.

"I've wanted you ever since I saw you," Ali said, wrapping his arms around me, kissing my hair and my neck. I pushed him away.

"Marina, it's fine. You know how long I've waited for this. You're finally mine, and I can touch you. There's no need to be afraid. I won't hurt you. I'll be gentle, I promise."

He unbuttoned his shirt, and, frozen with terror, I closed my eyes. Soon, I felt his fingers undoing the buttons of my manteau. I opened my eyes and tried to fight him, but his weight pinned me to the mattress. I begged him to stop, but he said he couldn't. He ripped off my clothes. I screamed. His bare skin touched mine, and the strange, unfamiliar warmth of his body pressed on me. He smelled of shampoo and soap. I gathered all my strength and struggled to push him away, but it was useless; he was too big and strong. Anger, fear, and a terrible sense of humiliation twisted, turned, and rose inside me like a storm that had nowhere to go, until I had no energy left, until I accepted that there was nowhere to run, until I surrendered. It hurt. The shocking pain wasn't the same as the pain of being lashed. When I was being tortured, I had managed to maintain a sense of authority, a strange kind of power that physical torment could never steal away. But now, I was his. He had me.

I cried all night. My insides were burning. Ali had his arms around me, holding me tight. Before dawn, he rose for *namaz*, and I stayed in bed.

He sat on the edge of the bed beside me and kissed my cheek and my arm. "I have to touch you to believe that you're my wife. Was it painful for you?"

"Yes."

"It will get better."

I fell asleep after he left the bed; sleep was my only escape.

\* \* \*

"Breakfast is ready," he called from the kitchen at about eight o'clock. The sun was shining through the sliding doors. I got up and opened them. A breeze swept through and brought in the song of the sparrows. The backyard was beautiful. The geraniums and marigolds were in full bloom. I felt as if I were living someone else's life. The next-door neighbor called her children in for breakfast. It was a perfect summer day, and there wasn't a cloud in the sky, but I wished for snow to cover the earth; I wished for its cold and honest touch to embrace my warm skin. I wanted my fingers to lose their sense of touch in deep frost and ache. I wanted all the shades of green and red to disappear under the weight of winter and its shades of white so I could dream and tell myself that when spring came, things would be different.

"There you are," I heard him say from behind me. "Breakfast is ready, and your tea is getting cold. There's fresh bread on the table."

I was in his arms again. "You can't imagine how happy I am," he whispered in my ear and told me that the first time he had seen me, I was sitting on the floor in a hallway, but unlike all the other women who were wearing black chadors, I had covered my hair with a beige cashmere shawl. Although he could see that I was small and slim, I had my back straight against the wall, looking taller than all the others around me. He said that with my head tilted toward the ceiling and my lips moving slightly in what seemed like a prayer, I had been calm in the middle of a world of fear and despair that surrounded me. He said he had wanted to look away, and he couldn't.

For the next few days, he pampered me to the point that I felt uncomfortable. I had always taken care of myself. I didn't want to be treated like a child. The girl I used to be was gone. I was a married woman. I couldn't hide under my bed as I used to. Maybe Ali was my cross and I had to accept him. Or, at least, I could try. I just wished he would leave me alone in bed. Every time he took off his clothes and touched me, I begged him to stop. He sometimes listened and sometimes didn't, telling me that I had to get used to it, that this was an important part of being married and that if I stopped resisting him, it would hurt less.

Finally, about a week after our wedding day, I rose from bed at dawn and decided to try to live my life and stop feeling sorry for myself. What was done was done, and I couldn't change it. I began by cleaning the house and making breakfast, and I told Ali that I wanted him to invite his parents and his sister for dinner. He thought I had lost my mind and told me he didn't think I knew how to cook. I told him I did, and he gave in.

"Okay, I'll call my parents and my sister," he said. "Then we'll go grocery shopping, and Marina?"

"Yes?"

"Thank you."

"For what?"

"For trying."

My heart felt a little warmer than it had in a very long time. I started working on dinner right after lunch. Ali was gone for a couple of hours, and when he returned, the house was filled with the smells of lasagna, beef and mushroom stew, and rice. I had just begun working on an apple cake. He came into the kitchen and told me that the smell of food had made him hungry. He wanted to know if my mother had taught me how to cook, and I told him that my mother was not patient enough to teach me anything; I liked to cook, so I had learned from cookbooks. He offered to make us tea and poured some water into the samovar. Then, after putting some loose tea leaves in a china teapot, he came toward me. I was breaking an egg into a bowl. He still terrified me. Every time he stepped close to me, every time I felt his breath on my skin, every time he touched me, I wanted to run away. He held my face in his hands and kissed my forehead, and I wondered if I was ever going to get accustomed to his touch.

Ali's parents, Akram, and Massood came and were all pleased with everything I had prepared. Ali's mother had a little bit of a cold, so after dinner and dessert, I made her some tea with lemon and brought her a blanket so she could rest on the couch. Akram came into the kitchen to help me with the dishes.

"Dinner was delicious," she said with a forced smile. I could feel the discomfort in her voice; she was trying to be kind to me, and I appreciated it.

"Thank you. I'm not a good cook, but I tried. I'm sure you can cook a lot better than me."

"No, not really."

Silence filled the space between us. I began putting the leftovers in the fridge.

"Why did you marry my brother?" she suddenly asked.

I looked straight into her eyes, but she looked away.

"Has your brother told you anything about what happened between us?" I said.

"He hasn't told me much."

"Why don't you ask him then?"

"He won't tell me, and I want to hear it from you."

"I married him because he wanted me to."

"That's not enough."

"Why not? Why did you marry your husband?"

"My marriage was arranged. My parents had made an agreement with my husband's parents when I was a child that I should marry their son as soon as I was old enough. You're from a different kind of a family, a different culture. If you didn't want to marry him, you could have said no."

"Why do you think I didn't want to marry him?"

"I just know. A woman can sense these kinds of things."

I took a deep breath. "Don't forget that I'm a prisoner. Ali threatened me that if I didn't marry him, he would hurt those who are dear to me."

"Ali would never do anything like this!"

"See, this is why I didn't want to tell you. I knew you wouldn't believe me because you love your brother."

"Will you put your hand on the Holy Koran and say that he did this?"

"Yes, I'm telling the truth."

She dropped in a chair and shook her head.

"This is terrible! Do you hate him for it?"

I didn't know what to say. This was not because I didn't want to tell the truth, but because I realized I didn't exactly know the true answer to this question. A few days earlier, I would have said, with conviction, that I hated him. But I wasn't so sure anymore. Something had changed, not fundamentally, but slightly, and I didn't understand why my feelings toward Ali were now different. But I had every right to hate him.

"No, I don't know. I did hate him, but not anymore. Hatred is a very strong word."

She looked into my eyes.

"Did you also convert to Islam because you had to?"

"Yes."

"So, you didn't really mean it?"

"No, but don't forget that I only told you because you insisted on knowing and I didn't want to lie. It's all over now. I'm a Muslim, I'm your brother's wife, and I've promised to be faithful to him and I will. I don't want to talk about it. What's done is done."

"May God give you strength," she said. "I know how difficult this must be."

"At least it's good to know that someone understands."

An honest, effortless smile brightened her face.

"How long have you been married?" I asked.

"Seven years."

"Do you love your husband?"

Surprised, she looked at me as if she had never considered her feelings toward him.

"Love is such a strong word," she said with a laugh, staring at her wedding ring, tracing its sparkling diamond with a finger. "I think it only exists in fairy tales. My husband is good and faithful to me, and I live a comfortable life. I guess you can say I'm happy, except . . ." Her gaze drifted away, and I recognized the nostalgic pain that loss leaves behind. It made my heart sink.

"Except what?" I whispered.

"I can't have children," she said and sighed as if this was the most difficult sentence she had ever spoken. "I've tried everything. In the beginning, everybody kept asking me if I was pregnant, but after a couple of years, they gave up. Now, I'm just the woman who can't have children. But as I told you, my husband is good to me. I know how important it is for him to have a son, but he's told me that he won't marry another woman."

"What are you ladies doing there? You're taking forever," Ali's mother said as she walked into the kitchen. "Your men would like some more tea."

As soon as we sat down in the living room, the phone rang. Ali answered it. I could tell it was from Evin. Listening most of the time, he looked concerned. Everyone was silent. I asked him what was wrong when the conversation was over.

"We've known for a while that the Mojahedin have plans to assassinate a few of the people who hold important jobs in Evin," he said. "We've been trying to find and arrest the ones involved. A few of them were arrested recently and have been interrogated. It was Mohammad on the phone. He called to let me know that the information he's obtained suggests that I'm on their assassination list. My colleagues and friends believe that it would be safer for Marina and me to stay in Evin for a while. I'm not worried for myself, but I don't want to put Marina's life in danger."

I had figured that he was important in Evin, and this confirmed it.

"I think staying in Evin is a good idea. It's better to be safe than sorry," said Mr. Moosavi. He looked worried.

I didn't know this at the time because I didn't have access to TV, radio, or newspapers, but a few government officials had been assassinated recently, and all the killings had been blamed on the Mojahedin.

"Marina, is it okay with you if we stay in Evin for a while? It will be a lot safer," Ali said.

"Sure," I said, knowing I didn't really have a choice.

"I'll make it up to you when things are better."


We went to bed after our guests left.

"Ali, do you see what violence does to people? You kill them, and they kill you. When is it going to end, only after everybody is dead?"

"You're naïve," he said. "Do you think that if we ask them nicely, they'll simply stop fighting the government? We have to protect Islam, God's law, and God's people from the evil forces that are at work against them."

"God doesn't need protection. I'm just saying that violence only brings more violence. I don't know what the solution is, but I know that killing is not the answer."

He pulled me into his arms. "Not everyone is as good as you," he said. "It's a cruel world."

"Yes it is, only because we're cruel to each other."

He laughed. "You don't give up, do you?"

"When are we going back to Evin?" I asked.

"Tomorrow morning. I hope you understand that once we go back to Evin, even though you're my wife, you won't be treated differently from before. You're still officially a prisoner. Do you want to stay in a solitary cell or do you want to go to 246?"

I said I didn't care which one, and he told me the solitary cells were a better choice because then he would be able to spend more time with me. I didn't argue. I still didn't want to explain anything to anyone at 246.

"Have there been many arrests lately?" I asked.

"Yes."

"Poor souls. They must feel terrified."

"Marina, many of these people are terrorists."

"Some of them, maybe, but you know that most of them are only children, and many of them haven't done anything wrong. If I stay in a solitary cell, will you let the younger ones come and stay with me during their interrogation period? There's enough room for two people in those cells. Ali, I hate being useless. I can help them feel better, and I'll feel better myself."

He smiled. "This is going to be interesting. Fine, you have a deal."

"Just don't tell them I'm your wife or they'll be scared of me."

If there wasn't any goodness around me, maybe it was up to me to do something good.

"Ali, where is Sarah Farahani?" I asked.

"She was in the prison hospital for a long time. Not the hospital you were in, though. There's another one for prisoners with psychological problems. Now she's in a cell at 209."

"She needs to go home. She's been through enough. She hasn't done anything. She just talked too much. She won't survive in Evin."

"Hamehd is the one who's in charge of her case, and you know how difficult he can be. I don't think Sarah will be going anywhere soon."

"Was her brother, Sirus, really executed?"

"Yes. He was an active member of the Mojahedin, and he didn't cooperate at all," he said matter-of-factly.

"So your policy is to kill whoever stands in your way."

"If Sirus had a chance, he would have shot me in the head."

"You could have kept him in prison instead of killing him."

"This wasn't my decision, and I'm not going to argue about it."

"Can I see Sarah?"

"I'll take you to her cell once we're back."

I had to ask him the question that had been on my mind for a while. There was no right time to ask it, and now was as good as ever.

"Ali, have you ever killed anyone? I don't mean at the front; I mean at Evin."

He stepped out of bed and walked to the kitchen. I followed him. He turned on the tap, filled a glass with water, and took a few sips from it.

"You have, haven't you?"

"Marina, why can't you let it be?"

"I hate you!"

I felt the terrible weight of my words, but I didn't regret them. I wanted to hurt him. This was revenge, and he deserved it. I had tried to accept my situation and to understand him, but I couldn't pretend I didn't know about the horrible things he had done.

He slowly put his glass on the table and stared at it. When he looked up, his eyes were dark with a strange combination of anger and pain. He came toward me. I took a few steps back and bumped into a cabinet. Even if I ran, I couldn't go far. He grabbed my arms, and his fingers dug into my flesh.

"You're hurting me," I said.

"Am *I* hurting *you*?"

"Yes. You've been hurting me since I first saw you. And you've been hurting other people, and you've been hurting yourself."

He lifted me off the ground and carried me to the bedroom. I kicked and screamed in vain.


The next morning, I refused to get out of bed. Ali called me from the kitchen three times, saying breakfast was ready. I pulled the covers over my head, sobbing. The bed creaked. I opened my eyes and, through the white veil of the thin cotton sheet, saw him sitting next to me. He sat sideways on the edge of the bed, his elbows resting on his knees and his hands clenched together. I didn't move.

"Marina?" he said after a few minutes.

I didn't respond.

"I'm sorry for getting mad at you. You have every right to blame me. But you have to understand that this is the way things are. I don't like what I do. The world is an unkind and violent place, and there are things we *have* to do. I know you disagree with me. But this is how it is, and I didn't make it this way. You can hate me if you want, but I love you. I didn't mean to hurt you last night. Come. Let's have breakfast."

I didn't react.

"Come on. Please. What can I do to make up for it?"

"Let me go home."

"Marina, you're my wife. Your home is where I am. You have to get used to it."

My sobs became heavier and louder. He peeled the sheet off me and tried to pull me into his arms. I pushed him away.

"You have to get used to the way things are now. Is there anything *reasonable* I can do to make you happy?"

I had to find some goodness in this pain or it was going to drown me.

"Help Sarah."

"I will."

Ali wore pajama pants but didn't have a shirt on. Narrow, white lines covered his bare back from side to side. Scars. There were many of them. Lash marks. I had not noticed them before because I always closed my eyes when he took off his clothes.

I touched his back.

"You have scars . . ."

He stood and put on his shirt.

For the first time, I felt a closeness between us, a connection. I didn't want it to be there. But it was as tangible as the sheet covering me, as real as his scars and mine. A sad understanding that didn't need words to exist, that delivered all it had to say in a silent glance or a light touch.

"Come. Let's go eat," he said.

We had breakfast.

About three hours later, I was back in my old solitary cell. I couldn't say I had missed it. Ali brought me a large stack of books—all about Islam—and told me he was going to be very busy. I reminded him that he had promised to take me to see Sarah, and he took me to her cell but warned me that Sarah was heavily drugged and was not going to be very responsive.

"You can stay with her for an hour or two but not more. I don't want to upset Hamehd."

Sarah was writing on the wall when I entered her cell. She had lost more weight, and her skin had turned yellow. I put my hands on her shoulders. She didn't react at all.

"Sarah, I missed you."

The walls were covered with words; they carried me back to our old lives: Sarah's house with its flower bed, her mother sitting on a swing in the yard, her father reciting Hafez's poems, Sirus playing soccer with his friends, our school with its tall windows, walking home from Agha-yeh Rostami's general store while licking an ice cream cone. It went on and on. She had even written about my pencil case. I didn't want to remember. Looking back made my heart ache with a terrible longing to go home. Home. It felt oceans and worlds away. But it was there. Somewhere beyond Evin. If my home were beyond Mount Everest, I would have climbed it. Even ten Mount Everests seemed possible to conquer.

"Sarah. I know you can hear me. Many of these are my memories, too. Our homes are still out there, and you have to survive Evin to go back. Your home is there, waiting for you. Don't forget that tomorrow always comes, but you have to be there to see it. Sirus wants you to see it. Fight this battle for him, for your mother, for your father."

I grabbed Sarah's shoulders and turned her around to face me.

"Hamehd wants you to be like this, to lose. Don't give him the satisfaction. You will go home. If you only knew what I've done. It's so hard sleeping in Ali's bed, but he isn't like Hamehd. There's goodness in him, and he loves me . . . but it's so hard. You can't imagine."

Sarah's arms went around me and became tighter and tighter. We held each other and cried.

After about two weeks, which I mostly spent reading except for when Ali was with me, I had my first cell mate, Sima. She had large hazel eyes, and although she didn't look more than thirteen, was fifteen years old. The guard who brought her to my cell told her to take off her blindfold before he locked the door behind him. She took it off, rubbed her eyes, squinted, and looked at me with round, terrified eyes.

She asked me who I was. I told her my name and that I was a prisoner. She looked slightly relieved and sat down, keeping a safe distance from me. Her feet were a little swollen. I asked if they hurt.

"They tortured me!" she cried.

I moved closer to her and told her that I had been tortured, too, more than she had been. She asked how long I had been in Evin, and I said, "Seven months."

"Seven months? That's too long! Have you been here in this cell the whole time?" she asked.

I explained that I had been at 246 and that after her interrogation period was over, she could be sent there as well to wait for her trial. She asked how long that would take, and I said it could take from days to months. She wanted to know if I had had a trial.

"Sort of," I said.

"What's your sentence?" she asked.

"Life in prison."

"Oh, my God!"

She said she couldn't imagine being in Evin for more than a week. I asked her who had interrogated her, and she said her interrogator was Ali and that he was very mean.

"He's mean sometimes," I said. "But there are others who are a lot worse than him."

Telling her the truth would have helped nothing.

Sima wanted to know everything about Evin's procedures and the 246, and I told her as much as I could.

Ali knocked on the door of the cell at about eight o'clock at night and called my name. I grabbed my chador and went to the door.

"What does he want from you?" Sima whispered.

"Don't worry; he won't hurt me," I said as I put on my chador and walked out of the cell.

Ali wanted to know how things were going with Sima, and I told him she was feeling a little better. I asked him why he had lashed her, and he said he hadn't had a choice; her brother was a member of the Mojahedin and was involved with the assassination of a government official. Ali had been trying to find and arrest him for months. He said he had to make sure Sima didn't know where her brother was.

"Please tell me you're not going to whip her again, are you?"

"No. She doesn't know anything. I'm sending her to 246. We'll let her go once her brother gives himself up."

I asked him where he was taking me.

"Just another cell. I'm exhausted. I really need you," he said.


After the morning prayer when I returned to my cell, Sima was fast asleep.

"When did you come back last night?" she asked as soon as she woke up. "I waited for you forever, and then I guess I fell asleep."

"I came really late."

"What were you doing all that time?"

"Nothing important."

"You don't want to talk about it, do you?"

"No. Don't worry about me."

She was crying. I embraced her and told her she would be all right as long as she didn't lose hope. I told her I had heard that Ali was sending her to 246, where she would meet my friends. They would help her. I asked her to tell them I was all right.

The next day, Sima was sent to 246, and my days became painfully boring and lonely. I asked Ali to bring me a few books of poetry, and he did. So I divided my days between reading and memorizing the works of Hafez, Sadi, and Rumi and sleeping.

A few days later, Ali picked me up at my cell in the evening to go to his parents' house for dinner. At the prison gates, we stopped, waiting for the guards to let the car through. Ali cranked down the window to greet the guards, who, although friendly toward him, always ignored me as if I weren't there. But this time, after wishing Ali a good night, the guard in charge nodded in my direction and said, "Good night, Mrs. Moosavi."

Confused, I looked around and, after a moment, realized he had addressed me.

Ali touched my hand. I jumped.

"You look shocked," he said.

"They always acted as if I was invisible."

"They're accepting you. They know we're married."

As soon as we arrived at Ali's parents' house, Akram and Ali's mother embraced me. "You're still skin and bone," Ali's mother complained, shaking her head. I followed her to the kitchen to help with dinner preparation. Akram began basting the lamb roast that was in the oven. Ali's mother poured some tea for the men and, on her way to the living room, asked me if I could make salad. There was some washed lettuce and a few tomatoes and cucumbers in a colander by the sink. I grabbed a knife, and as I was chopping, I remembered that I had had a dream about Akram the night before.

"I had a dream about you last night," I said.

"What dream?"

I paused, trying to decide whether to tell her or not.

"Come on, tell me! Did something bad happen?"

"No, no. Not at all."

"Then what was it? I believe in dreams. Do you remember it?"

I told her that it was a strange dream: she was in my church, lighting a candle, and she told me that I had told her to say the Hail Mary nine times a day for nine days to have a baby.

She was surprised and asked me what Hail Mary was, and I told her.

"You really believe that Mary was the Mother of God?" she asked after hearing the prayer.

I explained that Christians believed that God had willed his son, Jesus, to become flesh inside Mary's womb and that Mary was not an ordinary woman; she had been born for this.

"We believe that Mary was a great woman but not the mother of God!" said Akram.

"I'm not asking you to believe in anything. You asked me about my dream, and I told you," I snapped.

She looked down, trying to make up her mind. "I'll do it. I'll say this prayer. There's nothing to lose, is there?"

A couple of days later, early in the afternoon, Ali came into my cell. This was unusual; he always came in the evening. I was taking a nap and woke up startled. He sat next to me, leaned against the wall, and closed his eyes.

"Are you okay?" I asked.

"I'm fine."

He put his arms around me.

"What's wrong?"

"The guards brought in a girl a couple of nights ago. She's seventeen or so. She was caught writing DEATH TO KHOMEINI and KHOMEINI IS A MURDERER and other things like that with spray paint on a wall on Enghelab Avenue. When they arrested her, she said she hated the imam because he had killed her little sister. She's been saying the same things here. I think she's lost it. Hamehd beat her pretty bad, but she's still saying the same things. She'll be executed soon if she doesn't behave herself and cooperate. Will you talk to her? What she needs is a psychologist or something, but that's not going to happen." He sighed. "Don't say it. I know this isn't fair. And I know there's a good chance you won't be able to talk sense into her. I hate doing this to you. But I can't think of anything else."

"I'll talk to her. Where is she?"

"Interrogation building. I'll go get her."

About half an hour later, Ali pushed a wheelchair into my cell. The girl sitting in it was covered with a dark blue chador and was leaning to one side, her head resting against her shoulder.

"Mina, you can take off your blindfold now," said Ali, but she didn't move. Ali pulled off her blindfold, and she opened her eyes a little. Her right cheek was blue and swollen. I knew she couldn't see, hear, or understand much. Everything would seem like a senseless nightmare to her.

"My name is Marina," I said, kneeling in front of her. "I'm a prisoner. You're in a cell. I'll help you off the chair. Don't be afraid. I won't hurt you."

I pulled her up, and she fell into my arms. I helped her sit on the floor. Ali took the wheelchair and stepped out of the cell.

"Layla is dead," Mina whispered.

"What?"

"Layla is dead."

"Who's Layla?"

"Layla is dead."

While spreading a blanket on the floor so she could lie down, I saw her feet and gasped. They were even more swollen than mine had been.

"I'm going to take your slippers off. I'll do it very gently."

The skin on her feet felt and looked like an overblown balloon, but the slippers came off easily.

I poured some water into a plastic cup and put it to her dry, chapped lips. She took a few sips.

"Have more."

She shook her head, and I helped her lie down and took off her chador and scarf. She was shivering, so I spread a couple of blankets over her, and she soon fell asleep. I sat next to her. She was tall and thin. Her curly brown hair was dirty and stuck together from constantly being under a scarf since her arrest. I thought about her swollen feet, and my own feet began to throb. The pain I remembered from my first days in Evin was more than a memory. It lived inside me.

About four hours later, Mina began to moan. I grabbed a cup of water and helped her sit up.

"Listen to me. I know how you feel. I know everything hurts, but I also know it will get better if you drink this. Don't give up."

She had a few sips, and her eyes focused on me.

"Who are you?" she asked.

"I'm a prisoner. My name is Marina."

"I thought I was dead and you were an angel or something."

I laughed. "I promise you I'm not an angel—and you're very much alive. I have some bread and dates. You need to eat. Your body needs strength to recover."

She ate a few dates and a little bit of bread. There was a knock on the door of the cell as soon as she lay down again.

"Marina, put on your chador and step out," Ali's voice said from behind the door. He took me to another cell. We had some bread and cheese he had brought with him. He didn't ask me about Mina.

"Don't you want to know if I've talked to Mina?" I asked him.

"Frankly, I don't want to know anything right now. I need to switch off my brain. I just want to go to sleep."

* * *

When I returned to my cell at about four in the morning, Mina was still asleep. She woke when the sun came up.

"Who's Layla?" I asked her.

She wanted to know how I knew about Layla. I told her what she had said when she had come in.

"Layla is my sister."

"How did she die?"

"A protest rally. She was shot."

She said that a friend of Layla's, named Darya, had been attacked by the Hezbollah one day because her hair had been showing from underneath her scarf. Mina's mother had been on her way to the store and had witnessed the beating. Then the Hezbollah men had thrown Darya into a car and had driven away. Darya's parents had looked for her everywhere, every hospital and every Islamic committee, but she had disappeared. A couple of months after this, Layla heard of a protest rally and decided she had to go. She encouraged Mina to go with her. Mina tried to talk her out of it, but Layla said she would go whether Mina went with her or not. She asked Mina what if what had happened to Darya had happened to her. Mina finally gave in and decided to go with her. Layla made Mina promise not to tell their parents about the rally.

"So we went together," said Mina. "There were so many people. The revolutionary guards attacked and opened fire. Everyone began to run. I grabbed Layla's hand and tried to get us to safety, but she fell. I turned around, and she was dead."

I told Mina about the protest rally at Ferdosi Square, about the young man who was shot, and about my decision to commit suicide when I got home after the rally. And I told her that instead of taking my mother's sleeping pills, I decided to do something about what I had witnessed; I had decided to do the right thing.

"What did you do?" Mina asked.

"I wrote about the rally on a bristol board and put it on a wall in my school. Then, I started a school newspaper."

"I went out really late two or three nights a week and wrote about what had happened to Layla with spray paint on walls. I also wrote slogans against Khomeini and the government. They are all murderers."

"Mina, I came very close to execution. They will execute you if you keep saying things against Khomeini and the government. I've lost friends and I know how you feel. But your death won't solve anything."

"So, you cooperated and lived," she narrowed her eyes.

"It wasn't exactly like that. They threatened to hurt my family and loved ones. I could never put them in danger."

"I see. But my family is destroyed anyway. My father has diabetes and heart problems and has been in the hospital for a while. My mother hasn't talked to anyone since Layla's death. Lately, we've been staying at my grandma's house, and my grandma has looked after my mother. The guards can threaten me as much as they want. It can't get much worse. And some of it is my fault. I should have stopped Layla from going to that rally. Then she would have been fine. All of us would have been fine."

"You can't blame yourself."

"It's my fault."

"Would Layla want you to be executed?"

"She would want me to do the right thing."

"Is committing suicide the right thing?"

"I'm not committing suicide!"

"If you argue with guards and interrogators, they'll kill you. So, don't argue. A little bit of cooperation can save your life."

"I will not cooperate with the people who killed my sister."

"They'll kill you, too. And what will that accomplish?"

"I cannot live with a guilty conscience."

"Don't throw your life away."

"You can't change my mind. Do you really think this life is worth living?"

"You never know what tomorrow might bring, what will happen

in two, five, or ten months. You should give yourself a chance. God has given you life; live it."

"I don't believe in God. Even if there's a God, He's cruel."

"Well, I believe in God and I don't think He's cruel; *we* are sometimes cruel. Whether you existed or not, Layla would have lived and died the way she did. But God gave you the gift of being her sister, of knowing and loving her, of the good memories you shared. And now, you can remember her. You can live and do good things in her memory."

"I don't believe in God." She looked away from me.

Mina slept the rest of the day. I could understand her bitterness. Her anger had turned into hatred, consuming her. My faith in God had given me hope. It had helped me believe in goodness despite all the evil that surrounded me.

In the evening, Ali came to the door of the cell and called my name. Mina didn't move or open her eyes. Again, Ali took me to another cell. I tried to talk to him about Mina, but he didn't want to talk.

It was before the morning *namaz* and still dark when he returned me to my cell. After the door closed behind me, it became pitch-black. I couldn't see a thing. I sat on the floor right away so I wouldn't step on Mina. There wasn't a sound. I crawled ahead, feeling my way with my hands. Mina wasn't there.

"Mina?" I called.

The lights came on as the sound of the *moazzen* filled the air: "*Allaho akbar* . . ."

"Mina!"

"*Allaho akbar* . . ."

Mina was gone. *Ali was with me in the other cell all night. Dear God. Hamehd has taken her, and Ali doesn't know.* I tried to think. Maybe she was still alive. What could I do? I was sure Ali was on his way to the interrogation building. I could knock on the door of my cell and ask a guard to get him for me. On the other hand, this would only keep Ali away from the interrogation building. I had to wait.

I marched up and down my cell; it took only five or six steps to walk its length, and its width wasn't much more than three steps. Images from the night I had been taken for execution flashed in my head. I had witnessed the last moments of the lives of two young men and two young women. I didn't even know their names. Had their families been told that their loved ones had been executed? Where were they buried? The same thing could happen to Mina. I knocked on the door of my cell with my fists as hard as I could.

"Something wrong?" asked a man's voice.

"Can you please find Brother Ali and tell him I need to talk to him right away?"

He agreed.

I paced some more, my heart pounding. I didn't have a watch and couldn't tell how long I had waited. The *moazzen* had not announced the midday *namaz*, so it wasn't noon yet. I became dizzy and wobbled from side to side, hitting the walls. There had to be something more I could do. I began asking all the saints I knew for help. *Saint Paul, help Mina. Saint Mark, help Mina. Saint Matthew, help Mina. Saint Luke, help Mina. Saint Bernadette, help Mina. Saint Joan of Arc, help Mina.* When I couldn't remember any more saints, I knocked on the door again.

"I told him," said the same voice.

"What did he say?"

"He said he'd come as soon as possible."

I sat in a corner and sobbed.

*"Allaho akbar . . ."* the *moazzen* announced the time for the midday prayer. *"Allaho akbar . . ."*

The door of my cell opened. Ali came in and closed the door behind him. He stood there, staring at me for a few seconds.

"I was too late," he finally said. "She died last night during interrogation."

"How?"

"Hamehd said she was talking back, he slapped her, and she fell and hit her head somewhere."

"My God! Do you believe him?"

"It doesn't matter what I believe."

I wanted to cry, and I couldn't. I wanted to scream, and I couldn't. I wanted to stop terrible things from happening, and I couldn't.

Ali sat next to me.

"I tried," he said.

"Not hard enough," I cried.

He left.

Ali didn't come to see me for five or six days after this, and I spent most of my time sleeping, overwhelmed by Mina's death. Finally one morning, he brought a young woman named Bahar, who was holding a baby in her arms, to my cell. He still didn't say a word, but our eyes met, and I had a feeling that he wanted to talk to me, but he left right away.

Bahar's baby was five months old, a beautiful boy named Ehsan. Bahar was from Rasht, a city in northern Iran and close to the Caspian shores, not too far from our cottage. She had short wavy black hair, and although I could see the dark shadow of worry in her eyes, she moved and spoke in a calm, confident way. She and her husband had both been supporters of the Fadayian. They had been arrested in their home and brought to Evin. Bahar had not been lashed or hurt during her interrogation.

That night, Ali called my name from behind the closed door. Before I left, Bahar took my hands in hers and told me she knew I'd be all right. She had the largest hands I had ever seen in a woman, and they felt warm against my cold skin.

As usual, Ali took me to another solitary cell, but he was very quiet. He sat in a corner, watching me as I took off my chador.

"Don't judge me so harshly," he suddenly said.

"Mina is dead, I said. An innocent girl is dead, and you're worried about how I judge you? Of course I judge you harshly. What else can I do? You're the one who's in charge here."

226

"I'm not in charge. I've tried to be, but I'm not."

"Who's in charge then?"

"Marina, I'm doing all I can. You have to trust me. It isn't easy. And I want you to understand that I don't want to talk about it."


When I returned to my cell, it was four in the morning, it was very quiet, so I tiptoed to my spot.

"Are you okay?" Bahar's voice filled the darkness.

"I'm fine. Sorry if I woke you."

"You didn't. I was awake. Do you want to talk?"

"About what?"

"Anything that might be on your mind. So far we've mostly talked about me, now it's your turn, and don't tell me you're fine, because I know you're not."

I tried to fight my tears. She had caught me off guard. Where would I start?

"I want to tell you but I can't."

"Try. You don't have to tell me all of it."

"I'm Ali's wife."

"You can't be serious."

"I am."

"How is this possible? He arrested his own wife?"

"No. I didn't know him before I was brought here. He was one of my interrogators. When my other interrogator, Hamehd, took me for execution, Ali stopped it and then threatened me that if I didn't marry him, he would hurt my loved ones. I had no choice."

"This is rape!"

"Don't tell anyone about this. My friends at 246 don't know."

"Are you his *sigheh*?"

"No, he wanted permanent marriage."

"Under the circumstances, I don't know if permanent marriage is better or worse. With *sigheh*, at least you know he'll leave you alone after some time. But now—"

"I'm okay."

"How can you possibly be *okay*?"

That was it. I started sobbing. The baby woke up. Bahar picked him up, rocked him, and sang him a lullaby she had made up herself. It told of the Caspian Sea, the thick forests of the north, and the children who played there without care.

I found it easy to talk to Bahar. I told her about Gita, Taraneh, and Mina and how I hated myself for not having been able to help them. She told me that she had also lost friends and blamed herself for being alive.

I asked her how things had been outside Evin before she was arrested, and she told me that nothing much had changed during the last year or so. The Islamic government had successfully tightened its grip. Uneducated and undereducated people blindly followed Khomeini because they wanted to go to heaven, and the educated crowd remained silent to avoid imprisonment, torture, and execution. There were also the ones who didn't believe in the mullahs and their propaganda but, nevertheless, followed them in order to gain access to better jobs with higher pay.


Bahar went to 246 after spending three weeks in my cell, and I began feeling lonely. One night in mid-September, I asked Ali to let me go back to 246, and he agreed. He had brought some rice and roasted chicken, and we were having dinner.

"Tomorrow is the day of your retrial," he said.

This made me feel neither happy nor excited. I knew that even if I was acquitted, it wouldn't change much; I was married to Ali and I had to stay with him forever.

He told me I would be allowed to attend this trial.

"Will I have to say anything?"

"No, unless you're asked something. I'll be there, don't worry."

He had other news: Sarah was getting better and had been returned to 246. She had been sentenced to eight years.

"Eight years? You promised me that you would help her!"

"Marina, I did help her. It would have been much worse if I hadn't interfered. She's not going to stay here for all of it. I'll try to put her name on the parole list."

"I'm sorry, Ali. You're right. I really don't know what I would have done without you."

"I think this is the nicest thing you've ever said to me." He laughed, and I realized he was right.

The next morning, Ali picked me up at my cell. The courtroom was in another building, a ten-minute walk away. Employees and guards were rushing from one building to another, sometimes dragging a few prisoners behind them. Almost everyone we saw greeted Ali, bowing slightly, their right hands on their hearts. Then they nodded in my direction, looking down. Muslim women were not supposed to look men straight in the eyes, except for their husbands, fathers, and brothers, and a few other close relatives, and I followed this rule gladly. Ali also bowed to friends and colleagues and greeted them with kind words. We entered the courthouse, a two-story brick building with barred windows and dark hallways. Ali knocked on a closed door, and a deep voice said, "Come in." We stepped in. Three mullahs sat behind three desks and stood up and shook hands with Ali as soon as we entered the room. I looked down and only said *"salam aleikom"* when they greeted me. We were asked to sit down.

"In the name of God, the merciful and kind," said the mullah sitting in the middle, "this court of Islamic justice is now officially in session. Miss Marina Moradi-Bakht was condemned to death by execution in January 1982 but received Imam's pardon, and her sentence was reduced to life in prison. Since then, her condition has changed significantly. She has converted to Islam and has married Mr. Ali-eh Moosavi, who has always protected Islam to the best of his abilities and, on many occasions, has shown a great deal of personal sacrifice while serving the imam. In the light of all these changes, this court has reopened her case and has reduced her sentence to three years in prison, from which she has already served eight months."

All the mullahs stood up, shook Ali's hand again, and asked us to stay for tea. The retrial was over.


A few days later, I returned to room 6 on the first floor of 246. As soon as I entered the room, I found Sheida and Sarah standing in front of me. We embraced like long-lost sisters, and before I knew it, Sima and Bahar were holding us so tightly, we had to beg them to let go. I couldn't believe how much Sheida's boy, Kaveh, had grown; he was now about six months old.

"What are you doing downstairs?" I asked Sheida once we sat in a quiet corner.

"They moved me here a couple of weeks ago. Where were you?"

"The solitary cells of 209."

"Why?"

"I was getting a lot of migraine attacks and couldn't bear the noise here, so they moved me to 209."

"I see." I knew she had not believed me, but she didn't want to ask questions. She told me her sentence had been reduced to life, but her husband was still on death row.

"I'm thinking of sending Kaveh home to my parents. I'm allowed to keep him here with me until he's three, but I think it's selfish of me to keep him. He's never seen a tree, a flower, a swing, or another child," she said. It was true: Tall walls, barbed wire, and armed guards surrounded his world. He didn't deserve it. But every time Sheida thought of sending him to her parents, her heart nearly broke. She didn't know if she could let him go.


Sarah and I started working in a small sewing factory that had begun operating in the prison. We made men's shirts and liked the job, because it kept us busy all day. The guards told us we would get paid for our work when we were about to be released, but the wage was so low, it wasn't even worth a thought. Sarah seemed to be feeling better. Still, when she had the chance, she wrote on her body and on every surface it was possible to write on, but she concentrated on the job while at work.

Meanwhile, I hoped and prayed for Ali to get tired of me, but it didn't happen. My name was called over the loudspeaker about three nights a week, and after spending the night with him in a 209 cell, I would return to 246 in time for the morning *namaz*. Most of the girls never asked me where I went at night, but if someone did, I said I had volunteered to work at the prison hospital. Three or four other girls from 246 were also regularly called at night. Like me, they usually returned before sunrise. We avoided talking to each other. I could only guess that their situation was probably similar to mine.

Evin's daily routines carried us through days, weeks, and months. With each passing moment, our lives before prison slipped further away, but although the hope of going home became fainter and dreamlike, we secretly held it in our hearts and refused to let it die.

# Seventeen

"I have good news," Ali told me one night in February. He had a bright, boyish smile on his face. "Akram phoned me this morning. The doctor has told her she's pregnant!"

I was very happy for her.

"She also told me about your dream and the prayer. She believes she owes her happiness to you, and she made me promise to take you to her house right away."

I didn't say anything. Ali looked at me, smiling.

"What else have you been doing behind my back?" he asked.

"I haven't done anything behind your back."

"Why didn't you tell me about this?"

"It was a matter between two women."

"You aren't still afraid of me, are you?"

"Should I be?"

"No, never. It's true that we think differently, but, in a way, I trust you more than I trust myself. If this baby lives, Akram will consider herself in your debt forever."

"God answered Akram's prayers. It had nothing to do with me."

Akram was beside herself. I had never seen anyone so happy.

"When Ali called and said you were coming over, I told Massood to run to the bakery and get you some cream puffs. I remembered how much you liked them," said Akram while we were preparing dinner. She took two large white boxes out of the fridge.

"My goodness, Akram, you have enough cream puffs here to feed an army!"

"Massood is so happy he would have bought the bakery if I had asked him to."

"You told him about the prayer?" I asked, shocked that she would do so.

"I've told everyone!"

"He didn't get mad at me?"

"Mad? Why?"

"Well, you know, a Christian prayer?"

"He doesn't care! The prayer worked, didn't it? We're having a baby! This is all that matters. He says Mary has been mentioned as a great woman in the Koran, and there's nothing wrong with asking for her help."

Akram's happiness felt like a slap on my face. But I didn't want to feel upset because of her joy.

"What's wrong, Marina? Is Ali mad at you? Because if he is, I'll—"

"Ali isn't mad."

I began putting the cream puffs on a serving dish. They smelled fresh and sweet. Akram had no right to be so happy when young mothers like Sheida suffered in Evin. It wasn't fair.

"But you look so sad, Marina. What's wrong?"

"I'm sorry. I'm very happy for you, but I can't help but think about a friend of mine, Sheida. She was pregnant when she and her husband were arrested and were both condemned to death. She gave birth to her son, Kaveh, in prison. Kaveh will soon be one. He's adorable. Sheida's sentence has been reduced to life, but her husband still has a death sentence. Sheida wants to send Kaveh home to her parents, but she can't part with him. He's her life. But the poor little boy has been raised in Evin. He's never seen the outside world."

"This is terrible. Why is she in prison?"

"I don't exactly know. We don't talk about it, but I think she was a supporter of the Mojahedin."

"The Mojahedin are terrorists, Marina. They're evil."

"Sheida is not evil. She's a very sad woman, a mother. Believing someone is evil doesn't give us the right to do whatever we want to them, to do evil things ourselves. Wrong is wrong, no matter how you look at it. I'm sure Sheida doesn't deserve a life sentence."

"I'll talk to Ali. Maybe he can do something for her."

"Well, it doesn't hurt to ask him, but I don't think there's anything he can do. He isn't her interrogator. He's tried to help people, but he doesn't always succeed."

The samovar began to gurgle.

"Come, Marina, let's go have some tea and cream puffs."

I embraced her and told her she was very dear to me. I said that there was so much pain and sadness in Evin that I had forgotten how to be happy.

About four months later, on our wedding anniversary, Ali's parents invited us to their house for dinner. We had visited them about once every two weeks for the last eleven months, and they had always been kind to me. Akram's pregnancy had progressed very well. Her baby was due in about three months.

"Are you giving your wife a gift for your first anniversary?" Mr. Moosavi asked Ali after dinner that night.

Ali said he had decided to take me to the Caspian shore for a few days.

"But wouldn't that be dangerous?" I asked.

"Only my parents know where we're going. We'll be staying at my uncle's cottage in the middle of nowhere, and even he doesn't know we'll be there. He thinks my parents are going, and he won't be there himself because he's on a business trip. So, what do you say? Do you want to go?"

I nodded. He said we could leave right away; his mother had packed a suitcase for me.

We took Mr. Moosavi's car, a white Peugeot, and were on the road before ten o'clock.

"How did you come up with the idea?" I asked Ali.

"You had mentioned once that you loved the Caspian, and I wanted to spend some special time with you. We both needed to get away from Evin. The cottage used to belong to one of the shah's cabinet ministers before the revolution. This man left the country with his family around the same time as the shah. The Courts of Islamic Revolution confiscated his house, or I should say his palace, in Tehran and his cottage near Ramsar and put them up for sale. My uncle bought the cottage at a very good price."

"It must be beautiful."

"It is. You'll see. Tell me why you like the Caspian shores so much?"

I told him I had spent many happy summers there. Everything in Tehran was dull and colorless, but at the sea everything was full of life.

The cool air brushed against my face through the open window. At the beginning of the trip, I could smell only dust and exhaust fumes, but as the car continued on the winding road that climbed the Alborz Mountains, the night filled with the fragrance of clear streams and poplar and maple trees. For me, this was the scent of a lost world, of freedom, of happiness, and of all the good things that didn't exist anymore.

"When you were at the front and I was at 246, I found out that a friend of mine, Taraneh Behzadi, was sentenced to be executed," I said.

"Taraneh Behzadi? Doesn't sound familiar."

"You weren't her interrogator. She told me her interrogator's name was Hossein, from the fourth division. I thought you might be able to help her. I asked Sister Maryam if I could talk to you, and she said you were at the front."

"Marina, I can't interfere with the affairs of other divisions. Even though I was one of your interrogators, it still wasn't easy for me to reduce your sentence."

"She's dead. She was executed."

"I'm sorry."

"Are you?"

"Yes. I'm sorry that it had to come to this. But Islam has laws, she broke them, and she was punished."

"But were her crimes terrible enough to justify execution?"

"It's not my place to decide this. I didn't even know her. I don't know what she had done."

"God gives life, and He is the only one who can take it away."

"Marina, you have every right to be upset. She was your friend, and you wanted to help her. But even if I was here, it probably would have been impossible for me to save her. Interrogators and even courts do make mistakes. I have managed to help people who I believed received harsh sentences, but I don't always succeed. I tried to help Mina, didn't I? But it didn't work."

"Taraneh didn't deserve to die."

All I could see was Taraneh's large amber eyes and sad smile. Ali kept his eyes on the road.

"I've heard something terrible, and I have to ask you whether it's true or not!" I said.

"What?"

"Do you believe that virgins go to heaven when they die?"

"Marina, I know where you're going with this."

"Please, answer me."

"No, I don't believe this. And it's God's decision who goes to heaven and who goes to hell, not mine. Young girls are not raped before execution. You shouldn't believe everything you hear."

It was too dark, and I couldn't see his face clearly, but his breathing had become faster.

"*You* came close to execution. Were you raped?" he asked.

"No," I said and wanted to add, "not before it, but about six months after it, I was," but I decided against it.

"Marina, I understand how upset you are about your friend, but I promise you she wasn't raped."

I did not find much comfort in his words.


We arrived at the cottage at about two o'clock in the morning. Ali stepped out, opened a large wrought-iron gate, and, under a canopy of trees, we drove along a paved driveway. The wooded property was much larger than my parents' by the Caspian, but it was strangely similar to it. The song of crickets streamed in through the open windows. The wind swirled between leaves and branches, splashing waves of silver shadows against the windshield. It was only when we parked that I finally heard the sea; waves broke against the shore, filling the night with their familiar rhythm.

The white, two-story building was twice as big as my parents' cottage and had a stone lion the size of a large dog sitting on either side of its entrance. Ali unlocked the front door, and we walked in. The living room was furnished with French-style chairs and glass-top coffee tables, and all the floors were covered with silk Persian rugs. A wide stairway, which reminded me of *Gone With the Wind*, led upstairs, where there were six bedrooms. Ali chose the largest, which overlooked the sea. A king-size sleigh bed stood in the middle of the room. There was a large vanity table with drawers of different sizes, an armoire, and two bedside tables. Everything was free of dust and immaculately clean, so I guessed Ali's uncle and his family must have been there quite recently. I pushed aside the white, lacy curtains and opened one of the two windows, and the saltwater air brushed against my hair. I wondered what had happened to the original owners of the property. They must have loved it here, and wherever they were, were sure to miss it terribly.

"Your name is on the parole list," Ali said, standing behind me.

"What does that mean?"

"It means that you'll be officially free in about three months or so."

Officially free. What a strange term. Was I ever going to be truly free? I couldn't understand what the word "freedom" meant to him. He had taken my freedom away from me forever. I didn't say anything.

"Aren't you happy to hear this?"

"I don't know, Ali. I don't know what to think anymore. Even if I'm officially free, I won't be able to go anywhere."

"Yes, you will. We'll go home. Things are getting better. By the time you're released, it will be safe to go home."

He grabbed my shoulders, turned me around to face him, and touched my cheeks.

"Why are you crying?"

"I don't know. Memories, I guess. I can't help it."

His eyes were usually opaque but they sometimes melted into a strange, intense longing that terrified me. I looked down. When I looked up again, he was looking out the window with his back to me.

"Marina, do you still hate me?" he asked, turning to me.

"No, not anymore. I hated you at the beginning, but not now."

"Will you ever love me?"

"I don't know, but I know that as long as you work at Evin and a part of your job is hurting people, I won't be able to love you. And don't forget that you forced me into marriage. I'm your captive."

"I don't want you to think of me as your captor."

"But this is the truth."

"No, it's your perception of the truth."

"What do you mean?"

"Can't you see? You were almost dead, and I brought you back. Did you really think you could just walk away? Did you think that Hamehd and the others would have settled for that? You are naïve. I wanted you, but I'm not that selfish. If there was a way, I would have let you go, and then I would have probably killed myself with a clean shot in the head. In a way, we're both captives." He put his arms around me. "Before the revolution, I was a political prisoner for three years. I know what it means to want to go home. But let me tell you something: Your 'home' isn't the same as you left it, or even if it is, you are not the same. Your family will never understand you; you'll be lonely for the rest of your life. I'm probably wasting my time telling you all this, because you're still too young and too good. There's nowhere for you to go. The only place left for you in this world is with me, and the only place for me is with you."

We went to bed, but I couldn't sleep, watching the moonlight cross the floor. Ali slept with his back to me. His left shoulder rose and fell with each breath. I had told Taraneh that I had not been raped before they took me for execution, and this was the truth. But Hamehd and the guards knew I was a Christian, and in their opinion, virgin or not, I would have gone to hell anyway. And Taraneh knew this, but she had asked me this question, because although she had accepted her death sentence, she was desperate for even the tiniest bit of reassurance that she would die with dignity. Ali had told me that young girls were not raped before standing in front of firing squads. But he didn't believe he had raped me. From his perspective, he had forced me into marriage for my own good. Maybe he had raped girls under the name of *sigheh* without a second thought. I wanted to believe that he had never done anything like this, that I was the only one whom he had ever forced into any kind of marriage, but there was no way for me to know the truth.

I slipped out of bed and walked to the sea. Small waves whispered against the rocky shore, and stars floated in between silver-gray clouds, their pearly lights reflecting off the water's surface. The Caspian was calling me like an old friend. I thought that I was ready, that I could bear the weight of loss bearing down on me. But nothing felt right. Now, the sea was calling, and I wished to go. This dreadful need, this fierce desire to vanish. I stepped into the waves. They were as warm as I remembered them. Here, I could become a memory, but then all that I held in my heart would be lost.

*"Life is precious, don't let go, live again."* The voice of the angel.

"I needed you. I called you. You didn't come. And now you tell me not to let go? Not to let go of what?"

*"Life is precious, don't let go, live again."*

"What will you do if I go under and breathe water instead of air? Will you let me die this time and blame me for giving in to despair and grief? Or will you smile and make me feel guilty about all that I have or haven't done, sending me back to this torment?"

The wind brushed past me and flowed into the woods and into the valley of White River. Then it silently drifted through the stillness of the desert to find its way to the ocean.

I walked back toward the cottage, dripping. Ali was standing at the gate that opened to the beach. He was crying. Why couldn't I just love him and let go of the past? I had to surrender to the rhythm of existence, like a child discovering how to float in water for the very first time.

"I woke, and you weren't there," he said, lifting me off the wet sand and carrying me inside like a child.

\* \* \*

We returned to Evin after five days at the cottage. Nothing had changed. Four weeks went by, and then, in late August, I started to feel terribly sick. After I had vomited for a few days, Ali decided to take me to see his mother's physician. She ordered a few tests and later told me that I was eight weeks pregnant. It hadn't occurred to me that I might be expecting. When I agreed to marry Ali, I only considered the effects of my decision on my own life, my parents' lives, and on Andre. I had never thought about children. Now, there was another life that was affected: an innocent child. A child was going to need me, rely on me, and whether I liked it or not, was going to need its father.

Ali was waiting for me in the car. He was thrilled when I told him the news.

"Are you happy?" he asked me.

His question upset me. I was not happy, and this wasn't fair. The baby inside me didn't know anything about my life. All it needed was my love and attention. In a way, I was its angel. How could I possibly turn my back on it?

"I'm happy," I said, "but I'm also in shock."

"Let's go to my parents' house. I want them to know right away."

I knew that my parents needed to know, too, and so did Andre. Who was going to throw the first stone?

As soon as we arrived at his parents' house, Ali phoned Akram. His parents were overjoyed, and it pleased me to see them happy. All evening, his mother gave me advice concerning the stages of pregnancy. It already felt like I knew Ali's mother better than I knew my own mother. I was so desperate to find some normalcy and happiness that I wished I could forget myself and love Ali. But this was impossible. I could never forgive him for what he had done, not only to me but to others.

"You should stay here with us," Ali's mother told me. "You need rest and good food."

I refused the offer, but she insisted. Mr. Moosavi intervened.

"She'll stay where she wants," he said. "She's more than welcome to stay here. This is her home the same way it's Ali's, but maybe she wants to be with her husband. Pregnancy isn't an illness. She'll be fine."

Akram arrived and gave me hugs and kisses. She was due in about four weeks, and considering that she was a small woman, her belly looked too big. We went to her old bedroom so we could talk in private.

"Marina, I've never been this happy in my life! This is wonderful! Our children will grow up together. They'll be almost the same age."

I turned away from her.

"What's wrong?" she asked.

"Nothing. I've just been feeling nauseous all the time."

"Are you happy to be pregnant?"

I didn't want to hear that question, much less answer it. It broke my heart because I knew I wasn't happy. I had tried to be, but I wasn't. I didn't want the baby—and it hurt.

"You don't want the baby, do you?"

"No, I don't, but I don't want to feel this way. God knows I've tried."

"It's not your fault. You're scared. Come, feel the baby moving."

She put my hand on her belly, and I felt the baby kick.

"Your baby will grow and move inside you like this. It's the best feeling in the world. Give it a chance. I'm sure you'll love it more than you can imagine. I'll be here to help you with everything. There's no need to worry. And Marina, Ali really loves you, you're everything to him."

Akram had truly become my sister, and, whether I liked it or not, I had become a part of Ali's family. With them, I felt more loved and cared for than in my old life, and their love made me feel guilty because I realized I loved them in return. But love wasn't supposed to make one feel ashamed. Love was not a sin, and yet, for me, it had become one. Did this mean that one day I would love Ali, too? Did this mean that I had completely betrayed my parents and Andre?

In a cell that night, Ali and I both lay awake in darkness.

"Marina, I'm resigning from my job tomorrow," he said.

I was surprised to hear this, but it wasn't entirely unexpected. Even though Ali rarely talked to me about his job, I lived in Evin, and I had seen how frustrated he had become. I had especially noticed this after Mina's death. I blamed Ali for what happened to her, and I believed he should have done more to save her, but I had felt his helplessness, too. He had lost the battle to Hamehd.

"Why?" I asked.

He didn't want to talk about it, but I said I deserved to know. He told me he had gotten into a big clash with the prosecutor of Tehran, Assadollah-eh Ladjevardi, who was in charge of Evin. "Assadollah and I have been friends for years," he said. "He was also a prisoner in Evin during the time of the shah. But he's gone too far. I've tried to change things in Evin, and I haven't been able to. He wouldn't listen."

I had seen Ladjevardi twice. Once he had come for a tour of the sewing factory where I worked. And once when I was stepping out of Ali's car, Ladjevardi, who was getting into a car, had come up to us and greeted us warmly. Ali introduced me to him, and he said he had heard about me and was glad to meet me. He wished us happiness and said he was proud of me for converting to Islam.

"I promised you a good life when we got married," Ali said, "and that's what we're going to have, away from this place. I'll work with my father, and we'll have a normal life. You've been strong, patient, and brave, just as I knew you would. Now it's time to go home. I only need about three weeks to put everything in order."

Suddenly, leaving Evin was becoming a reality, but what I felt was not happiness. I knew that as Ali's wife, I would always be a prisoner.

"I'll have to tell my parents," I said. I couldn't keep my marriage a secret forever, especially with the baby on the way.

We heard a few gunshots in the distance. Ali told me he often thought of the night I had almost been shot.

"If I had gotten there only a few seconds later, you would have been dead," he said. "I've never told you this, but I sometimes have nightmares about that night. It's always the same: I'm there, and it's too late. I find you dead and covered in blood."

"That's what should have happened."

"No, it's not! God helped me save you."

"How about the others? There are people out there who loved them and didn't want them to die as much as you didn't want me to die."

"Most of them brought it upon themselves," he said.

I wanted to shake him. "No, you're wrong! You're only a human being. Can you say that you knew everything about them? Making decisions about life and death needs a complete understanding of the world that we don't have. Only God can make decisions like this because He's the only one who knows everything."

I was in tears and had to sit up to be able to breathe.

"I'm sorry," he said, "I'm not defending violence, but sometimes there's no other choice. If someone holds a gun to your head and you get a chance to shoot and defend yourself, will you do it, or will you die without fighting back?"

"I will not kill another human being."

"Then bad guys will win, and you'll lose."

"If winning involves killing, I'd rather lose. But then, others who witness my death or hear about it will know that I died because I refused to give in to hatred and violence, and they'll remember, and, maybe someday, they'll find a peaceful way of defeating evil."

"Marina, you live in your own idealistic world that has nothing to do with reality."

I stayed awake that night after he fell asleep. It seemed to me that Ali had begun to realize that violence was pointless—torturing and executing teenagers could never lead to any good and could never please God in any way. And, maybe, this was why he had saved me from death and married me; I was his strange, desperate way of rebelling against all that went on in Evin.

On Monday, September 26, Ali and I went to his parents' for dinner. Two weeks had gone by since his resignation, and, over dinner, he told me we would leave Evin in about a week and would move back to the house he had bought for us.

At about eleven o'clock, we said good night to everyone and stepped outside. It was a cold night, so Ali's parents didn't come out with us. The metal door connecting their yard to the street creaked as Ali pushed it open, and its lock clicked loudly as it closed behind us. We walked toward the car, which was parked about eighty feet away where the street was a little wider. A dog barked in the distance. Suddenly, the loud sound of a motorcycle filled the night. I looked up to see it come toward us from around the corner. Two dark figures were riding on it, and as soon as I saw them, I instinctively knew what was about to happen. Ali also knew, and he pushed me. I lost my balance and fell to the ground. Shots were fired. For a moment that stretched between life and death, a weightless darkness wrapped its smooth, silky body around me. Then a faint light spread into my eyes and a dull pain filled my bones. Ali was lying on top of me. Barely able to move, I managed to turn to him.

"Ali, are you okay?"

He moaned, looking at me with shock and pain in his eyes. My body and legs felt strangely warm, as if wrapped in a blanket.

His parents were running toward us.

"Ambulance!" I yelled. "Call an ambulance!"

His mother ran back inside. Her white chador had fallen on her shoulders, revealing her gray hair. His father knelt beside us.

"Are you okay?" Ali asked me.

My body ached a little, but I wasn't in pain. His blood was all over me.

"I'm okay."

Ali grasped my hand. "Father, take her to her family," he managed to say.

I held him close to me. His head rested against my chest. If he hadn't pushed me, I would have been hit. He had saved my life again.

"God, please, don't let him die!" I cried.

He smiled.

I had hated him, I had been angry with him, I had tried to forgive him, and, in vain, I had tried to give him love.

He struggled to breathe. His chest rose and fell and then was still. The world moved around us, but we had been left behind, standing on different sides of an unforgiving divide. I wanted to reach beyond the dark depths of death and bring him back.

The flashing lights of an ambulance . . . A sharp pain in my abdomen . . . And the world around me disappeared into darkness . . .

*I stood in a lush forest with my baby in my arms. He was a beautiful boy with large, dark eyes and rosy cheeks. He reached out with his little hand, grabbed my hair, and giggled. I laughed and, looking up, saw the Angel of Death. I ran to him. He smiled his warm and familiar smile, and his sweet fragrance surrounded me. It felt as though I had seen him just the day before, as though he had never left me.*

*"Let's go for a walk," he said and started down a path that disappeared into the forest. I followed him. It was a beautiful day, and it seemed like it had just stopped raining; the leaves of the surrounding trees were shimmering under swollen droplets of water. There were bushes of pink roses everywhere, and the air was sweet and warm. I had fallen behind. He disappeared behind a tree, so I walked faster to catch up with him and found him sitting on my Prayer Rock. I sat next to him.*

*"You have a beautiful son," he said.*

*The baby started to cry. I didn't know what to do.*

*"He's probably hungry. You should feed him," the angel said.*

*As if I had done it a million times, I put the baby to my breast, and he took it with his warm, tiny mouth.*

I opened my eyes. One by one, round droplets fell from a clear plastic bag into a tube. Drip. Drip. Drip. I followed the tube with my eyes; it was connected to my right hand. The room was dark except for the faint glow of a nightlight. I was lying on a clean white bed. There was a phone on a small table by my bed. I reached for it with my left hand, and a sharp pain filled my belly. I fell back and took a deep breath. The pain went away. I put the receiver to my ear. It was dead. Tears seeped from my eyes.

The door opened, and a blinding light expanded and reached me. A middle-aged woman wearing a white headscarf and a white manteau came in.

"Where am I?" I asked her.

"It's okay, dear. You're in a hospital. What do you remember?"

"My husband is dead."

*My husband is dead. Dear God, why does this hurt so much?*

The woman left the room, and I closed my eyes. *He's dead, gone, and I feel lonely. Terribly lonely. I almost feel the same as I did when I saw soldiers throw Arash's body onto a truck. But I loved Arash, and I never loved Ali. What's wrong with me?*

This was grief, denied, but present and strong.

Someone called my name. I opened my eyes to see a middle-aged man with a gray beard and a bald head. He said he was a doctor and asked me if I was in pain, and I said I wasn't. Then he told me I had lost my baby. Whatever was left of me crumbled.

For about two days, I drifted back and forth between nightmares, dreams, and reality, not knowing which was which. Somewhere in between blurry images and vague voices, I found Mr.

Moosavi sitting by my bed. I touched his shoulder, and he looked at me. The room was speckled with sunlight.

"This is too much for all of us," he said, crying. "But we have to surrender to God's will."

I wished I could understand God's will, but I couldn't.

Mr. Moosavi continued to talk, but his voice became fainter and fainter until it completely faded away. I dreamed that Andre and I were walking on the beach, holding hands. Taraneh was there, and so were Sarah, Gita, and Arash. A moment later, I was standing at the door of my parents' cottage, looking toward the driveway. Ali was walking away from me, waving good-bye. I frantically ran to catch up with him, crying out his name, but he had disappeared.

I woke with something cold on my forehead. Akram stood by my bed, and it was her cold hand I had felt. She had dark circles around her eyes and was crying quietly. I couldn't remember where I was. She reminded me that I was in a hospital. I asked her if Ali was truly dead, and she said he was. Sobbing, she crawled in bed beside me and put her arm around my shoulder.

When I was finally lucid enough, Mr. Moosavi told me he would make the arrangements for my release, but he had been told that he had to return me to Evin for the time being. He also said Ali had made a will a few days before his death and had left me everything he had. I told Mr. Moosavi I didn't think it would be right for me to take anything that belonged to Ali.

"You don't want to tell your family about your marriage, do you?" he asked.

I didn't respond.

"You made my son very happy," he said. "You deserve to start a new life."

He sat on a chair next to my bed, holding a string of amber-colored prayer beads in his hand. I recognized them; they were Ali's. I asked him how Fatemeh Khanoom was coping, and he said she had been very strong.

"How is Akram?" I asked.

"She came to see you a couple of days ago and tried to talk to you, but you weren't well."

"Yes, she was here . . ." I remembered.

"She has delivered her baby, a boy," Mr. Moosavi smiled a faint proud smile.

"When?"

"She went into labor after we told her about Ali."

Akram was in the same hospital I was in. She had had excessive bleeding, which was now under control, and the baby had been a little jaundiced but was getting better.

Before taking me back to Evin, Mr. Moosavi took me to see Akram and her little boy, whom she had named Ali. On our way to Akram's room, we walked by a large window, behind which about thirty babies slept or cried in small cribs. Mr. Moosavi pointed out a tiny baby with a red, wrinkled face, who was screaming angrily. It was little Ali. I asked to hold him, and the nurse brought him to me. He stopped crying as soon as I began rocking him in my arms and started sucking on my manteau; he was hungry. Unable to stop my tears, I took him to Akram, and she put him to her breast.

My baby was dead. I would have loved him if he had lived. But I was never going to feed him, change his diapers, play with him, or watch him grow.


When I walked into the 246 office and took off my blindfold, a guard I had never met before was staring at me. She was in her mid-forties, and had a mocking smile on her face.

"The famous Marina, or should I say Fatemeh Moradi-Bakht. We finally meet. Remember one thing: I'm the boss here now, and you are not going to receive any special treatment from now on. You are like everybody else. Understood?"

I nodded. "Where is Sister Maryam?"

"The Sisters of the Revolutionary Guards in Evin have been reassigned. I'm Sister Zeinab and I'm a member of the Islamic Committees, and we're in charge here. Any more questions?"

"No."

"Go to your room."

The world had its way of proving me wrong. Things could still get worse. But I was too tired to even shed another tear. In room 6, everyone gathered around me. Bahar's voice rose above everyone else's.

"Girls, give her some space. Marina, are you okay?"

I looked into her eyes, and all the voices faded away.

When I came to myself, I was lying on the floor in a corner with a blanket covering me, and Bahar was sitting by my side, reading the Koran.

"Bahar."

She smiled. "I thought you were in a coma or something. Where have you been?"

I told her about Ali's assassination. She was shocked.

"He got what he deserved," she said.

"No, Bahar. He didn't deserve this."

"Didn't you hate him for what he did to you?"

Why did everybody ask me this?

"He wasn't all evil. There was goodness in him. He was sad and lonely, and he wanted to change, to help people, but he didn't exactly know how, or maybe he did but couldn't, because people like Hamehd didn't let him."

"You're not making any sense. He raped you again and again."

"I married him."

"Did you want to marry him?"

"No."

"He forced you into it."

"Yes."

"Legal rape is still rape."

"Bahar, nothing makes sense. I feel like everything is my fault."

"Nothing is your fault."

I asked her about her son, Ehsan, and she told me he was taking a nap. She had not heard anything from her husband.

About two weeks later, my name was announced over the loudspeaker. Mr. Moosavi was waiting for me in the office. Sister Zeinab asked him to sign a piece of paper saying I had to be back before ten o'clock at night.

"I'm taking you to my house for dinner," he said as soon as we stepped out of the office.

"These new sisters aren't very nice."

"No, not at all."

Mr. Moosavi was distracted as we walked to his car.

When we cleared the gates, he asked me if I was feeling better, and I said I was. He said he and his family were doing better as well; God had given them strength, and Akram's baby had been keeping them busy. Then, he took a deep breath and said he'd received information that Ali's assassination had been an inside job. I couldn't believe it.

"Hamehd?" I asked.

"Yes. He's one of them, but it can't be proven."

I said Ali had told me that he had been having difficulties with Assadollah-eh Ladjevardi, and Mr. Moosavi said he believed Ladjevardi had ordered the assassination.

"Is there anything you can do to bring the ones responsible to justice?" I asked.

"No, as I said, nothing can be proven. Witnesses will never step forward."

Mr. Moosavi had lost his only son, and the killers, who were his son's colleagues, were going to walk away. This was terribly painful for him. I found it sadly ironic that Ali had died almost in the same way as the young men and women executed in Evin; members of the same firing squads who had killed Gita, Taraneh, and Sirus had pulled the trigger that had ended his life.

"There's something else you need to know, Marina," said Mr. Moosavi. "I've been trying to get you released and I haven't been able to."

"Why?"

"Because hard-liners, like Ladjevardi, who have a lot of influence in Evin, say you shouldn't be allowed to return to your old way of life. They say such a move will jeopardize your faith in Islam. They say that you're a martyr's wife, that your husband was murdered by the Mojahedin and that you should be protected against the infidel and marry a good Muslim man as soon as possible."

I couldn't believe what I was hearing. "I'd rather die," I said.

He shook his head. "There's no need to go that far, Marina. I promised my son I would get you home and I will. I'll have to go and see the imam. I'm sure I can convince him to give the order for your release. Some people will be upset, and they'll do their best to cause complications, so it could take longer than I had expected, but we'll be fine. You have to be strong. I might not be able to bring Ali's killers to justice, but I will protect you, because this is what he wanted me to do."

"Will you take me to Ali's grave?" I asked.

He promised he would.

"Marina, did you love him at all?" he suddenly asked.

I was surprised to hear this question. I had never expected him to be so open with me.

"He asked me not too long before he died if I hated him, and I told him I didn't. I can't say I loved him, no, but I cared about him," I said.

I had never been to Ali's parents' house without him. Every few minutes, I had a very strong feeling that he would walk into the room.

After dinner, Ali's mother told me she wanted to talk to me in private. We went to Akram's old bedroom. She closed the door behind us, sat on the bed, and motioned me to sit next to her. She told me Mr. Moosavi was doing his best to get me home to my parents, and I told her I knew this.

"I know he's told you, but I wanted to tell you myself," she said. "It was Ali's last wish for you to go home, and this means a great deal to us."

She said she had never expected Ali to survive when he was arrested by SAVAK and taken to Evin before the revolution. She knew it was an honor to be the mother of a martyr, but she had been terrified. She had not wanted to lose her only son. When he went to the front, she had been afraid again, and she had been relieved when he had returned, believing he'd be safe in Tehran.

"But look what happened," she sobbed. "The people he worked with stabbed him in the back. The people who were supposed to protect him. The ones he trusted. And nothing can be done. He survived the shah and the war to be killed like this. All we can do now is to honor his last wish. And we will, I promise you. And we know very well that Akram owes her baby to you. Little Ali is our miracle. He's our hope."

There was a knock on the door, and Akram came in with little Ali in her arms. He had grown since I had seen him at the hospital. He had big rosy cheeks and large dark eyes; he was beautiful. I held him and thought of my own baby. I was grateful that I had had a chance to hold my son, even if only in a dream.


A few days later, Mr. Moosavi took me to Behesht-eh Zahra cemetery, where Ali had been buried. Behesht-eh Zahra is located just south of Tehran, off the highway to Quom, a city famous for its religious Islamic schools. Akram had come with us. She sat in the backseat with me, and for the two hours of the journey, we held each other's hands in silence. The road was a dark, clean line cutting the desert in half. It had rained the night before, but now the sky was clearing. I rested my head against the back of the seat and let the waves of shadow and light wash over me. I had lost friends and loved ones before, but Ali didn't fit with them. He was unlike anyone else I had ever known. I couldn't change what he had done to me or what had happened between us. He died when he had begun to pull away from the person he had been. So many innocents had lost their lives behind the walls of Evin and were buried in unmarked graves, and Ali was accountable for the terrible things that had happened there. But the truth was that he had died unjustly. The hard-liners who were responsible for his death had murdered him because he had become a threat to them, because he had tried to make things better, because he had tried to break free.

In the cemetery, my mind refused to focus. The world had become a jumble of unrelated images. I came to myself when Akram told me we had entered Golzar-eh Shohadah, the part of Behesht-eh Zahra dedicated to martyrs. It was almost noon, and although a cool, gentle breeze had begun to blow, the sun was hot, and I was sweating. There were small trees here and there, but as far as the eye could see, the earth was carpeted with marble and cement tombstones placed horizontally on top of graves. Tin stands with glass windows, small shrines to the dead, stood all around us. Most of the dead buried here had been killed in the war, and most of them had been very young when they died.

Mr. Moosavi and Akram finally stopped. We had arrived at Ali's grave. His father dropped to his knees and put his hands on the white marble stone. His shoulders began to shake, and his tears fell onto the stone's sparkling surface, seeping into the engraved letters that read:

Seyed Ali-eh Moosavi
Islam's Brave Soldier
April 21, 1954, to September 26, 1983

Akram put her hands on her father's shoulders and pulled her chador over her face.

Inside the tin stand that stood at the head of the grave, there were three pictures of Ali. In the first one he was eight or nine years old, standing with his right foot on a soccer ball, his hands on his hips; he smiled at the camera. In the second one, he was about six-teen and had a thin beard, looking very serious. In the third, he was as I had known him: a dark-haired man with a thick, trimmed beard, a rather large nose, and sad, intense dark eyes. A few artifi-cial red roses were glued around the pictures, and on either side of the stand was a pot of red geraniums. Tears blinded me. I sat on the gravel-covered ground next to the grave and said tens of Hail Marys for him, for my husband, a Muslim man buried in Golzar-eh Shohadah, which means the flower garden of martyrs. I wanted him to have my forgiveness, and I knew that forgiveness didn't come at once and complete, beautifully packaged and tied with red ribbon, but it came little by little. And my forgiving him wasn't going to erase the pain he had caused me; this pain would remain with me as long as I lived, but my forgiveness would help me rise above the past and face all that had happened. I had to let him go so I could be free myself.

A few graves to our right, a small old woman with a hunched back scrubbed a marble tombstone with a yellow sponge dripping with soapy water. Then, from a bottle, she poured clean water over the tombstone and dried it with a white cloth. After the stone was spotless, she moved to the next grave and followed the same ritual. A thin old man wearing a white shirt and black dress pants sat on the dirt in between the two graves and chanted something, moving his prayer beads between his fingers and watching the woman.

No one was ever going to wash Taraneh's, Sirus's, or Gita's tombstones or build them tin shrines at the cemetery where friends, family, and strangers could stop, remember them, and offer a prayer. But I remembered them, and now that I had survived, I had to find a way to keep their memories alive. My life belonged to them more than it belonged to me.

I stood up, opened the glass window of Ali's memorial stand, took my rosary out of my pocket, and left it there for him.

Akram looked at the rosary.

"What is that?" she asked.

"My prayer beads."

"They're beautiful. I've never seen prayer beads like these before."

"They're for praying to Mary."

As we headed back to the car, I looked at the tombstones the old woman had cleaned so carefully. She and the old man were gone. One of the graves belonged to Reza Ahmadi and the other to Hassan-eh Ahmadi. They had been born on the same day and died on the same day; they were twins who had been killed at the front together.

I realized how accustomed to death I had become. And in my world, it happened to the young more than it did to the old.

After dropping Akram off at home, Mr. Moosavi took me back to Evin and told me he would do his best to get me home as soon as possible.

In late October, at a visitation, Sheida sent Kaveh home to her parents. He was about nineteen months old, an energetic, sweet toddler who had given us all a great deal of joy. He couldn't pronounce my name and called me Aunt Manah. When Sheida came back from her visitation without him, she looked like she had lost her soul. She sat in a corner and rocked herself back and forth for hours until she finally fell asleep.

A few days later, I gave all of Taraneh's belongings, which she had asked me to deliver to her parents, to a close friend whose eighteen-month sentence was close to completion. I was losing hope of ever going home.

On Christmas day of 1983, it snowed. Early in the morning, through the barred window of our room, I watched feathery flakes glide back and forth on the wind. Soon, the clotheslines and all the clothes hanging on them were frosted with white. When our time to use the yard came, most of the girls came back in immediately after collecting their laundry because it was too cold. Our rubber slippers didn't offer much protection against the elements. I volunteered to bring in Bahar's and Sarah's clothes. It was colder than I had thought, but I liked the touch of snowflakes on my face. There was no one outside. I took off my socks and slippers and stood as motionless as possible. The white curves of winter took me in, covering me, filling the small spaces between my toes. Christmas day. The day Christ was born. A day of joy and celebration, of singing carols, eating big meals, and opening gifts. How could the world go on as if nothing had happened, as if so many lost lives had never existed?

After a while, my feet began to hurt, and then they went numb. I could see myself on the night of the executions when I was supposed to die, tied up to a pole, waiting for death. Evin had taken me away from home, from who I had been; it had taken me to a realm beyond fear; it had shown me more pain than any human being should ever endure. I had experienced loss before; I had grieved. But here, grief became a never-ending, raging body of darkness that kept its victims in a perpetual state of suffocation. How was one supposed to live after here?

I had to stop thinking. These thoughts would bring me nothing but despair. I had to believe I would go home one day.

About three months later, on the morning of March 26, 1984, the loudspeaker crackled and I heard my name announced.

"Marina Moradi-Bakht, come to the office."

This could mean anything. They could let me go, put me in front of a firing squad—or Mr. Moosavi might have come to see me.

"Marina, you're going home, I know it," said Bahar.

"You can't predict anything around here."

"Marina, Bahar is right. This is it," said Sheida.

Sarah embraced me, laughing, tears running down her face. "Marina, talk to my mother. Tell her I'm okay. Tell her I'll come home one day," she said.

"Go Marina! Run!" the girls cried, pushing me along the hall-way.

I walked through the barred door and, before climbing the stairs to the office, looked back and saw the hands of my friends reaching out in between the bars, waving good-bye. I waved back. As soon as I stepped into the office, Sister Zeinab called the representative of room 6 over the loudspeaker, telling her to bring my belongings.

"You won," Sister Zeinab said. "I never thought they'd let you go home so soon."

"I've lost many friends, I've lost my husband, and I've lost my baby, and you think I've won?"

She looked down.

I was going home. Finally, I was going home.


Ali's father, mother, Akram, and the baby were waiting for me in a small room at the gates. Mr. Moosavi smiled at me.

"Did I keep my promise to you?" he asked.

"Yes, you did. How did you manage to do it?"

"I talked to the imam. Ladjevardi had spoken against you, but I finally convinced the imam that it was the right thing to let you go." He paused. "Will you remember me well?"

"Yes, I will. And how about you? How will you remember me?"

"As a strong and brave daughter," he said, wiping away his tears. He told me to phone him if anything went wrong. He said he would hold all the money Ali had left for me in the bank for a year, in case I changed my mind and decided I wanted it after all. He had tried to make it easier for me, but he explained that I still wouldn't be allowed to leave the country for a few years; this was the norm for people released from Evin.

I told Mr. Moosavi that Ali had promised me to help Sarah. I asked him to ask Mohammad to watch out for her, and he promised he would.

"I just have one piece of advice for you," Mr. Moosavi said.

"Don't go visiting all your prison friends' families. Maybe visiting one or two of them would be fine, but not more. Hamehd will be watching you, and if you give him the slightest reason to arrest you again, he will. And if this happens, I might not be able to help you. Stay home. Don't attract any attention."

"I'll stay home."

Mr. Moosavi offered to drive me to Luna Park, where my family would be waiting for me, but I thanked him for his kindness and said I preferred to walk. I needed some fresh air and some time to prepare myself to face my parents.

Luna Park, located about a mile and a half south of Evin, was an amusement park. The government had taken over a part of it for use as a base for shuttle buses for visitors to the prison. When a prisoner was being released, his or her family had to wait for their loved one at the park.

I stepped outside. It was the strangest feeling to know that I could simply walk home. I still didn't dare be happy. A gust of wind heavy with cold droplets of rain whipped against me. Adjusting my black chador, I carefully made my way down the few steps that led to the quiet, narrow street. Then, I paused, looked up, and watched the clouds move with the strong wind, and for a moment, a small patch of pale-blue sky was revealed, breathtaking. Although pale, it was still lively and beautiful against the different shades of gray. My eyes followed the road, and a white car appeared around the corner. The driver, a middle-aged man, slowed and stared at me but continued on his path. My socks were soaked inside my rubber slippers, and my feet were freezing.

An armed guard stood on top of a lookout tower, watching the street.

"Brother, which way is it to Luna Park?" I called out to him, and he pointed down the road.

There were puddles everywhere. Delicate ripples spread across their surface, making reflections quiver, blend, and dissolve. There weren't many pedestrians, but every once in a while, someone went by with quick, steady steps. A black umbrella danced in the air, moving purposefully away from me. At a corner, a thin, old man wearing a ragged suit stood in front of a decaying clay wall. His bony hands were open in prayer in front of his face.

What was I going to tell my parents? That within the past two years, I had been tortured, nearly died, been married, widowed, and had lost a child? How could I possibly put it into words? And Andre . . . Did he still love me despite the gap in time that separated us?

I noticed a girl walking not too far ahead of me. She carried a large plastic bag similar to mine, and her rubber slippers were at least three sizes too big. Every few steps, she stopped and glanced back at the mountains. She didn't seem to notice me. When she reached the highway and Luna Park came into view, although the pedestrian light was green, she didn't cross the road. I stopped a few steps behind her. She stood by the pedestrian crossing and watched the traffic light change from green to red and back again. Cars sped by, came to a stop, and moved again.

"Why aren't you crossing the road?" I asked. Startled, she turned around and stared at me through the rain. I smiled.

"I'm also going home from Evin. We can cross the road together," I offered.

She smiled an uncertain smile. Holding hands, we crossed the highway. Her hand was even colder than mine.

As soon as we arrived at the gates of Luna Park, a revolutionary guard stopped us. He was cursing at the cold rain. He asked our names, took a wet piece of paper out of his pocket, checked it, and let us through. We looked around. Except for a few large booths at the back, the place looked like an empty parking lot with revolutionary guards protecting it. I couldn't see any familiar faces, but my new friend ran toward a man and a woman who had just come in and were both crying. A few minutes later, I saw my parents. I ran, held them, and couldn't let go. As we walked to the car, my mother began struggling with her umbrella, which refused to open.

"Maman, what are you doing?"

"This stupid umbrella is stuck."

"We're almost at the car."

"You're soaked. I don't want you to catch a cold."

She wanted to protect me from the rain. For the last two years, there had been nothing she could have done to help me. She had been helpless, probably even more helpless than I had been. The umbrella finally opened, and although we were almost at the car, I took it.

Dripping, I stepped into my father's car to find Andre behind the wheel. He turned around and smiled. His presence meant that he had kept his promise and had waited for me; he still loved me. I finally felt happy. It was strange that before my arrest, we hadn't exactly known that we loved each other; we discovered this only after losing one another.

My mother's voice filled the car: "In this kind of weather why didn't they let us come to the prison gates? Look at you! You'll get sick for sure. Take off your socks."

"Maman, don't worry. I'm fine. Really. I'll change as soon as we get home."

"I've made you new clothes. They're all hanging in your closet."

While I was in prison my parents had moved to the house of an old friend, a kind woman named Zenia, who lived alone in a large five-bedroom, back-split bungalow in an upscale neighborhood. This arrangement was good for both parties. Zenia wasn't by herself anymore, and my parents no longer had to pay a high rent for a small space. The price of housing had dramatically increased during the years after the revolution, and many middle-class families who didn't own a house were having difficulties paying their rent.

"How did the moving go?" I asked my mother.

"Fine. We had to sell some stuff. Zenia has a lot of furniture, and there wasn't enough room for everything. Andre was an angel and helped us on the moving day. Thank goodness he has a station wagon. I don't know what we would have done without him."

"You still have the station wagon?" I asked Andre.

"Yes."

I was surprised he still had the same car, but then, I realized that although my time in Evin felt like a lifetime, it had only been two years, two months, and twelve days.

# Eighteen

I N ZENIA'S HOUSE, I had a bedroom with a window that covered almost an entire wall and overlooked the backyard. The walls and the curtains were pink, my favorite color, and two armchairs sat close to the window. Running my fingers over the soft fabric covering the chairs, I imagined myself sitting in one, reading a novel or a book of poetry. There was even a small vanity table, which was a part of a wall unit, and on it, in handmade frames from Isfahan, were two pictures of me. In one of them, I was about eight years old, leaning against my father's shiny blue Oldsmobile, wearing a white sundress, staring intently at the camera with an uncertain, questioning smile on my face. Had I ever been that young? In another, I was thirteen, on my bike in front of my aunt's cottage, wearing a blue T-shirt and a pair of white shorts, impatient to go to the beach to meet Arash. My brother had taken both pictures.

Instead of my old bed, a sofa bed covered with a tweedy brown fabric sat in a corner. I touched every piece of furniture. Everything seemed real. Why did I feel like I was dreaming? Somehow, my real life still existed in Evin, and this other world I had stepped into, this place I had called home and had longed to return to, was intangible and alien. *This is real. I'm home. I'm back. It's over. The nightmare is over. It's good that we've moved. This is a new beginning. I have to forget the past.*

I took my folded clothes out of the plastic bag I had brought from Evin. I thought of throwing all the contents of the bag into tha garbage, but I knew I couldn't. My white wedding scarf was on top of the pile; I had wrapped it around my wedding ring. Taking a deep breath, I unwrapped the scarf, opening each one of its silky folds. I could see Ali in my arms, struggling to breathe. Wishing the world were a simple place where people were either good or evil, I wrapped up the ring again and hid it in a dark corner of my closet. Then I went to the window. It had stopped raining, and sunlight streamed through the clouds in lacy golden ribbons. The backyard was very private, encircled by tall brick walls. Many bare rosebushes surrounded the empty swimming pool. There was a soft knock on my bedroom door.

"Come in." I kept my eyes on the peaceful garden.

Andre came in, stood behind me, and put his hands on my shoulders. I could feel the scent of his cologne and the warmth of his body.

"I was ready for you to come home with a baby in your arms, and I would have loved you just the same," he said. "Nothing would have changed for me."

I didn't move. He had no way of knowing about the baby, but

he had said what I needed to hear the most. I guessed he had heard that girls were raped in the prison. I fought my tears.

"I'm not pregnant."

"Were you tortured?"

"Yes. Do you want to know why I converted?"

I wanted him to know what had happened, but I didn't know how to tell him.

"It doesn't really matter to me, but I know you did it only because you didn't have another choice. Right?"

"Yes."

"I love you."

"I love you, too." I faced him.

This was the first time we had said this to each other.

He put his arms around me. His lips touched mine, and for a few moments, Evin became nothing but a memory, unable to keep me captive.


That night, we all sat around the dinner table. My mother had made beef and celery stew with rice. At the beginning, silence dominated the dining room, broken only by the sound of silver against china or a little cough.

"Thank God it rained today. It had been dry for too long. The lawn looked really sad but looks much better now," Zenia broke the silence with her warm, musical voice. She was about five feet one and a hundred and twenty pounds, with short blond hair and dark eyes.

"The more it rains now, the better the roses will bloom," added Hooshang Khan, a close family friend of Zenia's, who was eating with us.

Sisi, one of Zenia's three cats, was under the table, rubbing herself against my leg. I reached down, scratched her head, and she purred.

My father was looking at his food most of the time, but every once in a while, his gaze slowly moved around the table and lingered briefly on me. I tried to read the expression on his face. It was as blank as usual. He had looked devastated when he came for visitations, but now I was back and things had returned to normal. It was probably easier for everyone to pretend my imprisonment had never happened. But was this silence their way of protecting me or protecting themselves?

Ali's mother had made beef and celery stew and rice on the night of his assassination. How could I tell my family about Ali, about my marriage, and about his death? I felt like a stranger, a guest no one really cared about but had invited over to their house out of a sense of obligation. Once the visit was over, I was supposed to say good night to everyone and go home. But which home? To the Moosavis', or to Evin?

I couldn't sleep that night, watching the unfamiliar shadows on the walls. Ali saved me twice the night he died: once when he pushed me down, and then with his last words when he asked his father to take me to my family. If I didn't have Mr. Moosavi's support, I would either have spent the rest of my life in Evin, or much worse than that, as Mr. Moosavi had told me, Hamehd would have married me off to one of his friends, and I wouldn't have been able to do anything about it except commit suicide.

When he returned from the front, Ali had told me that if I didn't marry him, he would arrest Andre and my parents. I had believed him then, but now a whisper of suspicion spread inside me. What if it had just been a threat? If so, I could have refused him without putting anyone in danger. What would have happened if I had said no?

Now that I was lying safely in my bed, it had become much easier to be brave.

The next day, I searched the house for my books, most of which had been gifts from the old bookstore owner, Albert, and the golden box containing my grandmother's story. I couldn't find them. I went to my mother. She sat in the family room, smoking a cigarette.

"Maman, I can't find my books. Where are they?"

She shook her head and looked at me as if this was the most irrelevant question she had ever heard. "Your books. You still haven't learned a thing, have you? Your books were as dangerous as a ticking bomb. Do you know how terrified we were when you were arrested? I destroyed all the books the guards didn't take with them. It took me days, but I got rid of them." She couldn't burn them, because we didn't have a fireplace or a yard. So, little by little, she had ripped their pages, washed them into a paste in the wringer washer, and gradually mixed the paste with the garbage.

I dropped into a chair, thinking of beautiful words turning into an ugly paste.

Washed books. The written word drowned, silenced.

*The Chronicles of Narnia* were what I missed the most. Albert had signed them.

"There was a little golden box under my bed. What happened to that?" I asked my mother.

"Your grandmother's writings. Think, Marina! If the guards came to our house again and found them, papers with Russian writings, what do you think they would've thought? It would have taken us years to prove we weren't communists."

I didn't blame my mother; she had been scared. This was the doing of the Islamic revolution.

Grief was a strange thing. It had many shapes and forms, many varieties, and I wondered if anyone had identified them all and given them fancy names.


Soon it was my nineteenth birthday and my mother invited a few friends and relatives for the occasion. Before the guests arrived, I went through the clothes hanging in my closet: blacks, navies, and browns, and all long-sleeved and depressing. I wasn't eighty years old. I wanted a bright sleeveless dress; I wanted to slip into it, look in the mirror, and find the girl I used to be. I wanted to wear it and walk into my life where I had left it.

I went to my mother and told her that although the clothes she had made for me were very nice and I loved them, I wanted something brighter and more cheerful for my birthday. I asked her if I could borrow one of her old party dresses; she used to have a pink strapless one I adored. I knew it probably was a little too big for me, but I could fix it. I had learned how to sew in Evin. My mother agreed. After I spent about half an hour behind the sewing machine, the dress fit me just fine. I squeezed my feet into a pair of high heels. I was going to find my life and reclaim it.

The guests smiled, hugged, and kissed me and told me I looked great. I was happy to see them all, but there was a tangible distance between us, between the girl who had been gone and those who had lived a normal life. There were uncomfortable pauses in every conversation.

"Marina, you look lovely. How are you?" someone would ask.

"Very well, thank you," I would answer.

Then they would force a smile and try to hide the discomfort that was as visible as the color of their eyes.

"Oh, those pastries look delicious. Has your mother made them?"

It wasn't their fault. Everybody was polite and kind, but that was where it ended. No one wanted to know. One of the priests, Father Nicola, had joined us; he played Russian folk songs on the accordion, and my parents sang along. It was good to be surrounded by the smiling, familiar faces of friends and relatives and the melodies that had been the background of my childhood. Ali had been right. Home wasn't the same, because I wasn't the same. The comfortable, safe innocence of my childhood was lost for good.

After dinner, my godmother, Siran, sat next to me. She was a wise woman, and I had always liked to know her point of view.

"How are you?" she asked.

"Good as new," I answered.

"I'm happy you haven't lost your edge," she laughed. She was as elegantly dressed as always in a cream-colored blouse and a well-tailored brown skirt. "You have to be proud of yourself. Most people who are released from Evin lock themselves up in a room and don't talk to anyone for a long time. You've inherited your strength from your grandmother."

A waltz played and people danced around us.

"Why doesn't anyone ask me anything about the last two years?" I asked her.

"The answer is very simple. We're afraid to ask because we're afraid of knowing. I think this is some kind of a natural defense. Maybe if we don't talk about it, and maybe if we pretend it never happened, it will be forgotten."

I had expected my homecoming to make things simple again, but it hadn't. I hated the silence surrounding me. I wanted to feel loved. But how could love find its way through silence? Silence and darkness were very similar: darkness was the absence of light and silence was the absence of sound, of voices. How could one navigate through such oblivion?


After my birthday, I decided to work toward my high school diploma; I had to get on with my life. I could study at home and go for the exams. Although Andre was completing his bachelor's degree in electrical engineering, he came to see me every day and helped me with my calculus and physics. He told me about his classes, his professors, and his friends, and he sometimes took me to his friends' houses for get-togethers and birthday parties. In a strange way, this was our "dating" period.

At the time, the revolutionary guards had checkpoints throughout the city. They would stop cars at different times of day, but especially at night, and would conduct random searches. It was considered a crime for a man and a woman who were not closely related or engaged to be married to be in the same car alone together. So to be on the safe side, even though we had not discussed marriage, Andre asked the priests to give us a letter that explained he and I were engaged, and he always kept this letter in his car in case we were stopped and questioned.

I studied about ten hours a day, either in my room, or pacing, book in hand, around the empty swimming pool. Maybe I subconsciously filled my time with math and science to avoid thinking about the past. My father was at work all day, six days a week—he still worked as an office clerk for Uncle Partef—and my mother spent most of her time in lines for groceries, in the kitchen, or knitting, and I kept out of her way.

One warm day as we sat in the backyard, Andre moved his chair closer to mine and put his arm around my shoulder. Sparrows played around us, and red, pink, and white roses sweetened the air with their fragrance.

"When should we get married?" he asked.

In Evin, Mohammad had warned me that I was not allowed to marry a Christian. According to Islamic law, a Muslim woman isn't allowed to marry a Christian man, but a Muslim man is allowed to marry a Christian woman. The fact that I had converted to Islam by force and under extraordinary circumstances was irrelevant before the government. If I confessed that I had renounced Islam and returned to Christianity, according to Islamic custom, I deserved to die.

"You know that if we get married and they find out, I, and maybe you as well, will be condemned to death," I said.

The wind turned the pages of the math textbook on the table.

"Remember when we first met? That day at the church office?" he said. "It was love at first sight. From that moment, I knew you were the one for me. And I felt like I had to take care of you. And when they took you away, I knew you'd come back. We belong together. This is the way it was meant to be."

272

I touched his soft blond hair and his face and kissed him. "All those days in Evin, I wanted to come back to you. Although I knew it might never happen, I hoped for it."

Then, for the first time, he told me that on March 19, a week before I was released, my family had received a phone call from Evin early in the morning, informing them that they would let me go that day. He and my parents went to the prison immediately and waited all day but were turned away without any explanation. I was shocked to hear this; why hadn't anyone told me about it before? Had this delay been another result of the power struggle between Ladjevardi and Mr. Moosavi? If so, Mr. Moosavi had truly put up a fight, and I was sure he wouldn't have had a chance of winning it without Ayatollah Khomeini's support.

"We were so worried," said Andre. "We didn't know why they had changed their minds, and the guards wouldn't talk to us. Then they called again on March 26, and we rushed to the prison. At the gates, they told us to go to Luna Park and wait for you there. I parked the car in a parking lot close to Luna Park, and your parents walked from there. I waited in the car. I was really excited but I knew that nothing was certain, so I tried not to get my hopes up. A few minutes after your parents left, a bearded man in civilian clothes came up to the car and said "salam aleikom" to me. I greeted him back. I thought he probably needed directions or something. But the man bent close to me and said, 'Don't forget that you cannot marry Marina.' I asked him who he was and how he knew me, and he said it didn't matter. He said, 'I'm warning you: she's a Muslim and you are a Christian, so you cannot get married.' Then he turned and left."

After talking to the man, Andre had been shocked and worried. Although he knew that because he had come to the church at the time of my visit from Evin, the guards knew about our relationship, and it was only at that moment that he realized that the prison authorities had kept a close eye on him. Then his fear had turned into anger. It was not anyone's business whom he wanted to marry. He loved me and this was all that mattered.

"Marina, I understand the situation," he said. "I know that marrying you is dangerous. But I want to do it. We can't give in. We're not doing anything wrong. We're in love, and we want to get married. How far are we going to let them push us? We have to take a stand."

He was right.

I guessed Mohammad must have been the bearded man. I knew very well that this marriage could be my death sentence, but, ironically, I had to risk my life in order to make it mine again. In Evin, I came close to death, and Ali saved me. But he didn't give my life back to me; he kept it for himself. My life was the price I paid for staying alive, and I had to fight to retrieve it.

I told my parents about my decision to marry Andre, and they thought I had lost my mind. Even most of the priests believed we should not marry, but we set our wedding date for July 18, 1985, about sixteen months after my release from Evin. Friends and family repeatedly tried to change our minds. As a final attempt, my parents asked Hooshang Khan to speak to me. He was a kind, wise man and they knew I had great respect for him. When he knocked on my bedroom door one evening, I was sitting on my sofa bed, reading. He came in, closed the door behind him, and sat on a chair. Leaning forward, he rested his elbows on his knees and looked straight at me.

"Don't do this."

"What?"

"Don't marry Andre. I know you love each other, but these are difficult times. You could die for this. Give it time. Things could change. It's not worth losing your life."

His words unleashed the anger I had suppressed inside me.

"You have no right to tell me whom I can or cannot marry! Not you, nor my parents, and definitely not the government! I'll do what I want to do! I'll do what's right to do! Enough compromises!"

I had never raised my voice like that in my life. I had never been so rude to someone so much older. I knew I had behaved badly. Color left Hooshang Khan's face, and he walked out the door as I burst into tears. I was not going to let the government run my life. They had imprisoned me and tortured me emotionally and physically. I had been forced to convert to Islam and marry a man I didn't know. I had watched my friends suffer and die. What mattered now was doing the right thing, showing them that although I had been forced to convert, I would marry the man I loved, even if doing so would send me back to prison and put me in serious danger. This time, I was not going to compromise. They had not destroyed me, and they would never succeed in doing so.

The day Andre and I went shopping for wedding bands, I tried to tell him about Ali. I knew he would understand. We walked around the jewelry store, looking at the display windows. He deserved to know, and I wanted to tell him. A gold wedding band that looked like two rings welded together caught my eye, and I asked to see it. We both loved it. When we went back to the car, there was a parking ticket on the windshield. Andre told me that it was his very first ticket, and we laughed about it.

As we drove back home, I thought about where to begin. I had to start at the beginning, the very first moment I stepped in Evin. Then, I had to tell about every second, every single thing that had happened. No, I couldn't do this. I couldn't travel all the way back and live it again.


That summer, my parents went to the cottage for a few days, and Andre and I accompanied them. The cottage was as beautiful and peaceful as I remembered, but the joy that being there had always given me had become nothing more than a memory. Early the first morning, when everyone was still asleep, I ran to the Prayer Rock. Everything seemed the same. Ancient trees brushed the sky, and the rays of the rising sun saturated their leaves. My shoes and pants were wet from the dew. I lay on the rock and felt its rough, moist surface against my skin and thought of the day Arash and I had prayed here. So much had changed since then. I took my first wedding ring out of my pocket, knelt by the rock, and tried to pry out one of its stones, but it wouldn't budge. I tried and tried, but the stones were all cemented in. My fingers hurt. I ran back to the house. There wasn't a sound except for my father's snoring. I tiptoed into the kitchen, grabbed a knife, and rushed back to the rock. This time, I managed to take out three stones, put the ring inside the dark cavity, and put the stones back. I imagined the ring surrounded by thousands of prayers.

When we returned to Tehran, my mother told me that when I became a Muslim, my father had said that I wasn't his daughter anymore. She was washing the dishes and didn't even look at me as she spoke. I wasn't surprised, but I was hurt. I had expected to find shelter at home, but the doors were closed on me. The distance between us seemed to expand. She dried her hands and walked out of the kitchen. Even if I had told her my secrets, she wouldn't have been able to give me what I needed from her; I needed her understanding. She was the way she was. Her view of the world and what truly mattered was completely different from mine, and I didn't dare say that I was right and she was wrong. We were different, and I had to stop expecting her to think like me. I had to accept her the way she was, because that was what I wanted her to do for me. I couldn't understand why she had told me about my father's harsh reaction to my conversion. My father had not said a word about it to me, but I guessed she had decided I needed to know his true feelings on this matter.

My mother helped me with my makeup on the day of my wedding to Andre. One of my aunts had made my dress. I couldn't stop my tears as I took it from the closet. It was hard to believe that I had lived to see this day. I looked out the window of my bedroom and at the pink roses in the backyard, offering a prayer for each of the friends I had loved and lost. I missed them all.

Draping my dress over a chair next to the window, I thought of Ali and our wedding day, about how terrified I had been. Today was different; today was mine.

I wondered if Andre and I would ever have children. I was terrified of getting pregnant again. I often thought of the moments I had spent with my baby in my dream. His smiling eyes, his giggles, his little hand grabbing my hair, and his little mouth drinking hungrily from me.

Andre had gone out early in the morning to buy fresh fruit and soft drinks to take to the church. We had invited our guests to stay after the wedding ceremony and the mass to have some cake and refreshments at the church hall. In order not to attract too much attention, we had decided that I should go to the church early and change into my wedding dress there.

As the wedding march played, my father walked me down the aisle inside the full church, and I felt happier than I had ever felt in my life. Large flower baskets overflowing with white gladiolas sat on the altar, and smiling faces surrounded us.

We took pictures inside the church and in the church's backyard. We had cake and chatted with guests, and it was soon time to go home to the small condo Andre had rented after his father passed away and his aunt who had raised him left for Hungary. With a view of the Alborz Mountains, the condo was north of Tehran in a high-rise building on the Jordan Hills, facing the Jordan Highway. Just before stepping out of the church, I put on my scarf and Islamic manteau on top of my wedding dress, and then the two of us walked to Andre's navy blue Fiat. We were both happy and scared, and we hoped for the best, because we had to; we had decided to live our lives.

\* \* \*

Almost right after our wedding, Andre found a job at Tehran's electric facility, and a couple of months later, we rented an apartment with my parents to share expenses. The Iran-Iraq war, now in its fifth year, had begun to escalate. Since the beginning of hostilities in September 1980, the war had mostly skipped Tehran; the distance separating the city from Iraq had protected us. The names of streets in residential neighborhoods changed to the names of the young men killed at the front. Before my time in Evin, this name-change process had been slow and not very noticeable. But after my release, I could see that many street names served as a remembrance to the lives lost in the war.

Not too long before Andre and I got married, air attacks began to hit Tehran and a few other large cities. Without any warning, the first explosion came very early one morning; a missile blasted a residential neighborhood less than two miles from Zenia's house. It shook us with a big boom and woke me. Although at that moment I didn't know what the cause of the sound had been, I knew something terrible had happened. From then on, air-raid sirens screamed a few times a day and in the middle of the night, and although no one had a real bomb shelter and the government had never bothered to build any, people tried to take cover in safe spots, which were supposed to be far from windows. With each missile strike, broken glass killed and injured many.

Death had become part of daily life. The ones who could leave the city and go to small towns and villages did so, but most had nowhere to go. But like a river, which always finds its way to lower ground even if it has to dig through canyons, life managed to find the shortest route to "normalcy," stubbornly struggling against fear. Parents went to work and sent their children to school, but they embraced them a little while longer and said a more patient good-bye. A few schools had been demolished during the air attacks and hundreds of children had been killed as they sat behind their desks or played in their schoolyard. At the war front, Saddam Hussein had begun using chemical weapons such as sarin and mustard gas, killing thousands.

As Andre and I drove through the city to go to church or to a friend's house, we would see a large, lonely gap where a house had stood the day before. Sometimes, a stairway had refused to collapse in the ruins of a family's life, leading eerily to the emptiness behind it, or a wall covered with floral wallpaper cast its shadow over the dust of lost lives.

On a Wednesday morning about two years after I had been released from Evin, the phone rang. I was about to leave for the grocery store and had my purse in my hand.

"Can I speak to Marina?" said an unfamiliar voice.

"Speaking."

"Marina, I'm calling from Evin."

The world stopped. I put my purse on the floor and rested my weight against the wall.

"We want you to come to Evin on Saturday to answer a few questions. Be at the main front gate at nine in the morning, and don't be late."

"What questions?"

"You'll see. Remember, nine in the morning on Saturday."

I couldn't move. I couldn't even put the receiver down. My life after Evin was only a dream. It was time to wake from the dream and go back to reality. At least they hadn't asked for Andre. I finally hung up and went to our bedroom. No one was home, and I had time to pull myself together. I tried to think of what could happen. I tried to tell myself that it was okay and that they were just checking on me. But I couldn't. Feeling exhausted, I lay down on the bed and fell asleep. I woke with my mother calling my name and touching my shoulder.

"Why are you sleeping with your scarf and manteau on?" she asked.

For a second, I couldn't remember. Then I told her.

"What?" she looked as if she truly had not understood what I had just said.

I repeated myself, and her face turned white.

All I could do was sleep. I couldn't think about Evin. Thinking was not going to help. Sometimes, when I woke to go to the bathroom or to have a drink of water, I found Andre sitting next to me, his eyes staring into empty space, his face white and pale, and his body terribly still. He knew there was nothing he could do, that he had to let me go. There wasn't a sound in the house. Silence had swallowed us like a whale.

On Saturday morning, I said a brief good-bye to Andre without looking into his eyes. I didn't want to hold him, because I knew I wouldn't be able to let go. We had made a choice and had to stand by it. After all, I had known that it could come to this. My father drove me to the main gate of Evin; I had decided it was too dangerous for Andre to take me. My father was very quiet. I told him to leave right away and watched his car disappear around the corner. I wondered if they would torture me. But why would they? To them, I was a Muslim woman who had converted to Christianity and had married a Christian man, so I deserved to die. They didn't want to extract information from me; this was about capital punishment. "I will die with dignity," I thought, and only when this thought crossed my mind did I realize this was true as long as I did the right thing, as long as I followed my beliefs. And I had no doubt that no matter what was done to Taraneh, she had died with dignity, too.

Adjusting my chador, I went up to one of the guards standing in front of the gate and told him about the phone call. He asked my name and went inside. After a few minutes, he returned and told me to follow him. The heavy metal door closed behind me. We had entered a small room. He picked up a phone and dialed a number.

"She's here," was all he said.

This could be the last day of my life. Probably Hamehd was on his way to greet me. I promised myself to keep my head up. The door opened and Mohammad stepped in. I sighed with relief.

"Marina, it's good to see you again. How have you been?" he said.

"Very well, thank you, and you?"

"Thanks to God, I've been fine. Follow me."

I followed him. He didn't tell me to put on a blindfold. There were flowers planted everywhere, which seemed completely out of place in Evin. He led me into a building and into a room that was furnished with a desk and five or six chairs. A picture of Khomeini decorated the wall.

"Please, sit down," he said. "Tell me, what have you been doing since you got out of here?"

"Nothing much. I was studying most of the time and got my high school diploma."

"That's very good. Anything else?"

"Not really."

He smiled and shook his head. "You're in a lot of trouble again, and I think you know what I'm talking about, but you're very lucky to have a few friends around here. Hamehd had plans for you, but we've been able to stop him."

"What do you mean?"

"He found out about your second marriage and tried to have the Courts of Islamic Revolution condemn you to death. But you knew this could happen, didn't you?"

"I did."

"And you still did it?"

"Yes."

"Do you call this bravery or stupidity?"

"Neither. I just did what I believed was right."

"Well, this time, luck was on your side. Hard-liners like Hamehd have been losing support in Evin. I think Ali's assassination made people realize that hard-liners had gone too far. Ali had asked me to watch your back if anything happened to him, and although I'm against what you've done, I honored his wish. But I will not do this again. I asked you here to warn you to think a little before you act next time."

"I appreciate that."

"The Moosavis have been asking about you. I told them you'd be here today. They're here to see you."

The door opened, and they all walked in. I was glad to see them. Little Ali had grown; he was an adorable little toddler and stared at me suspiciously. Akram embraced me. We all sat down.

"I'm happy to see you well, Marina. Is everything okay with you?" asked Mr. Moosavi.

"Yes, thank you."

"So, you have married again. Are you happy?"

"Yes, sir."

"You're very stubborn. You could've been in a lot of trouble if we weren't watching out for you."

"I know, sir, and I thank you for it."

"I haven't touched your money, and if you want it, it's yours."

"No, thank you. I'm fine."

"This is your Aunt Marina, Ali. Go and give her a kiss," Akram said to her little boy. He slowly walked toward me.

"Come here, Ali," I said. "You're a big boy now!"

He came closer, kissed my cheek, and ran back to his mother.

Mrs. Moosavi was crying, and I embraced her. My life would have been very different if Ali hadn't died. Then they would have remained my family, the way they had been for fifteen months. I never wanted Ali to be harmed in any way. I felt guilty for not loving him and for not hating him, but it was over, and there was nothing I could do. My feelings toward him had always been and would remain a combination of anger, frustration, fear, and uncertainty.

From Evin, I walked to the highway and waved down a cab. I had lived. It was as if death were trying to push me away, to protect me, and I couldn't understand the reason why. The world moved and shimmered in front of my eyes. Why had I survived when so many had not? Sarah had not been released, and I should have asked Mr. Moosavi about her, but I had not been able to think straight. I wondered if he had been able to do anything for her.

At home, when I opened the door to the yard, I found myself in Andre's arms. He squeezed me tight, trembling.

"Thank God, thank God! Are you okay? I can't believe they let you go! What happened?"

I told him they were doing a routine check, the same way they did on everyone who had been in Evin.

"Did they ask if you had married?"

"No," I lied. "They either don't know, or they know and don't really care."

"Does this mean that they won't bother us again?"

"I don't know, but we should be okay at least for a little while. But don't forget that they're very unpredictable. It's hard to say what they'll do tomorrow."

I knew that if hard-liners like Hamehd gained more power and support in Evin, my situation would change dramatically.


I was terrified of the war, not only because of the missile attacks but because, in a few months, Andre had to leave for his mandatory military service. Then we heard of a special government program that allowed those with a master's degree to teach in universities in remote cities for three years instead of fulfilling their military duty. This was our only hope to keep Andre from the front; he had just received his master's degree. He applied to the program and was accepted.

We had to move to Zahedan, a city located in southeastern Iran close to the borders of Pakistan and Afghanistan. Andre was to become a lecturer at the University of Sistan and Baluchestan. He had to make a trip to Zahedan about a month before his starting date to attend to the paperwork and make the necessary arrangements. We went together, because I had never been to that part of the country, and I was curious to see my future home.

The flight from Tehran to Zahedan took about an hour and a half. As the plane began its descent, I looked out of my little window. It looked as if the earth had been laid to rest, covered with a shroud of sand. I noticed a small, mildly green dot in the distance and watched it grow amid the serenity of the endless desert. Clay and brick buildings had sprouted out of the sand, reaching toward the precious shade of scarce trees.

The plane landed, and we took a cab to see the city. The sunlight, which wasn't filtered by air pollution or humidity, was so intense it felt alien and hostile. The road connecting the airport to the city was in surprisingly good shape, splitting the flatness of the landscape like an old scar. In downtown Zahedan, small stores stood on both sides of narrow streets, and men and women wearing traditional garments—loose, baggy pants and long shirts for men, and ankle-length hand-embroidered dresses and loose scarves for women—filled the sidewalks. I had never seen a camel up close, and here, standing by the road, a camel was slowly and patiently chewing on something, watching the traffic with its large, bored eyes that seemed to have seen it all. In newer, more prosperous neighborhoods, large houses were built with high-quality bricks, but as we traveled north, buildings became smaller and were mainly made of mud bricks. At the northern borders of the city stood tall, rocky hills that seemed to have holes in them like openings to caves, and the cab driver told us that people had dug out those caves to live in them. I saw a group of barefoot boys running after a torn plastic ball under the sizzling sun, laughing. The cab driver asked us the reason for our visit, and Andre explained to him that he was to teach at the university.

"The shah built the university here," the driver said, "and it has been very good for us. Now well-educated people come here from Tehran and other big cities to teach our kids and the other kids who come here from faraway places," the driver said.

* * *

In March 1987, Andre and I put our belongings in our car and started our thousand-mile journey toward Zahedan. After a couple of hours, our small, yellow Renault 5 seemed to be alone in the world. Through the open windows, the hot wind whipped against my face. A sea of sand danced over the road in golden waves, and a little further toward the horizon, the earth vanished under the mirage of a quivering, silver ocean. For hours, the landscape didn't change and the road didn't curve. Sometimes, when we stopped to stretch our legs, I realized how quiet the desert was without the constant hum of the car. By the sea, even on a calm day, one could always hear the murmur of the water, and in a forest, even if all the animals had chosen not to make a sound, one could hear the leaves brushing against each other. But here, silence was absolute. At sunset, the sun dissolved into the sizzling, red end of the earth, and the night came slowly and silently, cooling the burning wind. I felt like I could touch the brilliant stars that filled the night sky with their tiny, pulsing bodies. Here, there were no reflections or echoes, a land so remote and forgotten that it seemed beyond the reach of time.

The University of Sistan and Baluchestan had built a residential area for its lecturers within its grounds. The houses were not luxurious but well built, comfortable, and clean. We had all the necessities of life. But here, tap water was heavy with minerals and wasn't drinkable, so two or three times a week, we had to drive to the water purification plant, which was about ten minutes away, to fill up large containers with drinking water.

Andre was very busy with his job. He was either teaching, or when he was home, he was preparing for his classes and correcting papers. The solitude and silence of the desert helped me push my past away. All day, I did ordinary things like cleaning and cooking, and when the work was done, I did it all over again. I rarely listened to the radio and didn't turn on the television or read any books. There weren't any books left for me to read, but strangely, I didn't miss them. I was simply exhausted, like a marathon runner who had run for hours, had managed to crawl through the finish line, and had finally collapsed. My mind only did the things it had to do. It reminded me to do my simple duties: the laundry was always done, the floors were spotless, and the food was on the table at the right time.

Andre had wonderful colleagues at the university. We sometimes got together with them and their families, and they were all very kind to us. They didn't know anything about my past, and I could chat with them about new recipes and decorating ideas.

The war had not touched Zahedan, which was quite far from the Iran-Iraq border, but the missile attacks on Tehran and seven other cities continued. I called my mother almost every day to make sure they were okay. Although it was good to sleep through the night without random explosions threatening to blow you into pieces, I felt like a traitor. I begged my parents to come stay with us in Zahedan for a while, but my father refused, saying he had to go to work. I asked him to at least let my mother come, and he said there was no need to worry; Tehran was a very large city, and the chances of getting hit by a missile were very slim. Then, my mother called me one morning.

"Maman, you okay?"

"I'm fine. I came to stay with Marie for a few days. It's safer here."

Marie lived in a high-rise condo building, not too far from my parents' apartment in Tehran. This didn't make sense.

"Maman, what are you talking about? It's safer *here* in Zahedan. Tehran is not safe, no matter where you are."

"Trust me. It's better here."

"Maman, tell me what's going on right now, or I'll get on the next plane and come and find out for myself."

"Our street was hit yesterday morning."

My parents lived on a small court. If a missile had hit their street when my mother was home, I couldn't understand how she wasn't hurt.

"Where did it hit exactly?"

"First house on the corner."

Four houses down the street, and she wasn't hurt?

"Their house is gone. Now it's just a big, dark hole as if it was never there. I didn't really know them. They were quiet people, our age. The man was at work. His wife and his grandson were killed. Two people going by in a car were killed, too. A few of the neighbors were hurt but not seriously. There was hardly anyone home; people were either at work or had gone shopping."

I tried to imagine the scene my mother had just described, but I couldn't.

"The man came home, and his family was gone," my mother continued. "There's only a hole. Just a couple of minutes before it came, the siren sounded. I was in the kitchen on the phone with your Aunt Negar. She said, 'There goes the siren. Hang up and go somewhere safe.' I squeezed myself between the fridge and the cabinet. And it came. It was loud. Boom! I thought I had exploded. But then, it was dead quiet, like I had gone deaf. I came out. There was glass everywhere. Some of it had turned into crunchy dust. And the larger pieces were lodged in the walls like arrows. The house was standing, but it was a mess. I found pieces of your closet door in the front yard."

The war finally ended in August 1988 when I was about four months pregnant. The government of Iran accepted a UN Security Council resolution, and a cease-fire was announced between Iran and Iraq. No one had won. More than a million people had been killed.

In the mid- to late 1980s, the Mojahedin-e Khalgh organization gathered about seven thousand of its members in Iraq to fight together with Saddam's army to weaken the government of Iran. I couldn't understand how the Mojahedin could stand beside a man like Saddam who had butchered so many Iranians. Soon after the cease-fire, the Mojahedin, who were based in Iraq, attacked the province of Kermanshah in western Iran, believing they could gather enough support to topple the Islamic regime, but the revolutionary guards easily defeated them. Many of them were killed, and the ones who survived retreated to Iraq. After this, hundreds of Evin prisoners who had been accused of sympathizing with the Mojahedin were executed.

I felt very sick for the first three months of my pregnancy and was frequently vomiting, but, from the fourth month on, I felt better. The baby was growing. I soon began to feel it move inside me and the experience made me cry, because I realized I loved it even more than I ever thought possible. I wanted to give Andre a healthy child.

My mother had offered to come and stay with me for a few days when the baby was born. The baby's crib was ready, and its little clothes were neatly folded in the closet.

I went to the hospital for an ultrasound at the end of my eighth month. Zahedan was a small city and my gynecologist happened to be there when my ultrasound was being performed. The baby's head was too big. The gynecologist believed that the baby was hydrocephalic, a serious condition in which water accumulates inside the skull of the fetus. The radiologist who performed the ultrasound, however, believed that the large size of the head wasn't enough to assume hydrocephalus. There should have been other signs, which were absent. I lay on the bed listening to the two doctors arguing about my baby.

"We should just drill a hole in its head and take the baby out; it's not worth a cesarean section," the gynecologist said.

Andre and I had had enough. I was scared and angry. I wasn't going to let my baby die, not ever again. I wanted to go to Tehran to get a second opinion, but my pregnancy was too advanced, and the airline wouldn't allow me to fly. Driving all the way to Tehran was far too risky. What if the baby decided to come in the middle of nowhere?

One of Andre's colleagues had a friend at the airline's office, and using his influence, he managed to buy us tickets. We were soon on our way to Tehran, where one of my cousins got her gynecologist to see me.

I went straight to the hospital from the airport. The doctor ordered another ultrasound, and after it, I was told that the baby was fine—it just had a big head. But a natural childbirth wasn't recommended, so we set a date for a cesarean section: December 31, 1988. I wasn't completely relieved. What if they were wrong? I desperately needed to hold this baby here, in this world. I needed to feed him and hear him cry. I needed this new life to be safe inside me, to be born, and to live.

Our son, Michael, was born on December 31, 1988. When I opened my eyes after the operation, I was in a lot of pain, felt nauseous, and my mouth was dry and bitter. Andre told me that the baby was fine. As I held my son in my arms, I thought of Sheida and her sadness after sending her son home to her parents. Now I understood how terrible she must have felt.


Ayatollah Khomeini died on June 3, 1989. He had been suffering from cancer and had just undergone surgery. People had known his death was imminent. I was sitting on my bed in Zahedan, breastfeeding Michael, who was about five months old, when I heard the news on the radio. The announcer was crying. My two years in Evin flashed in my mind. The revolution was supposed to be the end of Evin, but it wasn't. Instead, it strengthened the prison's silent horror and made it far bloodier than it had ever been. Khomeini was responsible for the terrible things that happened behind those walls. He was responsible for the deaths of Gita,

Taraneh, Sirus, Layla, Mina, and thousands of others. But somehow, I wasn't happy to hear he was dead. In a way, I pitied him. What was the point of placing judgment on a dead man? I was sure that like Ali, he wasn't all evil. I had heard that he enjoyed poetry and was a poet himself. He had changed the world, but no one was going to realize the depth of his impact until history had a chance to look back and analyze his actions and their outcomes from a safe distance. I prayed for the souls of those who had lost their lives after the revolution to find peace and for their families to find courage and strength to continue their lives and make Iran a better place.

Michael had fallen asleep. He was a beautiful baby. He had no idea that a man named Khomeini had changed the lives of his parents, and I wondered how Khomeini's death was going to affect us and Iran. Many believed that the Islamic government would not survive his death, that a power struggle between different factions of the government would bring an end to the Islamic Republic.

On the day of Khomeini's funeral, a scorching hot day, an ocean of about nine million people all dressed in black spilled onto Tehran's streets and funneled onto the highway that led to Behesht-eh Zahra cemetery. We watched the coverage on television. I had never seen such a large crowd—no one had. They cried, wailed, and slapped their chests the way the Shia mourn their martyrs. All I could think of was the innocent, young lost lives of the revolution, of Evin. But the mourners didn't seem to care about that. Khomeini was their imam, their leader, and their hero, the man who, in his signature defiant and unwavering way, had stood up to the West. "But why do they love him so much?" I tried to understand. Was their hatred of the Western world so deep that they didn't mind their innocent children being imprisoned and murdered? Maybe their relationship with him had nothing to do with love but was a fearful and awestruck admiration for a man from a poor family through whom they had found power and authority to stand up to a world that had bullied them for a very long time.

The crowd surrounded the truck that carried Khomeini's wooden coffin. Everyone wanted to take a piece of his shroud, to catch a last glimpse of him. The truck seemed to be drowning in the black crowd. Security forces struggled to keep the mourners away by spraying them with water from fire hoses, but it was useless. Under a veil of mist, dust, and heat, a helicopter's roar muffled the screams and wails as it neared the truck and landed in front of it. Khomeini's coffin was taken out of the truck to be moved into the helicopter, but the crowd got hold of the coffin, and it broke. Hands reached out and tore pieces of the white shroud, and one of Khomeini's legs became visible. His body was finally placed in the helicopter, which had to bob up and down to free itself from the people who were dangling from its skids.

A few hours later, a more organized attempt was made to put Khomeini's body to rest, and this time, it was successful. A few army helicopters neared the site. A metal casket was taken out of one of them. Khomeini's shroud-covered body was removed from it—in Shia tradition the body is put in the ground with only a shroud—and was finally buried among the country's thousands of martyrs.

Months went by, and the Islamic regime survived Khomeini's death. Ayatollah Ali Khamenei took Khomeini's place as the Supreme Leader of the country. He had already served as president for two terms. The reign of terror continued. The number of arrests decreased, not because there was more freedom, but because everyone knew the high price of speaking against the regime. The ones who dared to speak up were usually silenced immediately. Women went through "better" and "worse" times. Every couple of months, the revolutionary guards tightened their grip and showed no tolerance toward makeup or imperfect *hejabs*. Then came a period of a few weeks when one could get away with wearing lipstick and a few strands of hair showing.

\* \* \*

Although Andre and I knew we would never be safe in Iran, we had not been able to leave the country. When I was released from Evin, I had been told that I wasn't allowed to leave Iran for three years. The restriction wasn't automatically lifted because the three years were over. I first had to apply for a passport. The passport office would give me a letter to take to Evin to ask for permission to leave the country. Andre wasn't allowed to travel abroad until he had completed his three years of teaching in Zahedan. My situation was more complicated, but I wouldn't know for sure until I tried.

I applied for a passport and was denied, as I had expected. I took the letter they gave me at the passport office to Evin. There, I was told that I could leave the country only if I paid 500,000 tomans—about 3,500 American dollars—as a deposit to guarantee my return. If I returned within a year, the money would be refunded. If not, it would go to the government. At the time, Andre's salary was about 7,000 tomans a month—about sixty American dollars. We didn't have enough money.

I asked my father to lend us money. To help them out, we had paid half of my parents' rent even after moving to Zahedan. My father had sold the cottage and had twice as much as I needed in the bank.

"Papa, I'm only asking you to lend us the money," I said to him. "I've never asked you for money before. As soon as a free country accepts us and we find a job, we'll gradually pay you back."

"Do you think it's easy out there?" he asked. "Life is difficult. How do you know that you're going to make it?"

"I know it, because we're hardworking people, and because God is great. He'll help us."

My father laughed. "Let me tell you a little story," he said. "Two fishermen set out into the sea in a small boat. It was nice when they left the shore, and the waters were calm. Once they got far into the sea, the weather changed. They were soon caught in the middle of a big storm. 'What do we do now?' one of them asked the other as their boat was being tossed around. 'We have to pray to God to save us because He's great and powerful and can get us out of this mess,' said the other. 'God might be great, dear friend, but this boat is certainly small,' said the first one, and they both drowned at sea."

I couldn't believe what I had heard. Although he didn't know all that had happened to me in prison, he knew that I had been a political prisoner and that I didn't have a future in Iran. I had to live in fear, and, because of my political record, I wasn't allowed to go to university. I needed his help, and he was capable of helping me, but he denied me.

"You care more about money than you care about me!" I said. "I told you that I'll pay it back and I will. I wouldn't be asking you if I wasn't desperate."

"No," he said.

I finally had to face the bitter truth about my father: he would never make any sacrifices for me. I didn't know why he was the way he was. All my life I had felt a distance between us, but I had always ignored it, believing that he was simply not the kind to show his true feelings. I couldn't remember his showing love or affection toward anyone, not even to my mother or my brother. All my life, from the corner of my eye, I had watched fathers who loved their daughters and openly expressed their feelings, fathers who would make tremendous sacrifices for their children. I had dismissed the thought that my father was different. I had always pretended that he was kind, generous, and loving.

I thought of Mr. Moosavi. I knew I could pick up the phone and call him, and I had no doubt that he would give me the money Ali had left me. But I didn't want to do that; I needed that part of my life to be over. I wished my family would treat me the way Ali's family had. But I knew my wish would never come true.

Andre's father had worked at a furniture factory during the last few years of his life. With the help of the owner of the factory, he and a few other workers had invested in a piece of land to build a small condominium building. When Andre's father passed away, this project hadn't started yet, but Andre made more payments toward it. One day, we received a phone call from a lady who worked at the factory, and she informed us that the work on the building had begun. We told her we were planning to leave the country but had run into some financial problems. She offered to buy our share and to pay us 500,000 tomans more than what we had already invested. This was all we needed.

Andre received his passport as soon as our three years in Zahedan ended. I went to Evin, put in the deposit, and obtained mine. We had heard of a Catholic refugee agency in Madrid and decided to go to Spain. We bought our plane tickets, sold everything we had, which wasn't much, and bought American dollars. There was still no guarantee that we would be able to leave. At the airport, the revolutionary guards prevented many people who had valid passports from exiting the country. We weren't going to feel free until our plane crossed the Iranian border.

Our flight was early in the morning of Friday, October 26, 1990, and my parents were to drive us to Tehran's airport at around midnight. Michael, who was twenty-two months old, moaned and squirmed as I tried to put his clothes on him but slept comfortably in my arms as soon as the car began to move. The city was deserted. I watched the familiar streets go by. First, the narrow, residential streets of Davoodieh, where we lived after returning from Zahedan, and then the wide main streets lined with stores. I had memories from almost every street and every corner. My life in Iran had made me who I was. I was leaving behind parts of my heart and parts of my soul. This land was where my loved ones were put to rest—and I had to leave it. Here, there was no future for us, only the past. I wanted my children to see the home where I had once belonged. I wanted to show them the road that took me to school, the park where I played, and the church that gave me the gift of faith and peace. I wanted them to see the blue Caspian Sea, the bridge that connected the two sides of the harbor, and the rice fields that rested on the lap of the tall mountains. I wanted them to know the desert, its wisdom and its solitude. But I knew they probably never would. There was no return for us.

Once we passed Azadi Square with its tall white monument—a landmark of Tehran that had been built during the time of the shah and had become like a gateway to the city—I knew that this was a final good-bye. I took a last glance at the snow-covered peaks of the Alborz Mountains, which were barely visible against the night sky.

At the airport, we parked the car and walked toward the terminal in silence. Knowing that there were long security checks, we were hours early. Revolutionary guards opened every single piece of luggage and searched it thoroughly. It was against the law to take antiques, too many pieces of jewelry, or large sums of money out of the country. Everything went smoothly, and I waved good-bye to my parents. We were all crying.

Our Swissair plane took off in the cold, dark, early morning air. Before long, we crossed the border, and most women took off their *hejabs* and put on some makeup. Listening to the constant, soothing hum of the engines, I closed my eyes and wondered if heaven had a "lost and found." I had left many things behind. One of them was a silver jewelry box that my grandma, being the practical woman that she was, used for storing sugar and kept on the kitchen table. It had been a gift from her husband. I couldn't help but think that every time she sweetened her tea, it reminded her of all they had done together. There was also Arash's flute, the necklace he never had a chance to give me, and my first wedding ring. Maybe they weren't lost, and, someday, I would find them all under the moss-covered stones of my Prayer Rock in a strange forest where angels lived.

# Epilogue

O<small>N</small> A<small>UGUST</small> 28, 1991, after we had spent eight days in Madrid and then ten months in Budapest waiting for our paperwork, a Swissair plane took us to an airport in Zurich, where we stood in line, waiting to board our flight bound for Toronto. I had taught Michael some English and had told him about a beautiful country named Canada, where it snowed a lot in winter and we could build big snowmen and where summers were warm and green and we could go swimming in blue lakes. He stood close to me, clinging to my hand, his eyes wide with excitement. A few

Canadian students stood in the same line in front of us. I envied them and wondered what it felt like to be a Canadian.

"I can't wait to get to Toronto," said one of them.

"Me too," said another. "We had a great time here and everything, but there's no place like home."

I knew at that moment, as I watched those teenagers with their bright and carefree smiles, that we would be fine in Canada. It would be our new home where we would be free and feel safe, where we would raise our children and watch them grow, and where we would belong.

# Postscript

Z AHRA KAZEMI DIED in Evin on July 11, 2003.

On June 23, 2003, the Canadian-Iranian photojournalist had been taking photographs outside Evin during student-led protests when she was arrested. She was soon reported to be in a coma.

During the few days following her death, the Iranian President, Mohammad-eh Khatami, called for an internal investigation. Kazemi's son and Canadian foreign affairs officials demanded the return of her body to Canada. Iran admitted she had been beaten to death but, ignoring international pressure, buried her in Iran. No independent physicians were allowed to examine her body. Iranian authorities arrested a few security agents whom they said might have been responsible for Zahra's death, but they were all soon released.

At the end, an Iranian intelligence ministry interrogator named Mohammad Reza Aghdam Ahmadi was charged in her death and was put on trial but was acquitted. Kazemi's family's lawyers, including the Nobel Peace Prize winner Shirin Ebadi, believed that Aghdam Ahmadi had been a scapegoat.

On March 31, 2005, Dr. Shahram Azam, an emergency room doctor at Tehran's Baghiattulah Hospital, made public the horrific details he had told a Canadian foreign affairs official in Sweden a year earlier: Zahra had been brutally raped, scratched and bruised, had two broken fingers, a broken nose, three broken and missing fingernails, a skull fracture, a crushed left toe, and her feet had been flogged.


I didn't know Zahra Kazemi. In mid-July 2003, at around eight o'clock in the morning, I opened my front door to get my paper, which was lying on the porch. It was a beautiful day: the sun was shining and my roses and clematis were in full bloom, so I decided to read the paper outside. I took it out of its blue plastic bag and unrolled it to find the photo of a handsome woman with a big smile and lively eyes. I wondered who she was, and I read the article immediately. Each word felt like a rope tightening around my throat.

I had begun the work on my memoir in January 2002, and I had just written my third draft, so my memories of Evin felt quite fresh. I knew that what I had gone through in Evin was still happening behind its walls, but seeing Zahra's picture and her beautiful smile gave this knowledge a painful and shocking power that cut through me. She had died like Mina. But Mina's photo had never appeared on the front page of any newspapers. The world had now taken notice because Zahra was a Canadian. If the world had paid attention earlier, if the world had cared, Zahra would not have died; many innocent lives would have been saved. But the world had remained silent, partly because witnesses like me had been afraid to speak up. But enough was enough. I was not going to let fear hold me captive any longer.

On March 31, 2005, Michelle Shephard, a dear friend of mine who is a *Toronto Star* reporter and writes about Middle Eastern, terrorism, and security issues, called me in the morning. I was very glad to hear her voice, but she said she had bad news.

"You might want to sit down for this," she said.

I did. And she told me about Dr. Shahram Azam's report on Zahra's injuries. I wished I could have saved Zahra. I wished I had died with her. But my death wouldn't have helped anyone. I had a story to tell. Zahra had given Iran's political prisoners a name and a face; now it was my turn to give them words.

# Acknowledgments

Frankly, I don't know where or how to begin; maybe I should invent new words, because "Thank you" and "I'm grateful" sound too ordinary and inadequate and make me feel like I'm committing an act of treachery.

Andre, the love of my life: I strongly believe that you are the most honest and faithful individual God has ever created. Your goodness defies laws of nature. You stayed by my side and gave me hope and strength to survive. I know how difficult it was for you to accept that I had to follow my heart and write this book; however, you always supported me. Thank you for your unbending love, trust, and forgiveness.

Michael and Thomas: thank you for being there, for giving me the gift of motherhood and love. Through you, I became whole. Thank you for sharing your energy and wonder with me and for your patience during the long hours I spend writing.

Beverley Slopen, my amazing agent and miracle worker: you came to my rescue, made this book a reality, and opened the world to it. Your sound advice guided me through difficult times. I will never be able to express the depth of my gratitude to you.

My wonderful editors and publishers: Diane Turbide and David Davidar (Penguin Canada), Eleanor Birne and Roland Philipps (John Murray Publishers/U.K.), and Liz Stein and Martha Levin (Free Press/U.S.). Thank you for your tremendous support, thoughtful comments, and brilliant questions. You believed that I had to tell my story and guided me with your wisdom.

Jim Gifford: you miraculously appeared in my life, encouraged me, and became my teacher and friend. Because of you, my manuscript came a long way to become a book. I am forever in your debt.

Michelle Shephard: you made it possible for me to take a step back and look at my story through your words. You made me dig deeper into my memories and remember the details I believed were impossible to remember, helping me face what I had subconsciously tried to avoid. You have a special place in my heart.

Rachel Manley: it doesn't matter how hard I try to explain what you mean to me, I will fail. Yes, you are my mentor, but you are also a great deal more. You have been like a good mother, a best friend, and a favorite sister. I will always look up to you. Thank you for your support and for the most beautiful and amazing review I have ever received about this book. You are a great writer, poet, and teacher, and a truly free spirit.

Scott Simmie: we both know a great deal about loss, struggle, and grief, and we have both found freedom, happiness, and comfort in the written word and in the unexpected fragrance of roses and daffodils, fragrances that give life and warmth to the vast loneliness death leaves behind.

Joan Clark: you have to be an angel, because I cannot explain your kindness in any other way. Your attention to detail is phenomenal. You helped me organize my fragmented memories, making it possible for me to bring my manuscript a big step forward. Your friendship is a precious blessing.

Steven Beattie: when my hopes crumbled, you emerged from the ruins and gave me new hope. Thank you for believing in this work and my ability to get it done. Thanks for all your corrections, invaluable advice, and support.

Olive Koyama: thank you for asking me the right questions and for offering your encouragements.

Dear Father Nicola, Father Antoniazzi, and Father F.: knowing you is a gift. Thanks for remembering, for sharing what you remember, and for inspiring me with your words. And with special thanks to Father Nicola for inviting us to visit him in Bethlehem, which has become a highlight of my life, and for translating into Italian the article Michelle Shephard wrote about my story for the *Toronto Star*.

Lee Gowan: you taught me most of what I know about writing. I dream of being able to write like you. You lifted me when I was losing hope of ever getting this done. You opened the doors that led me here. Thank you for your never-ending kindness and generous friendship.

Gillian Bartlett: you helped me write with confidence. I have never known anyone as kind, energetic, generous, and wise as you. Your love of life touches everyone around you and makes the world a better, happier place.

Karina Dahlin, Kim Echlin, Kent Nussey, and all my friends and instructors at the School of Continuing Studies at the University of Toronto: without your help and support, this book would never have been possible. You are all as passionate as I am about the power of literature. You share my belief that speaking out is a step toward healing our violence-inflicted world.

Martha Batiz Zuk and Sonia Worotynec: thank you for your gift of friendship, for your confidence in my work, for all your valuable feedbacks that cleared my vision when I didn't know which way to go. And thank you for all your emails that kept me connected to the world as I worked on my manuscript. You are my saviors. Martha, you always lift me when I'm down. If I could ever choose a sister, you would be on top of my list.

The ladies of the book club: Romana Dolcetti, Karen Eckert, Neva Lorenzon, Flavia Silano, Joanne Thomson, and Dorothy Whelan. We have been reading together for fourteen years, and what a journey it has been! You welcomed me in your circle when I was lonely and a stranger; you treated me like your own, like I was your long-lost cousin; you shared your hearts, child-care tips, and best recipes with me. You read the very first draft of my manuscript, which was raw and distorted, and bestowed me with your kind, supportive words of encouragement.

Mary Lynn Vanderwielen: thank you for making me feel like I belonged and for your meticulous editing of my first draft.

Lynn Tobin: thank you so much for being like a sister to me. I cherish our friendship.

Also, many special thanks to my boss, coworkers, and regular customers at Swiss Chalet for their support, kindness, and understanding.

*And Zahra Kazemi. Your brutal death confirmed the fact that the story of political prisoners in Iran has to be told; you gave us a name and a face, and because of you, now, the world knows about the horrors of Evin. May you rest in peace.*

This book is for all my *hambands*.

I remember you all. I miss you all. I love you all.

Please forgive me for my long silence and many other faults.

# About the Author

Marina Nemat grew up in Tehran, Iran. In 1991, she emigrated to Toronto, Ontario, where she now lives with her husband, Andre, and their two sons.